Teach Your Children To Read Well

LEVEL 1B: GRADE K-2
INSTRUCTOR'S MANUAL

Michael Maloney
Lynne Brearley
Judie Preece

Teach Your Children Well Press

Belleville, Ontario, Canada

Teach Your Children Well
208-210 Front Street, Second Floor
P.O. Box 908, Belleville, Ontario K8N 5B6
Canada

ISBN 1-894595-17-3

INSTRUCTOR'S GUIDE

IMPORTANT NOTE:
A student should <u>not</u> start Level 1B until s/he has successfully completed the 30 Lessons of Level 1A.

For reasons of clarity, review and easy reference, the Instructor's Guide found in Level 1A is repeated below in its entirety.

Features of the Series

Teach Your Children To Read Well is a phonics-based series which teaches students everything they need to learn in order to read fluently. The series consists of four Levels - 1A and 1B, 2, 3 and 4 - which span the elementary school years. Each Level contains 60 lessons and covers approximately two grades of reading skills. Each of the four Levels has three texts - an Instructor's Manual, a Student Reader and a Student Workbook.

The *Teach Your Children To Read Well* series combines three highly successful educational technologies - Direct Instruction, Precision Teaching and Behavior Management.

Direct Instruction is based on the premise that quality teaching is a critical variable in student success. In over thirty years of educational research involving hundreds of thousands of children, Direct Instruction has been proven to be far and above the most effective teaching method. It looks carefully at how material is organized and presents concepts so that they will not be confusing to the student.

A measurement system, derived from Precision Teaching, quickly and easily determines the student's progress. It enables the instructor to gather data quickly and accurately and to make decisions immediately. It signals the need for review as well as the need for additional practice. It might even recommend skipping Tasks or Lessons.

Behavior Management is a method for getting the student under instructional control so that you can teach and s/he can learn effectively. No one teaches or learns well in the midst of chaos. Behavior Management strategies are included to motivate and reward the learner. This approach has been soundly supported by almost fifty years of empirical research.

Placement Tests

Each Level of the *Teach Your Children To Read Well* series contains a Placement Test which will assist the instructor in placing the student(s) in the appropriate program. The placement test is on the back cover of the Instructor's Manual for each Level.

Using the Instructor's Guide

It is important not to assume that you know all of the necessary skills to teach someone to read. Study the Instructor's Guide first. Do yourself and your student(s) a favor and master the Guide *before* you begin to teach. It will save time, effort and frustration for both you, as the instructor, and the student(s). There is a direct cause and effect relationship between how well the instructor is prepared and how well the student(s) learns to read. **<u>Remember: If the student didn't learn, the teacher didn't teach</u>**.

Learning Objectives

Learning objectives are the framework for the job of teaching someone to read. They are a list of the skills you want the learner to know when the program is completed. These objectives are specified so that the instructor can see the contents of each Lesson, the order in which new skills are introduced and the Lessons in which these skills will be reviewed. The learning objectives for Level 1 of *Teach Your Children To Read Well* are outlined in the Scope and Sequence Chart which follows.

SCOPE AND SEQUENCE CHART ~ Level 1A

Lesson Number	1	2	3	4	5	6	7	8	9
Skill									
Teaching Sounds	a	ē	d	h	n	g		w	u
	m	s	i	th	sh	e		wh	y
	t	r	c	f	ing	o		l	
Practicing Sounds	●	●	●	●	●	●		●	
Sounding Out Words	●	●	●	●	●	●	●	●	
Teaching/Practicing Alphabet Letters	●	●	●	●	●	●	●	●	●
Teaching/Practicing Vowels and Consonants	●	●	●	●	●	●	●	●	●
Sounding Out Words that Begin With Short Sounds			●		●	●	●		●
Reading Words				●				●	●
Reading Rhyming Words				●		●			●
Saying the Underlined Sounds and Reading the Words				●			●	●	●
Reading Sentences				●			●		
Teaching/Practicing Irregular Words						●	●		●
Sound Fluency Check						●	●	●	●
Word Fluency Check						●	●	●	●
Story Reading								●	
Vowel Letter Sounds									
Alphabet Letters Fluency Check									
Story Reading Fluency Check									
Teaching Quotation Marks									
Teaching/Reviewing the Final e Rule									
Workbook Exercises	●	●	●	●	●	●	●	●	●

10	11	12	13	14	15	16	17	18	19	20	21	22	23	24	25	26	27	28	29	30
ā																				
ĭ	k			b	x		j	qu		p				or			er			tch
ō	ck			v				ol						al			ir			
ū														ch			ur			

SCOPE AND SEQUENCE CHART ~ Level 1B

Lesson Number	31	32	33	34	35	36	37	38	39
Skill									
Teaching Sounds					ȳ z		ēā ai ou		ar oi/oy oo
Practicing Sounds		●				●			
Sounding Out Words		●	●			●	●	●	●
Sounding Out Words that End in e-d									
Sounding Out Words that Begin With Short Sounds									●
Reading Words	●		●		●	●		●	
Reading Rhyming Words			●			●	●		●
Saying the Underlined Sounds and Reading the Words		●	●	●			●	●	
Reading Sentences	●				●				
Teaching/Practicing Irregular Words	●			●					
Sound Fluency Check	●	●	●	●	●	●	●	●	●
Word Fluency Check	●	●	●	●	●	●	●	●	●
Story Reading		●		●		●	●	●	●
Story Reading Fluency Check	●	●	●	●	●	●	●	●	●
Teaching/Reviewing the Final e Rule	●				●				
Sounding Out Double Consonants					●				
Workbook Exercises	●	●	●	●	●	●	●	●	●

40	41	42	43	44	45	46	47	48	49	50	51	52	53	54	55	56	57	58	59	60

au   igh   wa   oa kn   ph   tion

aw   ea   gi,e   ly   sion

ould   ci,e

Tasks

Using *Teach Your Children To Read Well* is as simple as following a recipe. It provides a complete set of instructions that tells the instructor what to say and what to expect the students to respond. Each Lesson is divided into a number of Tasks. Each Task teaches a particular skill, such as learning new sounds. Each Task is carefully scripted. As the instructor you need only to follow the script and the objectives will be covered by the end of the program.

Instructions to the instructor are written in regular script.
Statements said by the instructor are written in bold face.
Responses of the student are written in italic print.

There are 14 major Task formats that the instructor needs to learn in order to teach this program. Once they are learned, the procedures can be applied to other Tasks. Samples of these major Task formats along with annotated instructions are included in this Guide. Like an actor in a play, it is critical that the instructor knows his/her part. It is well worth the time and effort involved to become thoroughly familiar with each format.

As the instructor you do not have to learn all 14 formats before beginning to teach the program. In the Instructor's Manual an asterisk indicates the first time a new Task is introduced. The new Task can be learned by the instructor before commencing that Lesson. Do not begin a new Lesson until you are thoroughly familiar with the material it contains. Each format should be learned so that it can be delivered at a normal speaking rate without hesitation or errors. Poorly presented formats create errors and attention loss for both the instructor and the student.

Most of the Task formats follow a procedure called "Model - Lead - Test." First the instructor models the Task so the student(s) can understand what the correct answer is, and equally important, what it is not, as well as the steps for arriving at the correct answer. After modeling the Task the instructor will ask the student(s) to repeat the procedure with him/her. This is known as the lead. When the instructor is satisfied that the student(s) knows the correct procedure or answer, the instructor gives the student(s) the chance to do it independently, thereby testing his/her ability to do the Task.

For the first several times they appear, the Tasks are very detailed. They become shorter as both you, as the instructor, and the student(s) become comfortable with them.

Correction Procedures

Specific Correction Procedure formats are scripted for each type of Task across all Levels of the series. It is critical for you as the instructor to listen for and correct every error that the student makes. The student should complete a Task quickly, completely and correctly before moving on to the next part of the Lesson. Sloppy error corrections allow students to progress when, in fact, they have not mastered the material. Instructors who either do not catch, or worse, neglect to correct errors, are setting the student up for future failure. **Every error must get corrected every time it occurs.** Most corrections follow the Model-Lead-Test-Repeat procedure.

Signals

Signals are a critical part of teaching these programs well. They are especially important when teaching a group of students. Signals are used in the same way a choir conductor uses them to keep everyone singing in unison. Signals tell the students when to respond. This is important in order to be sure that every student can do the task. Most groups have some students who are overeager to answer and some who are happy to stay in the background. If the overeager student gives the answer before the other students, the instructor never really knows if the quiet student knows the answer or is just copying the overeager student. To avoid this problem, saying "Ready," followed by a signal such as a tap on the table or a snap of your fingers, is used so that all of the students say the answer at the same time. The time frame between saying, "Ready," and giving the signal is about half a second. It is important that this remain consistent. When the students say the correct answer together, the response is clear. When one or more students respond slightly earlier or slightly later than the rest, the instructor hears a ragged jumble of answers. That tells you to do the Task again.

The following is a list of the 14 major Tasks to be mastered by the instructor:

1. Teaching Continuous Sounds and Sound Combinations
2. Teaching Short Sounds and Sound Combinations
3. Practicing Sounds and Sound Combinations
4. Sounding Out Words
5. Sounding Out Words that Begin with Short Sounds
6. Saying the Underlined Sounds and Reading the Words
7. Reading Rhyming Words
8. Teaching Irregular Words
9. Story Reading
10. Teaching the Final e Rule
11. Using the Final e Rule
12. Sounding Out Words with Double Consonants
13. Sound Fluency Check
14. Story Reading Fluency Check

Let's take a detailed look at each of these Tasks:

Teaching Sounds and Sound Combinations

Each letter or letter combination in the English language has one or more sounds. There are two types of sounds - continuous and short. Fifty of the sixty-six sounds and sound combinations taught in Levels 1A and 1B are continuous sounds. This means that you can say them for as long as you have breath. All vowels, most consonants and most sound combinations are continuous sounds. When they are introduced and practiced, they are marked with a dot under them. The student must be taught to hold continuous sounds for one second.

The 16 other sounds and sound combinations are short sounds. They cannot be said for more than a fraction of a second. The sounds b, c, d, g, g(i,e), h, j, k, p and t are short sounds, as are the sound combinations ck, ch, tch, ould, tion and sion. They are marked with an arrow under them. It is imperative that students be taught to differentiate between continuous and short sounds before they begin to blend these sounds into words.

In order to make learning easier for the student, some sounds and sound combinations have horizontal lines marked over them. For example, when a vowel letter says its name, a line appears over the sound. (Exceptions are long vowels in irregular words and in words with a final e. They are not marked. The student is taught to recognize these words without prompts.) In Levels 2, 3 and 4 these marks are faded out.

Listed below are the sounds and sound combinations taught in Levels 1A and 1B of the series. The sounds are organized and taught in such a way as to be most readily distinguished from other similar looking or similar sounding ones. This way they are least likely to be confusing for the learner.

Previously taught sounds and sound combinations are thoroughly reviewed in subsequent Lessons and in Fluency Checks at the end of each Lesson. The list below shows the sounds, the Lesson in which they are taught, what each sound says, an example of a simple word which contains that sound and whether the sound is a continuous or short sound.

Lesson	Symbol	Sound	As in	Short/Continuous
Level 1A 1	a	aaa	<u>a</u>m	continuous
1	m	mmm	a<u>m</u>	continuous
1	t	t	a<u>t</u>	short
2	ē	ēēē	m<u>e</u>	continuous
2	s	sss	<u>s</u>at	continuous
2	r	rrr	<u>r</u>at	continuous
3	d	d	ma<u>d</u>	short
3	i	iii	<u>i</u>t	continuous
3	c	c	<u>c</u>at	short
4	h	h	<u>h</u>im	short
4	th	ththth	<u>th</u>e	continuous
4	f	fff	<u>f</u>at	continuous
5	n	nnn	ma<u>n</u>	continuous
5	sh	shshsh	<u>sh</u>e	continuous
5	ing	ing	s<u>ing</u>	continuous
6	g	g	<u>g</u>as	short
6	e	eee	m<u>e</u>t	continuous
6	o	ooo	<u>o</u>n	continuous
8	w	wooo	<u>w</u>ing	continuous
8	wh	wooo	<u>wh</u>en	continuous
8	l	lll	<u>l</u>et	continuous
9	u	uuu	s<u>u</u>n	continuous
9	y	yēēē	<u>y</u>es	continuous
10	ā	āāā	<u>a</u>te	continuous
10	ī	īīī	f<u>i</u>nd	continuous
10	ō	ōōō	n<u>o</u>	continuous
10	ū	ūūū	<u>u</u>se	continuous
11	k	k	<u>k</u>ing	short
11	ck	k	ki<u>ck</u>	short
14	b	b	<u>b</u>at	short
15	x	ksss	o<u>x</u>	continuous
15	v	vvv	<u>v</u>an	continuous
17	j	j	<u>j</u>et	short
18	qu	cooo	<u>qu</u>ick	continuous

18	ol	ōlll	<u>ol</u>d	continuous
20	p	p	<u>p</u>ig	short
24	or	ōrrr	f<u>or</u>	continuous
24	al	olll	t<u>al</u>l	continuous
24	ch	ch	<u>ch</u>ip	short
27	er	rrr	t<u>er</u>m	continuous
27	ir	rrr	s<u>ir</u>	continuous
27	ur	rrr	t<u>ur</u>n	continuous
30	tch	tch	ma<u>tch</u>	short

Level 1B ....

34	ȳ	īīī	m<u>y</u>	continuous
34	z	zzz	<u>z</u>ebra	continuous
37	ēā	ēēē	m<u>ea</u>t	continuous
37	ou	owww	<u>ou</u>t	continuous
37	ai	āāā	s<u>ai</u>l	continuous
39	ar	orrr	<u>ar</u>t	continuous
39	oi/oy	ōyēēē	<u>oi</u>l / b<u>oy</u>	continuous
39	oo	ooo	c<u>oo</u>l	continuous
40	au/aw	ooo	<u>au</u>to/s<u>aw</u>	continuous
40	ould	ould	w<u>ould</u>	short
41	igh	īīī	h<u>igh</u>	continuous
41	ea	eee	h<u>ea</u>d	continuous
44	wa	wooo	<u>wa</u>ter	continuous
44	gi,e	j	<u>g</u>inger	short
44	ci,e	sss	i<u>c</u>e	continuous
46	oa	ōōō	b<u>oa</u>t	continuous
47	kn	nnn	<u>kn</u>ee	continuous
47	ly	lēēē	quick<u>ly</u>	continuous
49	ph	fff	<u>ph</u>one	continuous
51	tion/sion	shun	mo<u>tion</u>/ten<u>sion</u>	short

Learning these sounds and sound combinations is one of the two most important skills in learning to read. Before you can teach a student the sounds, you must have a thorough knowledge what sound each letter or combination of letters makes. Many individuals taught to read during the last 20 to 30 years were taught without an emphasis on phonics (recognizing individual symbols and the sounds they make). As a result, these instructors may not be completely fluent with the phonics used in this series. Fluency involves being able to recognize and correctly say the 66 sounds and sound combinations in one minute. On page 10 is a practice sheet of sounds and sound combinations taught in Level 1B. Again, a dot under the sound indicates that it is a continuous sound. Hold these sounds for one second. An arrow indicates a short sound. Do not hold these sounds. Use this sheet to practice and become thoroughly familiar with the sounds you will be teaching. Refer to the list of sounds on pages 8 and 9 to ensure that you are saying all the sounds and sound combinations correctly.

PRACTICE SHEET OF LEVEL 1B SOUNDS

ai	sh	$\bar{o}$	25 au	p	5
•	•	•	•	>	
qu	10 ar	w	x	ur	10
•	•	•	•	•	
i	ould	aw	z	35 kn	15
•	>	•	•	•	
sion	$c_{i,e}$	20 oy	oo	$\bar{a}$	20
>	•	•	•	•	
5 oa	$\overline{ea}$	ir	n	$\bar{e}$	25
•	•	•	•	•	
oi	i	tch	30 d	ph	30
•	•	>	>	•	
wa	15 ly	$g_{i,e}$	igh	ou	35
•	•	>	•	•	
ol	j	ea	tion	40 $\bar{y}$	40
•	>	•	>	•	

Now let's look at the scripted formats of the Tasks for Teaching both Continuous and Short Sounds and Sound Combinations as well as the Task for practicing these sounds.

TASK 1: TEACHING THE CONTINUOUS SOUND a as in am

Instructions to the instructor are written in normal script. The instructor's spoken instructions to the student are written in **bold script.**

→ Point to the sound a.

→ Say to the student, **I am going to touch this sound and say it.**
Listen. Touch the dot under the a and say **aaa** for one second. Lift your finger.
Say, **Listen again.** Touch the dot and say **aaa.** Lift your finger.

Model - First the instructor demonstrates the sound or sound combination twice.

The instructor says "Ready" and then touches the dot and holds his/her finger on it for one second while saying the sound with the student(s). Try to look at each student to see that they are saying the sound. If in doubt, do the lead again.

Say to the student, **Say the sound with me. When I touch the sound, we will both say it. We'll keep on saying it as long as I touch it.**

→ **Ready.** Touch the dot under the a and say **aaa** with the student for one second.
Lift your finger and stop saying the sound.

Be sure to reinforce correct answers with positive comments.

→ Say, **Good saying aaa. Let's do that again. Remember, when I touch the sound we both say it. We'll keep on saying it as long as I touch it.**
Ready. Signal.
Repeat the task until the student does it as instructed.

Lead - The instructor then says the sound or sound combination with the student two or more times.

Listen carefully to hear if all of the students respond at the same time. Be particularly attentive to any student who responds late.

Say, **Now it is your turn to say the sound. When I touch the sound, you say it. Keep on saying it as long as I touch it.**

Student responses are written in *italic script.*

→ **Ready.** Touch the dot under the a and listen to your student say *aaa.*
Lift your finger after one second. Student stops saying the sound.

It is important to vary your praise statements so as not to become repetitive and tedious.

→ Say, **Great! Do that again. Remember, when I touch the sound, you say it.**
Keep on saying it as long as I touch it.
Ready. Signal.
Repeat the task until the student does it as instructed.

Test - The instructor then listens to the student say the sound or sound combination on his/her own.

There is a dot under the sound a because a is a continuous sound which the student should say for one second. With a sound combination such as shshsh, there will also be a dot because it too is a continuous sound.

→ a
•

All Correction Procedures are indicated with a check mark.

✔ Correction Procedure
If the student does not say the sound correctly or does not hold the sound for one second, say, **I'll say this sound. Listen.** Touch the dot under the sound and say **aaa** for one second.
Say, **Do that with me. Ready.** Signal. Repeat the task. When the student has said the sound correctly with you, say, **Nice going! You got it. Now say that sound all by yourself when I touch it. Ready.**
Touch the dot under the sound and listen to the student say *aaa.*

Correction Procedure - If any student makes an error, use the Correction Procedure in a step-by-step fashion to correct it. Then redo the entire Task with the whole group.

TASK 2: TEACHING THE SHORT SOUND t as in at

Instructions to the instructor are written in normal script. The instructor's spoken instructions to the student are written in **bold script**.

→ Point to the sound t.

→ Say to the student, **This is a short sound. I am going to touch this sound and say it. Listen.** Tap the arrow under the t and lift your finger immediately as you say **t. Listen again.** Tap, lift and say **t.**

Model - First the instructor demonstrates the sound or sound combination twice.

The instructor says "Ready," then taps the arrow and lifts his/her finger while saying the sound with the student(s).

Do that with me. When I touch the sound, we will both say it.

→ **Ready.** Tap the arrow under the t and say **t** with the student.

Try to look at each student to see that they are saying the sound. If in doubt, do the lead again.

Good saying t. Let's do that again. Remember, when I touch it we both say the sound. Ready. Signal. Repeat the task until the student does it as instructed.

Lead - The instructor then says the sound or sound combination with the student two or more times.

Listen carefully to hear if all of the students respond at the same time. Be particularly attentive to any student who responds late. Student responses are written → in *italic script*.

Say, **Now it's your turn. Say the sound when I touch it. Ready.** Tap under the t and listen to the student say *t.* Say, **Super! Do that again. Ready.** Signal. Repeat the task until the student does it as instructed.

Test - The instructor then listens to the student say the sound or sound combination on his/her own.

There is an arrow under the sound t because t is a short sound which the student should not hold. With a sound combination such as ck, there will also be an arrow because it too is a short sound.

✔ Correction Procedure

If the student does not say the sound correctly or holds the sound, say, **I'll say this sound. Listen.** Tap the arrow under the sound, say the sound and lift your finger.

Say, **Do that with me. Ready.** Signal. Repeat the task.

When the student has said the sound correctly with you, say,

All right! You got it. Now say that sound all by yourself when I touch it. Ready. Tap the arrow under the sound, lift your finger and listen to the student say *t.*

Correction Procedure - If any student makes an error, use the Correction Procedure in a step-by-step fashion to correct it. Then redo the entire Task with the whole group.

Be sure to reinforce correct → answers with positive comments.

TASK 3: PRACTICING SOUNDS

In this format, only sounds and/or sound combinations which have been taught in previous Lessons are grouped together for review. See Correction Procedure below. →

Say, **Now let's see if you can remember all of the sounds you have learned.**
I am going to touch each of the sounds.
When I touch the sound, you say it. If you make three mistakes, we will practice the sounds and then try again.

The instructor uses the Ready signal and touches each continuous sound for one second. ⟶

Put your finger on the first sound.
Say, **What's this sound?**
Ready. Signal. Student says, *mmm.*

The instructor uses the Ready signal and taps each short sound, quickly lifting his/her finger. ⟶

Next sound.
Ready. Signal. Student says, *t.*

Repeat for each sound in the list. Remember to touch and hold the dot under the continuous sounds for one second and to tap the arrow under the short sounds.

Continuous sounds and sound combinations will have a dot under them. Students will hold these sounds for one second. ⟶

Short sounds and sound combinations will have an arrow under them. Students should not hold these sounds. ⟶

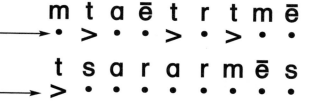

 Correction Procedure
If the student is not able to say all of the sounds in the list with fewer than three errors, change the task. Model the sounds in the first row and have the student practice only that row three or four times.
Then model the sounds in the next row and have the student do it three or four times. Do not spend more than one minute practicing each row. If the student is still having difficulty, take a short break and repeat the Lesson from the beginning.

If an error occurs, the instructor follows the Model-Lead-Test-Repeat Correction Procedure.

Sounding out Words

Once the student can attach a sound to a symbol, s/he must then be taught to blend those sounds together to produce a word. This is undoubtedly the most important part of the program. The critical aspect in teaching blending skills is to make sure the student does not stop between the sounds in a word. S/he must be taught to go from one sound to the next without gaps between the sounds. This is particularly difficult to achieve with words such as "cat" which begin with a short sound. There is a natural tendency to say the sound c and then stop. The student needs to be taught to blend the c into the aaa and say *"caaa"* without a break between the two sounds. Learning proper blending skills allows the student to decode the thousands of phonetically regular words in the English language.

To help students sound out words, lines with dots and arrows appear under them. The big dot at the front of the line is where the instructor puts his/her finger to focus the student's attention on the word. (It is suggested that for teaching one student the instructor sits on the student's left. Place the Manual on the table between you. Touch the bullets with your left index finger to easily follow the scripted format. Use your right index finger to touch the dots and arrows. For groups, the instructor will sit in front of the students with the Manual held up so that each student can see it.) To sound out the word, the instructor says **"Ready,"** then slides his/her finger along the line to the dot under the first sound. Dots along the line signify continuous sounds or sound combinations that must be held for one second. Arrows denote short sounds or sound combinations. They indicate that the student should say but not hold the sound and keep moving along the line to the next sound. These dots and arrows help the instructor and the student to determine which letters to hold and which to blend into the next sound. Step-by-step procedures for sounding out a word starting with a continuous sound and a word beginning with a short sound are shown in the diagrams on page 15.

Sounding out a word that starts with a continuous sound.

Focus student's attention on the word by putting your finger on the big dot. Say, **"Ready."** Wait for half a second.

s   t   i   ff

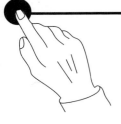

Slide to the dot under s. The student says *sss*. Hold for one second.

Slide right past the arrow under the t as the student says *t* to the dot under the i.

Hold the i for one second as the student says *tiii*.

Slide to the dot under the ff. Hold for one second as the student says *fff*.

Slide along the arrow.

Sounding out a word that starts with a short sound.

Focus student's attention on the word by putting your finger on the big dot. Say, **"Ready."** Wait for half a second.

c   a   s   t   ing

Slide right past the arrow under the c as the student says *c* to the dot under the a.

Touch the dot under the a for one second as the student says *caaa*.

Slide to the dot under the s. Hold for one second as the student says *sss*.

Slide right past the arrow under the t as the student says *t* to the dot under the ing.

Hold for one second as the student says *ting*.

Slide along the arrow.

Thoroughly learn the formats on pages 16 and 17 for teaching students how to sound out words.

TASK 4: SOUNDING OUT WORDS
THAT BEGIN WITH CONTINUOUS SOUNDS

Most students who have difficulty learning to read cannot blend sounds together without stopping between the sounds, despite knowing their phonics. It is critical that students do not stop between the sounds. Even very slight pauses can create errors.

Say, **Now we are going to learn to sound out words. When we sound out words, we say the sounds in the words without stopping between the sounds.**
Put your finger on the dot in front of the first word.
Say, **My turn. I'm going to say the sounds in the word mat. Listen.** Slide to the dot under the m and say **mmm** for one second.
Slide to the dot under the a and say **aaa** for another second.
Slide through the arrow under the t and say **t.**
Keep on sliding along the arrow.
<u>Do not stop between the sounds.</u>

Model - The instructor demonstrates how to sound out the word twice.

The instructor says, "Ready," pauses briefly and then slides along to the dot under the first sound. ⟶

Put your finger on the dot in front of mat.
Say to the student, **Do that with me. Say the sounds in mat. Ready.** Slide through the dots and arrows as above as you and the student say **mmmaaat.**
Say, **You got it. Good sounding out mat. Let's do that one more time. Ready.** Signal.

Lead - The instructor then sounds out the word with the student two or more times.

Listen carefully to hear if all of the students respond at the same time. Be particularly attentive to any student who responds late.

Say, **Now do that all by yourself. Say the sounds in mat. Remember, when I touch the sounds, you say them. Keep on saying them as long as I touch them. Don't stop between the sounds.
Ready.** Put your finger on the dot in front of mat and slide through the dots and arrows as the student sounds out *mmmaaat.*
Repeat.
Say, **What's that word?**
Ready. Signal. Student says *mat.*
Say, **That's right. You sounded out mat. Nice work.**

Test - The instructor then listens to the student sound out the word on his/her own.

Focus the student's attention by putting your finger on the big dot in front of the word. ⟶
Lines with dots and arrows are provided under the words to show the instructor where to pause while the student says the sounds in the word.

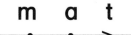

✔ **Correction Procedure**

If the student does not say the sounds correctly, does not hold the sounds a or m for one second, holds the sound t, or stops between the sounds when you touch them, say, **Listen. I'll show you how to sound out this word.** Model the task for the student by sliding through the dots and arrows without stopping.
Then say, **Do it with me. Ready.** Signal.
When the student says the sounds correctly with your assistance, say, **Now it's your turn. Say the sounds in mat all by yourself. Remember not to stop between the sounds. Ready.** Slide through the dots and arrows and listen to the student say the sounds.
Say, **Great job! Let's do that one more time.** Repeat.

The Correction Procedure follows the Model-Lead-Test-Repeat format.

TASK 5: SOUNDING OUT WORDS THAT BEGIN WITH SHORT SOUNDS

Students with weak blending skills have particular difficulty with these types of words. Such words are hard because the student naturally stops after having said a short sound.

Now we are going to sound out some words. These words begin with short sounds. We have to put the sounds together without stopping.

I will show you how to do that.
Listen. Put your finger on the dot in front of cat. Slide past the arrow under the c to the dot under the a and say **caaa.**
<u>Remember not to stop between the c and the a.</u> Hold the **aaa** for at least one second, then slide past the t and say **t.**
Say to the student, **Listen while I do that again.**
Repeat task.

The instructor models the correct response so that students can hear how to blend an initial short sound into the nearest continuous sound.

Say, **Do that with me. When I touch the sounds, say them with me.**
Ready. Signal. Repeat the task.
Say, **Good sounding out cat. You didn't stop between the sounds.**

Lead - The instructor then sounds out the word with the student two or more times.

Pay particular attention to errors where the student fails to blend the initial short sound into the next available continuous sound.

Now try it all by yourself.
Ready. Signal. Student sounds out *caaat* while you slide along the dots and arrows with your finger.
Say, **Do that for me one more time.**
Ready. Signal.

Test - The instructor then listens to the student sound out the word on his/her own.

What's that word?
Ready. Signal. Student says *cat.*

An arrow indicates that the instructor should slide past the short sound until s/he reaches the first continuous sound that the student can hold. This shows the student how to blend the two sounds into one. It helps to teach him/her how to successfully sound out words that begin with short sounds.

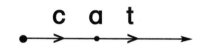

✓ **Correction Procedure**
If the student miscalls a sound or stops between the sounds, say, **My turn.** Slide along the dots and arrows as you sound out the word.
Then say, **Do that with me. Ready.** Signal. Sound out the word with the student.
Say, **Good work! Now it's your turn to sound out the word.** Slide your finger along the dots and arrows as the student sounds out the word.

The Correction Procedure follows the Model-Lead-Test-Repeat format.

Reading Words

Once students have practiced sounding out phonetically regular words, they are soon able to read the entire word without sounding it out first. This allows them to read thousands of phonetically regular words as sight words. If they should have difficulty remembering the word, they can revert to a reliable strategy for sounding it out. Approximately four-fifths of the thousand most commonly used words in the English language are phonetically regular and can be sounded out. Estimates suggest that more than eighty percent of our reading and writing consists of these most frequently occurring thousand words. At the end of Level 1 students will have mastered many of these words.

This format teaches students to recognize sounds they have learned when those sounds are embedded in words.

The student isolates the sound and decodes it. ——→

Then the student says the entire word without sounding it out.

TASK 6: SAYING THE UNDERLINED SOUNDS AND READING THE WORDS

Put your finger on the underlined sound in the first word.
Say, **Tell me the sound that is underlined.**
Ready. Signal. Student says, *aaa*.
That's right, aaa.

Now tell me the word.
Ready. Signal. Student says, *rat*.

Repeat Task for each of the words in the list.

r<u>a</u>t	m<u>ē</u>	r<u>i</u>d
s<u>i</u>t	<u>c</u>at	<u>d</u>im
a<u>m</u>	s<u>a</u>d	<u>th</u>ē
	tr<u>i</u>m	

✓ **Correction Procedure**

If the student makes an error saying the sound or the word, say, **The underlined sound is (correct sound).**
Do that sound with me. Ready. Signal. Student says, (*correct sound*) with you.
Your turn. Tell me the underlined sound. Ready. Signal.
Good. Now sound out the word. Ready. Slide your finger along the arrow as the student sounds out the word.
Say, **That's right. Now say the word.**
Good. Let's start that row over again. Go back to the beginning of the row and redo the row before going on to the next one.

If the student is having difficulty reading the word, have him/her sound it out first.

Repeat the entire row before continuing on with new words.

The Correction Procedure follows the Model-Lead-Test-Repeat format.

TASK 7: READING RHYMING WORDS

Say, **Now we are going to read some words that rhyme with at.**
Touch the dot in front of the word at. Slide your finger along the line and say **at**.

Say, **What's that word?**
Ready. Signal. Student replies, *at*.

Touch the dot in front of the next word, **fat.**
Say, **This word rhymes with at.**

My Turn. Listen. Slide your finger along the line and say **fat.**

Do that with me.
Ready. Signal. Repeat task with student.

Say, **Your turn to rhyme with at.**
What's this word?
Ready. Slide your finger along the line under fat and listen to the student say *fat*.

Repeat for each word.

Teaching rhyming words is a fast way to expand reading vocabulary. By pairing previously learned sounds with a rhyming word, the student learns many new words with minimal effort.
Don't sound the word out. Read it as you slide your finger along the line.

Model the rhyming word.

Lead - Read the word with the student.

Test - Have the student read the word alone.

at ———▶

fat ———▶

cat ———▶

hat ———▶

rat ———▶

mat ———▶

that ———▶

sat ———▶

✓ **Correction Procedure**
If the student does not say the word correctly, say,
This word is (correct word). What word?
Repeat Task from beginning.

Correct the misread word and repeat the entire list.

Teaching Irregular Words

Approximately one-fifth of the most frequently used one thousand words in English are phonetically irregular. That means that they can not be reliably sounded out. (e.g. was, his, friend) Students need to be able to decode irregular words as well as phonetically regular words in order to become good readers. Approximately 144 of the most frequent irregular words in English are taught in Levels 1A and 1B of the series. They are taught as sight words. Irregular words are introduced in small numbers and continually practiced in other formats throughout the program. Other irregular words are systematically presented and taught in Levels 2, 3 and 4.

TASK 8: TEACHING IRREGULAR WORDS

Say, **Here are some new irregular words. First I will read the word, then you will read the word and spell it.**

Listen. The first word is his.
What word?
Ready. Signal.
Yes, his.

Spell his.
Ready. Signal.

Repeat for each word.

This is the third most important format for teaching students to be able to crack the reading code. It completes the strategies for word reading and allows students to read any word they might encounter.

By definition irregular words can not be easily sounded out, so another strategy is required. Students learn to spell these words as a means of helping them to remember them.

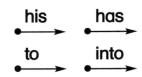

✓ **Correction Procedure**
If the student does not say or spell a word correctly, model it for them, have them repeat it and start at the beginning of the Task.

Reading Sentences and Stories

Starting in Lesson 4 of Level 1A, students begin to read sentences in the Student Reader. To reduce errors and prevent guessing, sentences are constructed only from words that have been previously taught. In Lesson 8 the first brief story is introduced. Story reading is an essential part of each Lesson in all Levels of the series. In Level 1 stories begin with simple sentences and build in complexity and length as more sounds, sound combinations and words are learned.

TASK 9: STORY READING

Say to the student, **Now you are going to read a story.
Turn to Lesson 11 on page 13 in your Reader.**

Say, **The title is written at the top of the story.
What does the title tell you?
Ready.** Signal.
That's right, the title tells you what the story is about.
Ask the student to read the title.
Say, **So what do you think this story is about?**
Accept reasonable answers.

Titles, quotation marks, contractions and the past tense are taught when they appear in the Reader.

Say, **Good. Now let's read the story. Read as well as you can.
If you make an error, I will help you. If you make more than 7
errors, we will go back to the beginning and read the story
again.**

The instructor needs to monitor student reading to make sure that the student stops at the ends of sentences and does not add, delete or miscall words.

**Put your finger on the first word.
Now read the sentence.
Ready.** Signal.

Students read stories aloud so that the instructor knows that the student is able to read quickly and accurately.

Lost in the fog

Fred and Edith got on a red raft to fish.
The red raft had a mast.
Fred got a fat cat fish with a rod and a frog.
Then the mist got thick.
Fred and Edith got lost in the fog.
Fred and Edith can not see land.
The raft is rocking.
The deck is slick and wet.
Fred lands on his hands on the deck.
He has a cut on his left hand.
Edith is wishing that some one will come.
A craft with three men finds them.
Now Fred and Edith are glad.
Fred thanks the three men.
            This is the end

Sentences and stories in the Student Reader begin at 30 point font, are reduced to 24 point in Lesson 31, then to 20 point from Lessons 46 to 60. The stories appear in a smaller font in the Instructor's Manual so that the instructor can follow along as students in a group read the story in their Reader.

 Correction Procedure
Say to the student, **Wait. That word is (correct word).
What is that word? Ready.** Signal.
Good. Now read that sentence again.
Count each error. If the student makes 7 errors, reread
the story from the beginning.

Teaching Rules

In Level 1 students learn a few rules. These rules give them a strategy to easily decode hundreds of new words. Two particularly important rules are the Final e Rule and the Doubling Rule.

TASK 10: TEACHING THE FINAL e RULE

Point to the first word in the list below and say to the student, **Read this word for me.**
Ready. Signal. Student reads, *rob.*
Say, **Yes, that word is rob.**

Now read the rest of the words in the list.

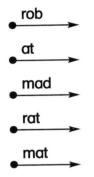

This rule allows students to discriminate between many similar looking words. Knowing that an e at the end of the word makes the vowel say its name gives them a strategy for sounding out hundreds of new words that end in e.

With a pencil add an e to the end of each of the words in the list.

Then say, **We are going to learn a rule about words that end with an e.**
Listen. An e at the end of a word makes the vowel say its name.
Listen again. An e at the end of a word makes the vowel say its name.

The exceptions to the rule (some, come, live, love, etc.) are taught as irregular words.

Say that rule with me.
Ready. Signal.
Repeat the rule with the student until the student can state the rule with you.

Students must be taught the rule verbatim and must be able to say the rule as well as being able to apply it.

Then say, **Your turn to say the Final e Rule.**
Ready. Signal.
Repeat until student says the rule correctly.

The instructor needs to make sure that every student can repeat the rule as a first step in using it.

✔ **Correction Procedure**
If the student is unable to say the rule correctly, model the rule for the student two more times. Say the first part of the rule and have the student repeat it. Then say the second part of the rule and have the student repeat it. Then see if the student can repeat the whole rule with you. Pay careful attention to see which words in the rule the student is unable to repeat. Say that part of the rule with the student two or three times, then try the entire rule.

TASK 11: PRACTICING THE FINAL e RULE

Point to the list of words below and say to the student, **You're going read this list of words for me.**

First word.
Ready. Signal. Student reads, *tap.*

Now read the rest of the words in the list.
Ready. Signal.

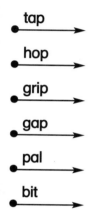

tap

hop

grip

gap

pal

bit

With a pencil add an e to the end of each of the words in the list.

Say, **Remember the rule about words that end with an e.**
Listen. An e at the end of a word makes the vowel say its name.

What's that rule?
Ready. Signal.

That's right. Now read these words all by yourself.
Ready. Signal.

If the student makes an error, review the Final e Rule and begin the Task again.

Once the student can repeat the Final e Rule, they need to learn to apply it consistently when they encounter words which end in e.

To assist the student, non-examples are changed into examples of the rule by adding a final e. Or examples of final e words are changed into non-examples by removing the final e. In either case students are forced to discriminate between words which follow the final e rule and words which look similar but do not follow the rule.

Instructors must be willing to provide enough practice and correction to make sure the student can reliably determine when the rule does and does not apply.

TASK 12: SOUNDING OUT WORDS WITH DOUBLE CONSONANTS

Say, **In some words you must double the final consonant before you add an ending.**
You are going to sound out some of these words.

Put your finger on the first word.
Sound the first word out.
Ready. Signal. Student sounds out, *rrruuunnning*.
Yes, running.

Sound out the next word.
Ready. Signal.

Repeat for all of the words in the list.

Some words double the final consonant before adding an ending. These words sound out the doubled consonant as if it were a single one. The doubled consonant avoids having the word look like an example of a final **e** word and being miscalled.

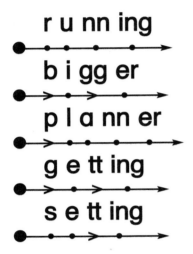

✓ **Correction Procedure**
If the student miscalls the word by making the first vowel long, cover up the ending and the 2nd consonant of the pair so that only the root word is visible. e.g. run[ning].
Say, **My turn. Sound out, rrruuunnn.**
Say that with me. Ready. Signal. Student sounds out, *rrruuunnn* with you.
Your turn to sound out run. Ready. Signal. Student sounds out, *rrruuunnn*.
Uncover the ending and the second consonant and say,
Now let's look at the whole word.
My turn. Listen. rrruuunnning.
Do that with me. Ready. Signal.
Your turn. Ready. Signal.
Say, **Now let's go back to the top of the list and start again.**

The key to success with this format is to learn the Correction Procedure well.

Fluency Checks

One of the major breakthroughs of Precision Teaching lies in its development of the concept of fluency. Fluency is that level to which a skill is learned so that it is performed almost automatically and is not lost during periods of non-use. Students learn at different rates. Some learn easily; some need more instruction and more practice. Fluency checks of sounds, words and stories are the quality control checks for each block of five Lessons. Unless students are fluent with the material in those Lessons, they will almost certainly have great difficulty with new work if they keep moving ahead in the program.

Students should be able to identify sounds quickly and easily. The fluent range is 50-60 sounds per minute. That means that they should be able to say one sound per second. Students should not do more than one sound per second because it will cause them not to hold the continuous sounds. Rushing will teach them to treat all sounds as short sounds. This will dramatically affect their blending skills.

Students are expected to read over 60 words in a list in a one-minute timing with no more than two errors.

Fluency in story reading is over 200 words per minute with fewer than three errors.

The scripted formats for Sound and Word Fluency Checks are practically identical. Once you learn one, the other is easy. The Story Reading Fluency Check format is slightly different. Samples of the Sound and Story Reading Fluency Check formats, plus an actual sample of one of the student's Sound Fluency Checks, follow on pages 26 and 27. They will help you to familiarize yourself with measuring a student's skills in this manner. All scores are entered into the Fluency Charts found in the Student Workbook. A sample of how scores are recorded on this chart is shown on page 28.

TASK 13: SOUND FLUENCY CHECK 1

Sample of a Sound Fluency Check

When teaching a group, do the Fluency Checks with one student at a time.

Students should be timed for 30 seconds. Saying sounds for longer periods is almost punishing.

Pay particular attention to this.

A skipped sound counts as a mistake. Mistakes are recorded as Learning Opportunities.

Keep these instructions consistent. Go! and Stop! tend to send kids into panic mode.

See sample of Sound Fluency Check on page 27.

Many students will want to keep trying to better their score. Encourage the extra practice but don't let them wear themselves out. Set a time limit for Fluency Checks and stick to it.

To be done with one student at a time.

Say to the student, **Turn to page 2 in your Reader.** Help student to find the correct page. **This is a list of all the sounds you have learned so far. I want to find out how well you know these sounds. I am going to time you for 30 seconds now to see how many of these sounds you can say correctly. We will practice this list for five Lessons. You must be able to say at least 25 sounds correctly in the 30-second time period. If you are unable to do this, I will reteach you the first five Lessons. Remember to hold each sound with a dot under it for one second. Remember not to hold the short sounds. They have an arrow under them. You will have 30 seconds to say as many sounds as you can. Try not to make mistakes. If you do not know a sound, go to the next one.**

You may go down the columns (indicate down) **or across** (indicate across). **Which way would you like to go in this list?** Student chooses down or across. **O.K., you are going to go (down** or **across).**

Remember, I will say please begin when you are to start and thank you when you are to stop.

Put your finger on the first sound.
Ready. Please begin. Time student for 30 seconds.
Say, **Thank you.**

Make a pencil mark in the list where the student ended. Determine the number of errors and/or skipped sounds. Subtract the number of errors from the total sounds said. Put a star to makr the total number of sounds the student said correctly on this attempt.

Say to student, **To know how many sounds you said in one minute, I will multiply your scores by 2 and we will record them in the back of your Workbook. This time you said (number) sounds per minute with (number) errors.**

Using a pencil, record sounds said correctly per minute in the Sounds Said Correctly column for Day 1 of Sound Fluency Check 1 on page 122 of the Student Workbook.

Record number of errors and/or skipped sounds per minute in the Learning Opportunities column.

If the student wants to do the task again, give him/her the opportunity to improve his/her score. Record the best score of the day as today's score.

Only sounds learned to this point in the program are included in the Check.

Fluency Checks are a part of every Lesson.

To be unable to say 25 sounds in 30 seconds indicates that the student has not mastered the material. Further instruction and review are imperative. Do NOT move on to the next Lesson.

Each student has his/her own learning style. Give him/her a choice here. However, once a choice is made, it must be done that way for each attempt at that particular Fluency Check.

Fluency scores are always recorded as a per-minute count.

See sample of Fluency Chart on page 28.

26

The Student Workbook

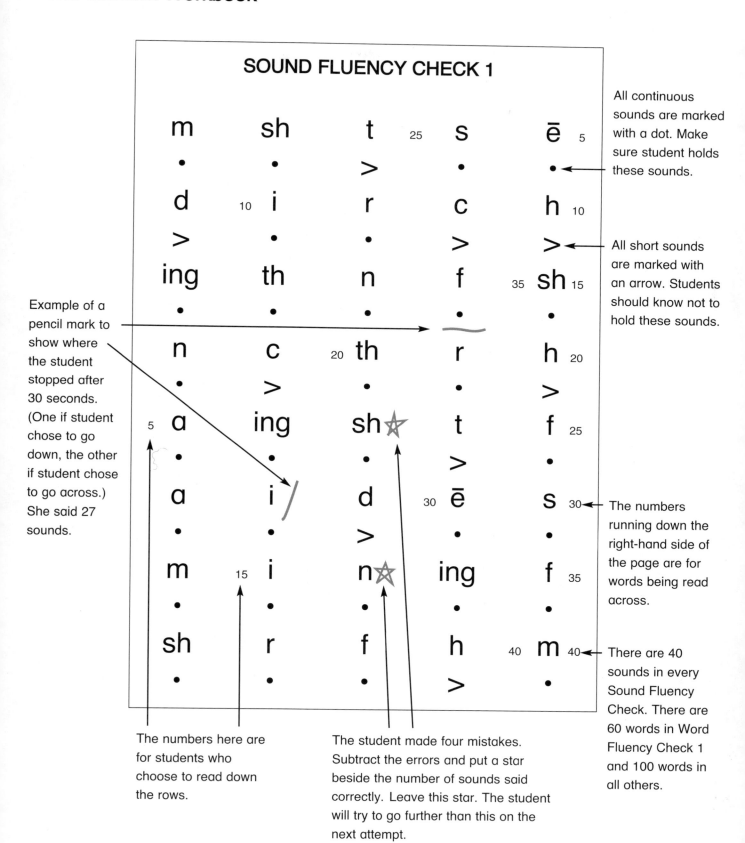

SOUND FLUENCY CHECK 1

All continuous sounds are marked with a dot. Make sure student holds these sounds.

All short sounds are marked with an arrow. Students should know not to hold these sounds.

Example of a pencil mark to show where the student stopped after 30 seconds. (One if student chose to go down, the other if student chose to go across.) She said 27 sounds.

The numbers running down the right-hand side of the page are for words being read across.

The numbers here are for students who choose to read down the rows.

The student made four mistakes. Subtract the errors and put a star beside the number of sounds said correctly. Leave this star. The student will try to go further than this on the next attempt.

There are 40 sounds in every Sound Fluency Check. There are 60 words in Word Fluency Check 1 and 100 words in all others.

Alphabet Letters Fluency Chart

Fluency Check ☞ 1
Number

Sound Fluency Chart

1 2 3 4 5

Find the Fluency Check that the student has been timed on.

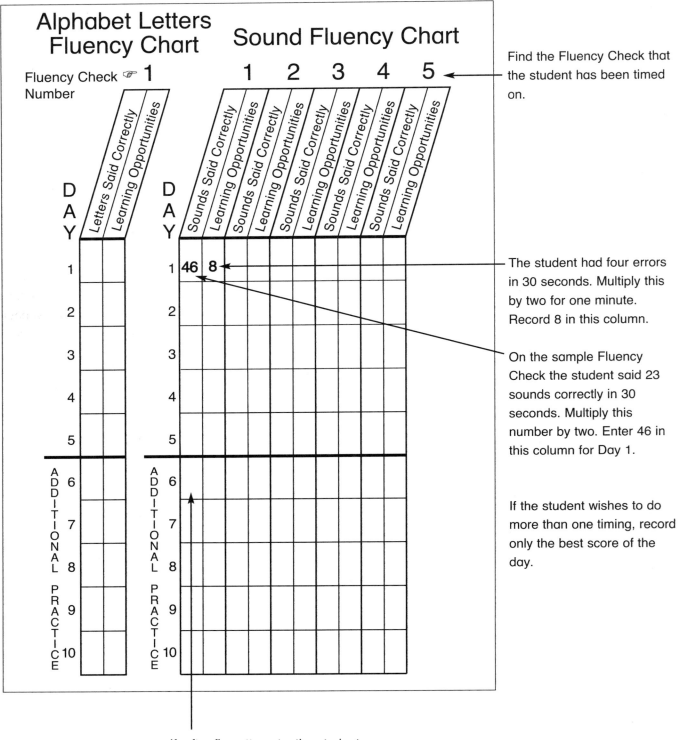

The student had four errors in 30 seconds. Multiply this by two for one minute. Record 8 in this column.

On the sample Fluency Check the student said 23 sounds correctly in 30 seconds. Multiply this number by two. Enter 46 in this column for Day 1.

If the student wishes to do more than one timing, record only the best score of the day.

If, after five attempts, the student has not yet reached fluency, review the previous five Lessons and enter scores for additional practice in these columns.

TASK 14: STORY READING FLUENCY CHECK

Work with one student at a time. Say, **Now we are going to do another kind of Fluency Check. This time you are going to read a story.**
After five days of practice you must be able to read at least 200 words correctly in a one-minute time period. If you are unable to do this, you will continue to practice each day until you can.
When I say please begin, you are going to start reading the story as quickly as you can. You will have one minute. When the time is up, I will say thank you.
Try not to make mistakes. If you do not know a word, skip it and continue reading.

Get set to read the title and then the story.
Ready. Please begin. Time student for 1 minute.
At the end of 1 minute say, **Thank you.**

Make a pencil mark where the student read to. Determine the number of errors and/or skipped words. Subtract the number of errors from the total words read. Put a star to mark the total number of words the student read correctly on this attempt.
Record words read correctly in the Words Read Correctly column for Day 1 of Story Reading Fluency Check 1 on page 124 of the Student Workbook.
Record errors and/or skipped words in the Learning Opportunities column.
As with the Word Fluency Check allow the student the opportunity to do the task again to try to improve his/her score if s/he so chooses.

Each of these stories is different and includes words learned in the program up to that point.

Unlike the Sound and Word Fluency Checks, the number of words read in a story is timed for one minute.

Miscalled, skipped and/or added words are counted as errors.

The title is an important part of the story. Always have the student read it. It is counted in the total number of words.

Follow the same procedure to record scores as in the Sound and Word Fluency Checks.

If a student achieves fluency before five attempts, s/he should be timed on a story of his/her choice in the Student Reader. All stories there are also numbered.

The exercises in the Student Workbook practice the skills learned in each Lesson. Material from previous Lessons is also included to provide continual review. As with the Student Reader, the Workbook Exercises contain only material which has been previously taught. It is not assumed that a student begins this program with a prelearned skillset. Therefore, how to print letters is taught, as are numbers to twenty and letters of the alphabet.
The Workbook offers the student a wide range of activities. Many are fun and entertaining, as well as being valuable learning tools. Sounds are practiced by both printing and reading them. Sentences or stories from the Lesson are reviewed

with a variety of questions. Regular and irregular words are also practiced in puzzles, riddles and mazes. There are even a few drawing and coloring exercises which most young students enjoy. In all, there are approximately 20 different Workbook Exercise formats. Most of them reoccur often throughout the 60 Lessons. These formats are quite straightforward. You need only to read the instructions and monitor the student's responses. As with the Task formats in the Instructor's Manual, the Workbook formats become less detailed as you and the student become comfortable with them. Exercises found in the Workbook include:

1. Printing Sounds/Words
2. Circling and/or Crossing out Sounds, Vowels or Consonants
3. Matching Sounds and Words
4. Joining Dots/Numbers to Make a Picture
5. Unscrambling Letters to Make Words
6. Making New Words from the Letters in a Word
7. Practicing Numbers
8. Putting Letters and Words in Alphabetical Order
9. Vowel Power!
10. Rhyme Time!
11. Filling in the Blanks
12. Answering Questions on Sentences and Stories in the Reader
13. Practicing Rules
14. Word Search Puzzles
15. Crossword Puzzles
16. Drawing and Coloring Pictures
17. Solving Codes
18. Mazes

Praise and Points

Praise is a powerful reinforcer of many behaviors. It is critical to encourage the student's efforts and improvement. Praise should be as specific as possible so that it describes what the student did that pleased you. It is important to vary your praise statements. Using the same words over and over again weakens the effectiveness and can become tedious.

Ultimately we want the child's improved skills to be the reward for all the hard work s/he is doing. For some children the reading activities are rewarding enough to keep them engaged in learning. For others, however, intervening rewards may have to be provided. When students are working hard and are not yet competent readers, the incentive of collecting points to earn something special is a very good motivator. Points are like putting money into a bank account. They can be saved up and used to "buy" things the student might want.

The points system is optional. Whether or not to use it is a decision made by the instructor or parents or both. If you do choose to award points, tell the student, before you begin the program, that points will be awarded for working hard, paying attention, following instructions, completing Workbook Exercises and doing well on Fluency Checks. Then determine what the points can be used for. One option is to make up a menu and allow the students to select from it. The menu should include suggestions from the student and should pay reasonably well for hard work insofar as the parent can afford it. Students need to know the value of items. For smaller things a penny-a-point seems to work well. Determining equivalent points for larger items or ones without monetary value is left up to the parent's discretion. Examples of rewards that could be "purchased" with earned points include: a special event (visit to a restaurant or museum, bowling or a camping trip to name just a few), renting a video, treats (chocolate bars, Lifesavers, pizza), cards, inexpensive toys or even the privilege of staying up later, having a sleepover or extra time on the computer. For nutritional and health reasons some people might not wish to use food items. Every situation is different in terms of family values and practices. Parents have to determine what kinds of rewards they are willing to make available.

Points are awarded at the end of every Lesson. There is a Points Chart after the exercises of each Lesson in the Student Workbook. After the student has completed the Lesson, determine and circle the number of points earned in each category. Add the scores and enter the total for that Lesson on the chart provided on page 125 of Workbook Level 1A and page 141 of Workbook Level 1B. A sample of this chart and how to use it is illustrated below.

Points Chart ~ Lessons 1 - 30

LESSON	Points Earned	Running Total	Points Spent	Balance	LESSON	Points Earned	Running Total	Points Spent	Balance
1	30	30	0	30	16				
2	29	59	0	59	17				
3	34	93	0	93	18				
4	40	133	0	133	19				
5	39	172	125	47	20				
6					21				
7					22				
8					23				
9					24				
10					25				
11					26				
12					27				
13					28				
14					29				
15					30				

Pace of the Lesson

The pace at which the teaching occurs is a major factor in how students learn. Too slow a pace allows student's attention to wander, creates boredom, disinterest and even behavior problems. Too fast a pace forces students into errors that they would not usually make. A proper pace keeps the student engaged and attentive without forcing them into unnecessary mistakes. Presentations should be made at a pace with which the weakest student in the group is able to do each format competely and correctly.

Each Lesson is designed to take approximately 30 to 60 minutes to complete. If for some reason the student is having difficulty in finishing the material within this time frame, take a break and continue later. Spending too much time on the same Task will only create fatigue and frustration for the student.

Getting started

All families have busy lives but it is important to try to establish a consistent schedule for teaching the student to read. As much as it is possible, try to sit down with the student at the same time each day, preferably before one of his/her favorite activities. This will motivate him/her to do the work quickly and well.

Most people like consistent and familiar places. If possible the learning setting should have its own specific location. Remove or minimize as many sources of distraction as possible to assist the student to do his/her best.

You should now be all set to begin Level 1B of *Teach Your Children to Read Well.*

REVIEW LESSON

- Say to the student, **We have completed the first 30 Lessons of Level 1. You have become a very good reader.**
- **Now we are going to begin the next 30 Lessons.**
- **Before we start Lesson 31 we are going to do some Fluency Checks which will review some sounds and words that you already know.**

TASK 1: SOUND FLUENCY CHECK 6

- Say, **Turn to page 1 in your Reader. There is a list of sounds from Lessons 1 to 30.**
- **You are going to say these sounds as quickly as you can, remembering to hold the sounds with the dots under them for one second.**
- **Which way would you like to do this list?** Student chooses down or across.

- **Put your finger on the first sound.**
- **Ready. Please begin.** Time student for 30 seconds.
- Say, **Thank you.**

- Record sounds said correctly per minute in the Sounds Said Correctly column for Day 1 of Sound Fluency Check 6 on page 138 of the Workbook.
- Record number of errors and/or skipped sounds per minute in the Learning Opportunities column.

TASK 2: WORD FLUENCY CHECK 6

- **Now let's do a Word Fluency Check. On page 2 there is a list of words found in Lessons 1 to 30.**
- **You are going to read these words as quickly as you can. Which way would**

you like to read this list? Student chooses down or across.

- **Put your finger on the first word.**
- **Ready. Please begin.** Time student for 30 seconds.
- Say, **Thank you.**

- Record words read correctly per minute in the Words Read Correctly column for Day 1 of Word Fluency Check 6 on page 139 of the Workbook.
- Record number of errors and/or skipped sounds per minute in the Learning Opportunities column.

TASK 3: STORY READING FLUENCY CHECK 5

- Say, **Now we are going to do a Story Reading Fluency Check. Turn to page 3 in your Reader.**

- **Put your finger on the title. Get set to read the story.**
- **Ready. Please begin.** Time student for 1 minute.
- At the end of 1 minute say, **Thank you.**

- Record words read correctly per minute in the Words Read Correctly column for Day 1 of Story Reading Fluency Check 5 on page 140 of the Workbook.
- Record number of errors and/or skipped sounds per minute in the Learning Opportunities column.

End of Review Lesson

INSTRUCTOR'S MANUAL
LESSON 31

TASK 1: PRACTICING THE FINAL e RULE

- Point to the list of words below and say to the student, **You're going to read this list of words for me.**

- **First word.**
- **Ready.** Signal. Student reads, *cut*.

- **Now read the rest of the words in the list.**
- **Ready.** Signal.

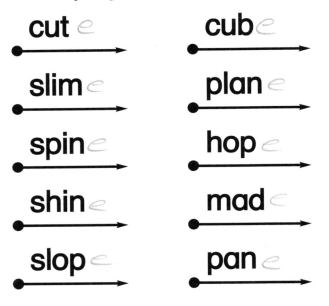

cut e   cube

slim e   plan e

spin e   hop e

shin e   mad e

slop e   pan e

- With a pencil add an e to the end of each of the words in the list.

- Say, **Now read these words all by yourself.**
- **Ready.** Signal.

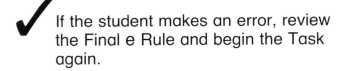

✓ If the student makes an error, review the Final e Rule and begin the Task again.

TASK 2: READING WORDS

- Now you are going to read some words. Some of these words will follow the Final e Rule, some will not.

- Put your finger on the first word.
- **What's that word?**
- **Ready.** Signal.

- Repeat for each word in the list.

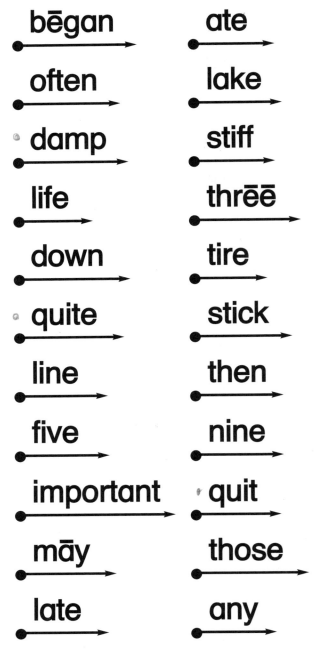

bēgan   ate

often   lake

damp   stiff

life   thrēē

down   tire

quite   stick

line   then

five   nine

important   quit

māy   those

late   any

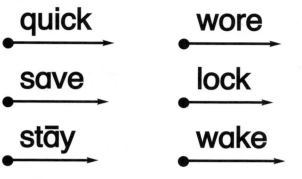

quick →   wore →

save →   lock →

stāy →   wake →

✓ If the student makes an error where the Final e Rule applies, use the Final e correction procedure as in previous Lessons.
For other words, use the model, lead, test correction procedure and begin the row again.

TASK 3: PRACTICING IRREGULAR WORDS

- You are going to read some irregular words you have already learned.

- **Read the first word and spell it.**
- **Ready.** Signal.

- Repeat for each word.

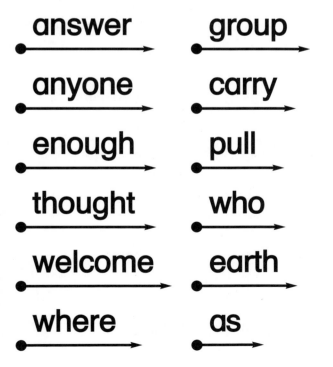

answer →   group →

anyone →   carry →

enough →   pull →

thought →   who →

welcome →   earth →

where →   as →

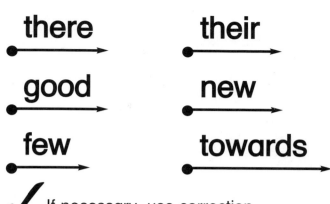

there →   their →

good →   new →

few →   towards →

✓ If necessary, use correction procedure from previous Lessons.

TASK 4: TEACHING IRREGULAR WORDS

- Say, **Here are some new irregular words. First I will read the word, then you will read the word and spell it.**

- Listen. The first word is **country**.
- **What word?**
- **Ready.** Signal.
- **Yes, country.**

- **Spell country.**
- **Ready.** Signal.

- Repeat for each word.

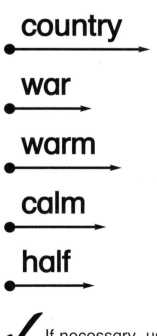

country →

war →

warm →

calm →

half →

✓ If necessary, use correction procedure from previous Lessons.

TASK 5: READING SENTENCES

- **Now you are going to read some sentences made up of words that you know.**
- **Turn to Lesson 31 on page 6 in your Reader.** Check.

- **Read the first sentence.**
- **Ready.** Signal.

- Repeat for each sentence in the exercise.

1. The paper plane began to spin and fall down.
2. Turn the cube when it is time.
3. The damp cub went into the pond.
4. Often the three cubs left and ran up the slope.
5. We play the game and hope to win the gold.
6. A quick plan can cut the cost.
7. Quit jumping along with that stiff stick.
8. The spine is important to keep your back stiff.
9. That cute girl is slim.
10. Then he got mad when the slop fell.
11. Is he an important person?
12. Do not catch the little ball.
13. After she left, we felt sad and down.

 If necessary, use correction procedure as in previous Lessons.

TASK 6: SOUND FLUENCY CHECK 6

- **Time for another Sound Fluency Check. Turn to page 1 in your Reader.**
- **In this list you are reading (down or across). Let's see if you can say more than you did the last time.**

- **Finger on the first sound.**
- **Ready. Please begin.** Time student for 30 seconds.
- **Thank you.**

- Record sounds said correctly per minute in the Sounds Said Correctly column for Day 2 of Sound Fluency Check 6 on page 138 of the Workbook.
- Record number of errors and/or skipped words per minute in the Learning Opportunities column.

TASK 7: WORD FLUENCY CHECK 6

- **Time for another Word Fluency Check. Turn to page 2.**
- **In this list you are reading (down or across). Let's see if you can read more than you did the last time.**

- **Finger on the first word.**
- **Ready. Please begin.** Time student for 30 seconds.
- **Thank you.**

- Record words read correctly per minute in the Words Read Correctly column for Day 2 of Word Fluency Check 6 on page 139 of the Workbook.
- Record number of errors and/or skipped words per minute in the Learning Opportunities column.

TASK 8: STORY READING FLUENCY CHECK 5

- Say to the student, **We are now going to do our second Story Reading Fluency Check. Turn to page 3 in your Reader.**
- **Remember to read as quickly as you can without making mistakes.**

- **Put your finger on the title. Get set to read.**
- **Ready. Please begin.** Time student for 1 minute.

- At the end of 1 minute say, **Thank you.**

- Determine and mark the words read correctly with a star.
- Record the number of words read correctly in the Words Read Correctly column for Day 2 of Story Reading Fluency Check 5 on page 140 of the Workbook.
- Record errors and/or skipped words in the Learning Opportunities column.

TASK 9: WORKBOOK EXERCISES

- Say, **Now we are going to do the Workbook part of the Lesson.**
- **Open your Workbook to Lesson 31 on page 1.**

Exercise 1: Practicing the Final e Rule

- **Find Exercise 1. In this exercise you are going to practice the Final e Rule.**
- **Read the list of words in Column A** (point to words).
- **Ready.** Signal. Student reads from hug to at.
- **Good. Take your pencil and add an e to each word. Now read the words.**
- **Join each word in the first list with its matching word in the second list.**
- When the student has joined each word have him/her read both words to make sure they are the same.

Exercise 2: Printing Words

- **In Exercise 2 you are going to print some words in the blanks. These words will be the opposite of the word in Column A. The words you will use are in the box** (point to box).
- **Remember, opposite means completely different. The first word is stop. Go is the opposite of the word stop. Number 1 is done for you.**

- **Look at number 2. The word is ask. What six-letter word in the box is the opposite of the word ask?**
- **That's right, answer. Print answer in the blanks. Check it off in the box.**
- **Repeat for each word.**
- Then say, **Now print the circled letters in the blanks to find out what you call a hole in the ground. What's that word?**
- **Ready.** Signal. Student says, *a well.*
- **Good work!**

Exercise 3: Filling in the Blanks

- **Find Exercise 3. Here you see some pictures. There are blanks beside each picture. You must fill in the blanks to print the word which matches the picture. The words you will use are in the cloud.**
- **Look at the first picture. What is it?**
- **Ready.** Signal. Student says, *a plane.*
- **Good! Now find the word plane in the cloud. Print the word plane in the blanks under the picture of the plane.** Check.
- Repeat for the rest of the pictures.
- **Now read each word. Circle any vowel that says its name.**

Exercise 4: Completing Various Tasks on Sentences from the Reader

- **In Exercise 4 you need your Reader. Find the sentences in Lesson 31 on page 6.**
- **Read the first sentence in your Workbook. Cross out any word that begins with a short sound or short sound combination.** Check.
- **Read sentence 2. Fill in the blanks with the correct words from your Reader.** Check.
- **Read sentence 3. Fill in the blank with the correct word from your Reader.** Check.
- **Read sentence 4. Fill in the blanks with**

the correct words from your Reader.
Check.

- Read sentence 5. Circle the vowels that say their name. Check.
- Read sentence 6. Fill in the blanks with the correct words from your Reader. Check.
- Read sentence 7. Circle all the sound combinations in this sentence. Check.
- Read sentence 8. Cross out any word that ends in a short sound or a short sound combination. Check.
- Read sentence 9. Fill in the blanks with the correct words from your Reader. Check.
- Read sentence 10. You are going to circle all the vowels. Check.
- Read sentence 11. Fill in the blank with the correct word from your Reader. Check.
- Read sentence 12. Cross out all the short sounds or short sound combinations in this sentence. Check.
- Read the last sentence, number 13. Circle the two words that have the same letters in them. Check.

Exercise 5: Word Search Puzzle

- Find Exercise 5. It's a word search puzzle.
- In this puzzle words can go across, up, down or backwards. The fingers beside the words tell you what direction those words go in the puzzle. Read the first word in the list of words that you will be looking for.
- **Ready.** Signal. Student reads, *quick.*
- Look in the puzzle. Go through each row until you find the letters q-u-i-c-k going across.
- That's right. Draw a circle around the word **quick**. Put a check mark beside the word **quick** in the list so that you know you have found it.
- If the student is having problems finding the word, repeat steps above for each

word in the list. If s/he can do the puzzle independently, allow him/her to do so.

```
TASK 10:
AWARDING POINTS
```

- Determine and circle the number of points the student has earned in each category.
- Record the total points for Lesson 31 on page 141 of the Workbook.

End of Lesson 31

LESSON 32

- Now let's see if you can remember all of the sounds you have learned.
- Say the sound when I touch it. If you make a mistake, we will practice that sound and then do the row again.

- What's the first sound?
- Ready. Signal.

- Repeat for each sound in the list.

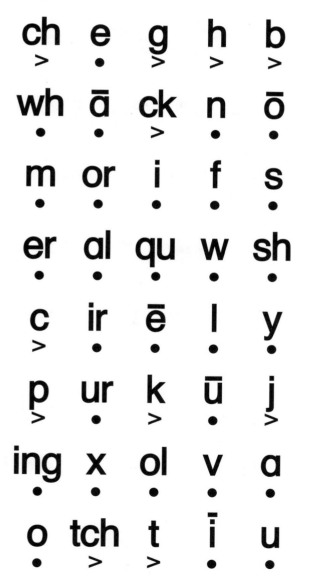

th   d   r

✓ If any error occurs, use correction procedure (my turn, do it with me, your turn) as in previous Lessons and repeat the row.

TASK 2: SOUNDING OUT WORDS

- Now you are going to sound out some words. As I touch the sounds, you say them.

- First word.
- Ready. Signal. Student sounds out word.

- Good work. What's that word?
- Ready. Signal.

- Repeat for each word in the list.

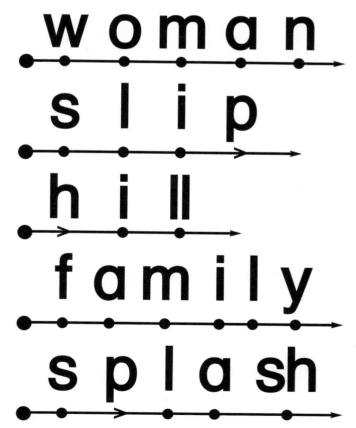

woman

slip

hill

family

splash

39

t o p

s t ēēp

e v er y

sh i p

n e v er

s u dd e n

al m ōs t

s t e p

TASK 3: READING WORDS

- Turn to TASK 2 in this Lesson. Say,
  **Now you are going to practice reading
  the words you sounded out.**

- **First word.**
- **Ready.** Signal. Student reads word.

- Repeat for each word in list.

TASK 4: SAYING THE UNDERLINED SOUNDS AND READING THE WORDS

- Touch the underlined sound in the first
  word.
- Say, **Tell me the underlined sound.**
- **Ready.** Signal.

- **Now tell me the word.**
- **Ready.** Signal.

- Repeat for each of the words in the list.

tru<u>ck</u>	<u>w</u>ent	t<u>a</u>ke
<u>d</u>own	<u>b</u>ōth	r<u>e</u>d
ba<u>ck</u>	fish<u>ing</u>	m<u>a</u>d
m<u>a</u>de	st<u>or</u>e	<u>th</u>en
h<u>o</u>me	<u>sh</u>ore	p<u>o</u>nd
w<u>o</u>ke	<u>up</u>	th<u>o</u>se

wh̲ip   **st̲ate**   **su̲c̲h̲**

ru̲sh   **anyt̲hing**   **c̲h̲eck**

 Use correction procedure (my turn, do it with me, your turn) as in previous Lessons if student makes an error.

TASK 5: READING WORDS

- Turn to TASK 4. Say, **Now we are going to read these words.**
- **First word.**
- **Ready.** Signal.

- Repeat for each word in the list.

 If the student makes an error reading a word, use the correction procedure as in previous Lessons.

TASK 6: STORY READING

- **Now you are going to read a short story.**
- **Turn to Lesson 32 on page 7 in your Reader.**

- **Put your finger on the title.**
- **Read the title please.**
- **Ready.** Signal.

- **Now read the story.**
- **Ready.** Signal.

<u>The big truck</u>

A big red and green truck went up a hill.
The hill was steep.
The truck just made it to the top of the hill.
But then it slid back down the steep hill.
It went splash into a pond.
A woman was fishing at the shore of the pond.

The woman who was fishing got mad at the man in the truck.
She made the truck man take her to the fish store to get some fish.
Then they both went home.
The end

 Use correction procedure as in previous Lessons if necessary.

TASK 7: SOUND FLUENCY CHECK 6

- **Time for another Sound Fluency Check. Turn to page 1 in your Reader.**
- **In this list you are going (down** or **across). Let's see if you can say more than you did the last time.**

- **Finger on the first sound.**
- **Ready. Please begin.** Time student for 30 seconds.
- **Thank you.**

- Record sounds said correctly per minute in the Sounds Said Correctly column for Day 3 of Sound Fluency Check 6 on page 138 of the Workbook.
- Record number of errors and/or skipped sounds per minute in the Learning Opportunities column.

TASK 8: WORD FLUENCY CHECK 6

- **Time for another Word Fluency Check. Turn to page 2.**
- **In this list you are reading (down** or **across). Let's see if you can read more than you did the last time.**

- **Finger on the first word.**
- **Ready. Please begin.** Time student for 30 seconds.
- **Thank you.**

- Record words read correctly per minute in the Words Read Correctly column for

Day 3 of Word Fluency Check 6 on page 139 of the Workbook.

- Record number of errors and/or skipped words per minute in the Learning Opportunities column.

TASK 9: STORY READING FLUENCY CHECK 5

- **Time for another Story Reading Check. Turn to page 3 in your Reader.**

- **Put your finger on the title. Get set to read.**
- **Ready. Please begin.** Time student for 1 minute.
- At the end of 1 minute say, **Thank you.**

- Record the number of words read correctly in the Words Read Correctly column for Day 3 of Story Reading Fluency Check 5 on page 140 of the Workbook.
- Record errors and/or skipped words in the Learning Opportunities column.

TASK 10: WORKBOOK EXERCISES

- Say, **Now we are going to do the Workbook part of the Lesson.**
- **Open your Workbook to Lesson 32 on page 5.**

Exercise 1: Practicing the Final e Rule

- **Find Exercise 1. In this exercise you are going to practice the Final e Rule. You are going to print the words which follow the Final e Rule in this box** (point to box on the left) **and the words which do not follow the Final e Rule in this box** (point to box on the right).
- **Read the first word.**
- **Ready.** Signal. Student reads, *rob.*
- **Does rob follow the Final e Rule?**

- **Ready.** Signal. Student says, *no.*
- **You're right. So print rob in this box** (point to box on the right). Check.
- Repeat for each word in the list.

Exercise 2: Filling in the Blanks

- **You need your Reader for Exercise 2. Turn to Lesson 32 on page 7 of your Reader.**
- **You are going to fill in the blanks in Exercise 2 with the correct word from the story** <u>The big truck</u>.
- **Read the first sentence in your Workbook.**
- **Ready.** Signal.
- **Find the correct word that completes that sentence and print that word in the blank.** Check. **Now read the whole sentence.**
- Repeat for each sentence.

Exercise 3: Making New Words

- **Find Exercise 3. You are going to make some new words by changing one letter at a time. The list has been started for you. Read those words.**
- **Ready.** Signal. Student reads, *wet, pet, pot, not.*
- **What letter can you change in the word not to make a new word?**
- **Good! Print that word on the line under not.** Check.
- Monitor the student as s/he prints new words. Be ready to make some suggestions.

Exercise 4: Solving Codes to Answer a Riddle

- **Let's look at Exercise 4. You are going to solve a code to answer a riddle. Read the riddle.**
- **Ready.** Signal. Student reads, *What do you get if your dog falls into a pond?*

- Let's figure out the sound that goes in each set of words. Have the student read the words in each box, then print the missing sounds in each shape.
- Good! You have figured out what each shape's sound is. Now solve the code to answer the riddle by printing the correct letter in the blanks below.
- So what do you get if your dog falls into a pond?
- That's right! A wet pet!

Exercise 5: Using Instructions to Draw and Color a Picture

- Now let's look at Exercise 5. Read the first sentence.
- **Ready.** Signal. Student reads, *The truck is green.*
- What colour will the truck be?
- **Ready.** Signal. Student says, *green.*
- That's correct. Color the truck green.
- Have the student read each sentence and then draw or color each part of the picture.

TASK 11: AWARDING POINTS

- Determine and circle the number of points the student has earned in each category.
- Record the total points for Lesson 32 on page 141 of the Workbook.

End of Lesson 32

LESSON 33

TASK 1: SOUNDING OUT WORDS

- Now you are going to sound out some words. As I touch the sounds, you say them.

- First word.
- **Ready.** Signal. Student sounds out word.

- Good work. What's that word?
- **Ready.** Signal.

- Repeat for each word in the list.

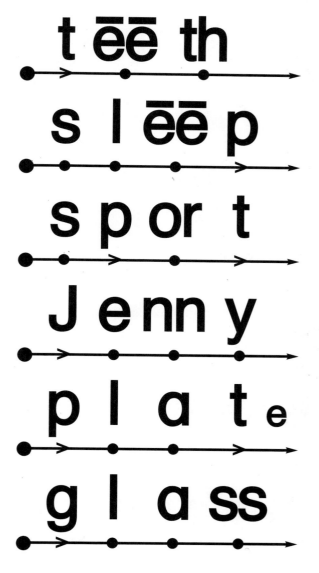

43

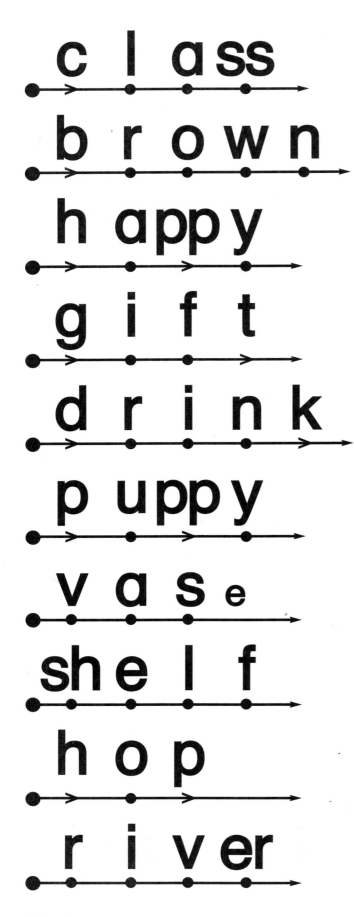

class

brown

happy

gift

drink

puppy

vase

shelf

hop

river

vest

torn

cup

several

✓ If any error occurs, use correction procedure (my turn, do it with me, your turn) as in previous Lessons.

TASK 2:
READING WORDS

• Turn to TASK 1 in this Lesson. Say, **Now you are going to practice reading the words you sounded out.**

• **First word.**
• **Ready.** Signal. Student reads word.

• Repeat for each word in list.

✓ If necessary, use correction procedure (my turn, do it with me, your turn) as in previous Lessons.

TASK 3: SAYING THE UNDERLINED SOUNDS AND READING THE WORDS

• **Now we are going to read some words that have the sound combination e-r, i-r or u-r.**

- First word.
- What sound?
- Ready. Signal.

- What's the word?
- Ready. Signal.

- Repeat for each word in the list.

p<u>er</u>son	d<u>ir</u>t
stick<u>er</u>	ch<u>ur</u>ch
aft<u>er</u>	diff<u>er</u>ent
lett<u>er</u>	f<u>ur</u>
mist<u>er</u>	f<u>ir</u>st
numb<u>er</u>	st<u>ir</u>
s<u>er</u>ve	th<u>ir</u>d
<u>u</u>nd<u>er</u>	wint<u>er</u>
t<u>ur</u>n	ent<u>er</u>
h<u>er</u>	b<u>ir</u>th

✓ If the student makes an error reading a word, use the correction procedure as in previous Lessons.

TASK 4: READING RHYMING WORDS

- **Now you are going to read some words that rhyme with lake.**
- **Touch the dot in front of the word lake.** Slide your finger along the line and say **lake**.

- What's that word?
- Ready. Signal.

- All the words rhyme with lake.

- Look at the next word.
- What's that word?
- Ready. Signal.

- Repeat for each word in the list.

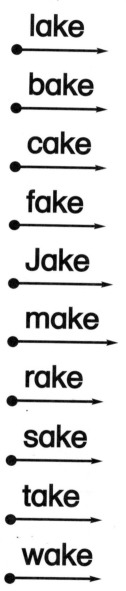

lake
bake
cake
fake
Jake
make
rake
sake
take
wake

✓ Use correction procedure as in previous Lessons if student makes an error.

- **Now you are going to read some words you have learned before.**
- **First word.**
- **Ready.** Signal.

- Repeat for each word in the list.

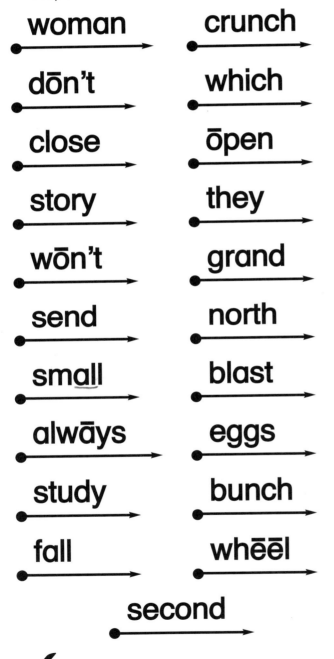

woman

dōn't

close

story

wōn't

send

small

alwāys

study

fall

crunch

which

ōpen

they

grand

north

blast

eggs

bunch

whēēl

second

✓ If the student makes an error reading a word, use the correction procedure as in previous Lessons.

NOTE: If the student has said 50+ sounds correctly in 1 minute for three consecutive days, s/he may discontinue timings on Sound Fluency Check 6 if s/he so chooses.

- If not, say, **Time for a Sound Fluency Check. Turn to page 1 in your Reader.**
- **In this list you are going (down** or **across).**

- **Finger on the first sound.**
- **Ready. Please begin.** Time student for 30 seconds.
- **Thank you.**

- Record sounds said correctly per minute in the Sounds Said Correctly column for Day 4 of Sound Fluency Check 6 on page 138 of the Workbook.
- Record number of errors and/or skipped sounds per minute in the Learning Opportunities column.

NOTE: If the student has read 60+ words correctly in 1 minute for three consecutive days, s/he may discontinue timings on Word Fluency Check 6 if s/he so chooses.

- If not, say, **Time for a Word Fluency Check. Turn to page 2.**
- **In this list you are reading (down** or **across).**

- **Finger on the first word.**
- **Ready. Please begin.** Time student for 30 seconds.
- **Thank you.**

- Record words read correctly per minute in the Words Read Correctly column for

Day 4 of Word Fluency Check 6 on page 139 of the Workbook.
- Record number of errors and/or skipped words per minute in the Learning Opportunities column.

TASK 8: STORY READING FLUENCY CHECK 5

NOTE: If the student has read 200+ words per minute in the story three consecutive times, s/he has reached fluency and does not need to try again on this Lesson unless s/he chooses to do so. Have the student do a one-minute timing on the story The big truck on page 7 of the Reader.

- If the student has not yet reached fluency, say, **Time for another Story Reading Fluency Check. Turn to page 3 in your Reader. Let's see if you can read more words than you did the last time.**

- **Put your finger on the title and get set to read the story.**
- **Ready. Please begin.** Time student for one minute.
- Say, **Thank you.**

- Record the number of words read correctly in the Words Read Correctly column for Day 4 of Story Reading Fluency Check 5 on page 140 of the Workbook.
- Record errors and/or skipped words in the Learning Opportunities column.

TASK 9: WORKBOOK EXERCISES

- Say, **Now we are going to do the Workbook part of the Lesson.**
- **Open your Workbook to Lesson 33 on page 9.**

Exercise 1: Filling in the Blanks

- In Exercise 1 you see some pictures. There are blanks in the words under each picture. You must fill in the blanks with some double letters to print the word which matches the picture.
- **Look at the first picture. What is it?**
- **Ready.** Signal. Student says, teeth.
- **Good! Sound out the word teeth. What double letters will you print in the blanks to complete the word teeth?**
- **That's right, e-e. Print those letters in the blanks.** Check.
- Repeat for the rest of the pictures.

Exercise 2: Putting Words in Alphabetical Order

- Find Exercise 2. In this exercise you are going to print some words in alphabetical order. **First say the alphabet.**
- **Ready.** Signal.
- **Now read the words.**
- **Ready.** Signal. Student reads from mine to enter.
- **You must look at the first letter in each word. What first letter in these words** (point to list) **comes first in the alphabet?**
- **Ready.** Signal. Student answers, came.
- **That's right! Print came in the blanks. Put a check mark beside it.**
- **What is the word with a first letter that comes next in the alphabet?**
- **Ready.** Signal. Student says, enter.
- **Well done. Print enter on the second set of blanks.** Check.
- Repeat for the rest of the words. When the student has finished doing all seven of them, say, **Good work! You just put those seven words in alphabetical order.**

Exercise 3: Answering a Riddle

- Put your finger on Exercise 3. It's a riddle. You are going to print the letters that are circled in Exercise 2 to find out who the Mississippi River is married to. Check as the student prints the circled letters in the blanks.
- So who is the Mississippi River married to?
- That's right, Mr. Sippi!

Exercise 4: Following a Maze

- Find Exercise 4. Read the question.
- Ready. Signal. Student reads, *What is another word for little kids?*
- Good reading! You are going to take each letter through the maze to a box below. The unscrambled letters will spell the answer to that question.
- Put your pencil on the first letter. Follow this letter's path to the end. Check that the student is following the correct path.
- Now print that letter on the line in the box.
- Repeat for each letter.
- So what is another word for little kids?
- That's correct, children.

Exercise 5: Printing Words

- Look at the next page for Exercise 5. You have to print some words that have the sound rrr in them. The words are inside the frame. Read those words.
- Ready. Signal. Student reads the 15 words inside the frame.
- Touch the first word you need to print. This word has three letters and ends in e-r. The clue beside this word says, not him. Look in the word list and find a three-letter word with e-r at the end that means not him. What word did you find?
- Ready. Signal. Student says, *her.*

- Right. Print h in the box for the first word. Put a check mark beside the word her so that you know you have used it.
- Repeat for each word.

Exercise 6: Word Search Puzzle

- Find Exercise 6. It's a word search puzzle.
- In this puzzle all the words rhyme with take. The words can go across, up and down or backwards.
- Read the first word in the list of words that you will be looking for.
- Ready. Signal. Student reads, *bake.*
- The arrow beside the word tells you whether the word goes across, up, down or backwards. Bake goes across. Look in the puzzle. Go through each row until you find the letters b-a-k-e.
- That's right. Draw a circle around the word bake.
- Put a check mark beside the word bake in the list so that you know you have found it.
- If the student is having problems finding the word, repeat steps above for each word in the list. If s/he can do the puzzle independently, allow him/her to do so.

TASK 10: AWARDING POINTS

- Determine and circle the number of points the student has earned in each category.
- Record the total points for Lesson 33 on page 141 of the Workbook.

End of Lesson 33

LESSON 34

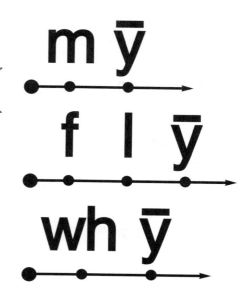

TASK 1: TEACHING THE SOUND ȳ as in my

- Today we're going to learn a new sound.
- **Listen.** Touch the dot under the ȳ and say iii for one second. Lift your finger.
- Repeat.

- **Say the sound with me.**
- **Ready.** Signal.
- Repeat.

- **Your turn.**
- **Ready.** Signal.
- Repeat the task until the student does it as instructed.

✓ If any error occurs, use correction procedure (my turn, do it with me, your turn) as in previous Lessons.

TASK 2: PRACTICING THE SOUND ȳ

- Now you are going to sound out some words that have the sound you just learned. As I touch the sounds, you say them.

- **First word.**
- **Ready.** Signal. Student sounds out, *mmmiii.*

- **Good work. What's that word?**
- **Ready.** Signal.

- Repeat for each word in the list.

✓ If any error occurs, use correction procedure (my turn, do it with me, your turn) as in previous Lessons and begin the list again.

TASK 3: TEACHING THE SOUND Z as in zebra

- **Let's learn another new sound.**
- **Listen.** Touch the dot under the z and say **zzz** for one second. Lift your finger.
- Repeat.

- **Say the sound with me.**
- **Ready.** Signal.
- Repeat.

- **Your turn.**
- **Ready.** Signal.
- Repeat the task until the student does it as instructed.

z

✓ If any error occurs, use correction procedure (my turn, do it with me, your turn) as in previous Lessons.

- Now you are going to sound out some words that have the sound you just learned. As I touch the sounds, you say them.
- **First word.**
- **Ready.** Signal. Student sounds out word.

- **Good work. What's that word?**
- **Ready.** Signal.

- Repeat for each word in the list.

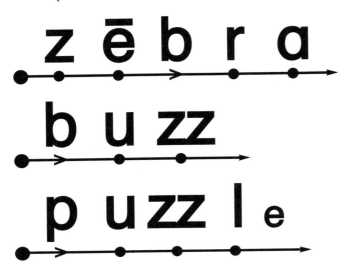

 If any error occurs, use correction procedure (my turn, do it with me, your turn) as in previous Lessons and begin the list again.

TASK 5: PRACTICING IRREGULAR WORDS

- You are going to read some irregular words you have already learned.

- **Read the first word and spell it.**
- **Ready.** Signal.

- Repeat for each word.

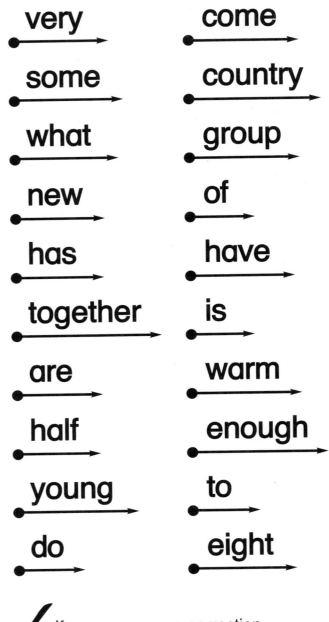

very → come →
some → country →
what → group →
new → of →
has → have →
together → is →
are → warm →
half → enough →
young → to →
do → eight →

✔ If necessary, use correction procedure from previous Lessons.

TASK 6: TEACHING IRREGULAR WORDS

- Say, **Here are some new irregular words. First I will read the word, then you will read the word and spell it.**

- **Listen. The first word is friend.**
- **What word?**
- **Ready.** Signal.
- **Yes, friend.**

- Spell friend.
- Ready. Signal.

- Repeat for each word.

friend

picture

quiet

today

 If necessary, use correction procedure from previous Lessons.

games	home
Jenny	children
licks	play
happy	asking
lots	day
puppy	cake
gifts	also
box	girl
say	bring

 Use correction procedure (my turn, do it with me, your turn) as in previous Lessons if student makes an error.

TASK 7: SAYING THE UNDERLINED SOUNDS AND READING THE WORDS

- Touch the underlined sound in the first word.
- Say, **Tell me the underlined sound.**
- **Ready.** Signal.

- **Now tell me the word.**
- **Ready.** Signal.

- **Next word. What sound?**
- **Ready.** Signal.

- **What word?**
- **Ready.** Signal.

- Repeat for each of the words in the list.

class   brown

fell   birthday

TASK 8: READING WORDS

- Point to words in TASK 7. Say, **Now you are going to read these words.**
- **First word.**
- **Ready.** Signal.

- Repeat for each word in the list.

 If the student makes an error reading a word, use the correction procedure as in previous Lessons.

TASK 9: STORY READING

- Now it's time to read a story. Turn to Lesson 34 on page 8 in your Reader.

- Put your finger on the title.
- Read the title please.
- **Ready.** Signal.

- Now read the story.
- **Ready.** Signal.

A birthday for Jenny

Today is Jenny's birthday.
She is asking eight friends from her class to come to her home.
They will play lots of games and have cake.
The children bring little gifts for Jenny.
One girl gives her a kite.
Another hands Jenny a big box.
Jenny opens the box.
She finds a puzzle.
There is a very big cake.
The children have lots of fun and make Jenny feel very happy.
For her birthday Jenny also gets a new puppy.
The puppy is brown and black and has big feet.
He licks all of the children.
Then the puppy licks some cake that fell from a dish.
Now the puppy is also happy.
                    The end of the story

 If the student has a problem with any word, have him/her sound it out, say it and then start at the beginning of that sentence again. If the student makes 7 errors, reread the story from the beginning.

TASK 10: SOUND FLUENCY CHECK 6

REMINDER: If the student has said 50+ sounds correctly in 1 minute for any three days of the last four, s/he may discontinue timings on Sound Fluency Check 6 if s/he so chooses.

- If not, say, **Time for a Sound Fluency Check. Turn to page 1 in your Reader.**
- **In this list you are going (down or across).**

- **Finger on the first sound.**
- **Ready. Please begin.** Time student for 30 seconds.
- **Thank you.**

- Record sounds said correctly per minute in the Sounds Said Correctly column for Day 5 of Sound Fluency Check 6 on page 138 of the Workbook.
- Record number of errors and/or skipped sounds per minute in the Learning Opportunities column.

REMINDER: If the student has been unable to say at least 50 sounds correctly per minute at least one time in Sound Fluency Check 6, finish and correct the Workbook Exercises for Lesson 34 but do not proceed to teach new material. Instead, reteach Lessons 31 through 34. Include daily practice and timings on Sound Fluency Check 6 on page 1. Circle and practice any sounds the student is having difficulty with. Record scores in the Additional Practice columns for Sound Fluency Check 6 on page 138 of the Student Workbook. Students should continue to be awarded points for working hard, paying attention, following instructions and doing well on fluency checks. When the student is able to say 50+ sounds from the list in 1 minute, begin Lesson 35.

TASK 11: WORD FLUENCY CHECK 6

REMINDER: If the student has read 60+ words correctly in 1 minute for any three days of the last four, s/he may discontinue timings on Word Fluency Check 6 if s/he so chooses.

- If not, say, **Time for a Word Fluency Check. Turn to page 2.**
- **In this list you are reading (down** or **across).**

- **Finger on the first word.**
- **Ready. Please begin.** Time student for 30 seconds.
- **Thank you.**

- Record words read correctly per minute in the Words Read Correctly column for Day 5 of Word Fluency Check 6 on page 139 of the Workbook.
- Record number of errors and/or skipped words per minute in the Learning Opportunities column.

REMINDER: If the student has been unable to read at least 60 words correctly in 1 minute at least one time in Word Fluency Check 6, finish the Workbook Exercises for Lesson 34 but do not proceed with new material. Instead, redo Lessons 31 through 34. Include daily practice and timings on Word Fluency Check 6 on page 2. Circle and practice any words the student is having difficulty with. Students should continue to be awarded points for working hard, paying attention, following instructions and doing well on fluency checks. When the student is able to read 60+ words from the list in 1 minute, continue in the Reader with Lesson 35.

TASK 12: STORY READING FLUENCY CHECK 5

REMINDER: If the student has read 200+ words per minute in the story for three of the last four attempts, s/he has reached fluency and does not need to try again on this Lesson unless s/he chooses to do so. Have the student do a timing on the story from Lessons 32 or 34.

- If the student has not yet reached fluency, say, **Time for another Story Reading Fluency Check. Turn to page 3 in your Reader. Let's see if you can read more words than you did the last time.**

- **Put your finger on the title and get set to read the story.**
- **Ready. Please begin.** Time student for one minute.
- Say, **Thank you.**

- Record the number of words read correctly in the Words Read Correctly column for Day 5 of Story Reading Fluency Check 5 on page 140 of the Workbook.
- Record errors and/or skipped words in the Learning Opportunities column.

NOTE: If the student has not yet reached fluency at 200+ words a minute in the same story on at least one timing, finish and correct the Workbook Exercises for Lesson 34, but do not proceed with new material. Instead, have the student practice reading the first half of the story until s/he can read it with fewer than 3 L.O.s in 30 seconds. Then practice the next half in the same manner. Combine the two sections and practice until the student can read them fluently in a minute. Record scores in the Additional Practice columns for Story Reading Fluency Check 5. Award points for working hard, paying attention, following instructions and doing well in fluency checks. When the student has reached fluency, begin Lesson 35.

- Open your Workbook to Lesson 34 on page 13.

Exercise 1: Matching Rhyming Words

- **Find Exercise 1 on your worksheet. It's a Rhyme Time! exercise. You are going to draw a line to match rhyming words.**
- **Read the first word.**
- **Ready.** Signal. Student reads, *to.*
- **Now touch the second group of words. Read the first word there.**
- **Ready.** Signal. Student reads, *mall.*
- **Does mall rhyme with to?**
- Repeat until student finds the correct rhyming word, do.
- **Good. Now draw a line to join the words to and do.**
- Repeat for the rest of the words in the list.

Exercise 2: Printing Sounds

- **In Exercise 2 you are going to practice printing the letter for the sound zzz.**
- Have the student use the ball and arrows to trace all six of the sound zzz.

Exercise 3: Filling in the Blanks

- **You need your Reader for Exercise 3. Turn to Lesson 34 on page 8 of your Reader.**
- **You are going to fill in the blanks in Exercise 3 with the correct word from the story <u>A birthday for Jenny</u>.**
- **Read the first sentence.**
- **Ready.** Signal.
- **Find the correct word that completes that sentence and print that word in the blanks.** Check. **Now read the whole sentence.**
- Repeat for each sentence.

Exercise 4: Vowel Power!

- **Now let's look at Exercise 4. It's a Vowel Power! exercise.**
- **Tell me the five vowel letters.**
- **Ready.** Signal. Student answers, *a, e, i, o and u.*
- **Right! Now you must fill in the blanks with one of those vowels to make a word that you know. The words are in the box beside the chef.**
- **Touch the first word. What vowel goes in that blank?**
- **Ready.** Signal. Student responds, *a.*
- **Yes, a. Print a in the blank.**
- **Now read that word.**
- **Ready.** Signal. Student reads, *catch.*
- Repeat for each word.

Exercise 5: Circling the Word that Doesn't Belong

- **In Exercise 5 each line has a list of four words. Three of the words have something the same. One word does not. You are going to circle the word in each sentence that doesn't belong.**
- **Finger on number 1. Read each of those words.**
- **Ready.** Signal. Student reads, *gas, green, drag, grim.*
- **Which of those words does not belong?**
- **Ready.** Signal. Student answers, *drag.*
- **That's right because all the other words begin with the short sound g and drag begins with the short sound d.**
- Repeat for numbers 2 to 6.
- If the student is having difficulty, give him/her a hint or tell him/her the answer and ask for the reason that that word does not belong.

Exercise 6: Answering a Riddle

- **Exercise 6 is a riddle. Read the riddle.**
- **Ready.** Signal. Student reads, *What do you get when you cross a bunny with a*

puppy?

- To answer the riddle you are going to print the letter that is in one word but not in another.
- Read number 1. What letter is in the word chop but not in cop?
- **Ready.** Signal. Student answers, *h*.
- Yes, **h**. Print an **h** in the first blank below.
- Repeat for numbers 2 to 6.
- **So what do you get when you cross a bunny with a puppy?**
- **A hop dog! Great work!**

TASK 14: AWARDING POINTS

- Record the total points for Lesson 34 on page 141 of the Workbook.

End of Lesson 34

LESSON 35

TASK 1: PRACTICING THE FINAL e RULE

- Point to the list of words below and say to the student, **You're going to read this list of words for me.**

- **First word.**
- **Ready.** Signal. Student reads, *pal*.

- **Now read the rest of the words in the list.**
- **Ready.** Signal.

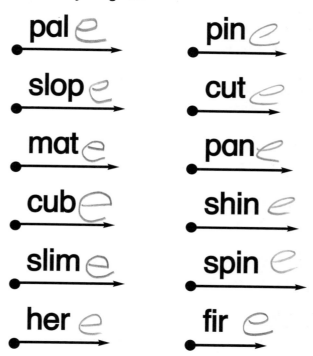

pal e   pin e

slop e   cut e

mat e   pan e

cub e   shin e

slim e   spin e

her e   fir e

- With a pencil add an **e** to the end of each of the words in the list.

- Say, **Now read these words all by yourself.**
- **Ready.** Signal.

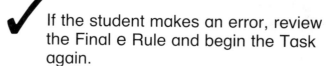 If the student makes an error, review the Final e Rule and begin the Task again.

- Now you are going to read some more words. Some of these words will follow the Final e Rule, some will not.

- Put your finger on the first word. Say, **What's the first word?**
- **Ready.** Signal.

- Repeat for each word in the list.

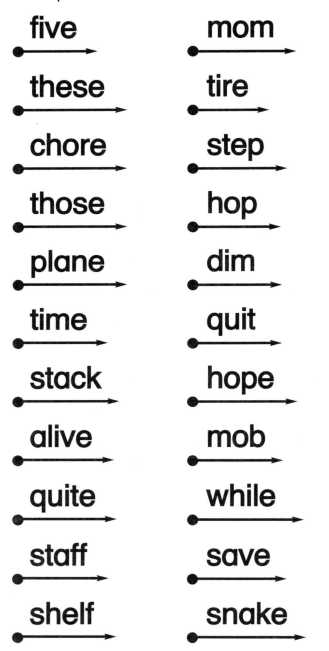

five →	mom →
these →	tire →
chore →	step →
those →	hop →
plane →	dim →
time →	quit →
stack →	hope →
alive →	mob →
quite →	while →
staff →	save →
shelf →	snake →

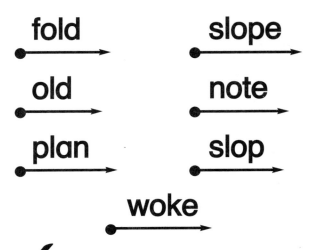

fold →	slope →
old →	note →
plan →	slop →
	woke →

✓ If the student makes an error where the Final e Rule applies, use the Final e correction procedure as in previous Lessons.
For other words, use the model, lead, test correction procedure and begin the row again.

╭──────────────────────────────╮
│ ***TASK 3: SOUNDING OUT**   │
│ **WORDS WITH DOUBLE**   │
│ **CONSONANTS**   │
╰──────────────────────────────╯

- Say, **In some words you must double the final consonant before you add an ending.**
- You are going to sound out some of these words.

- Put your finger on the first word. Say, **Sound out this word.**
- **Ready.** Signal. Student sounds out, *rrruuunnnning.*
- **Yes, running.**

- Repeat for all of the words in the list.

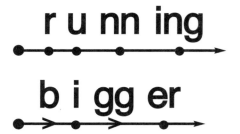

r u nn ing →

b i gg er →

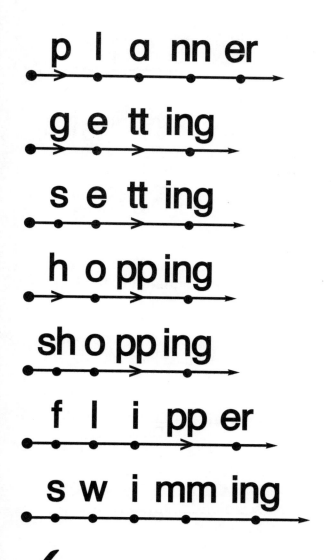

p l a nn er

g e tt ing

s e tt ing

h o pp ing

sh o pp ing

f l i pp er

s w i mm ing

 Correction Procedure
If the student miscalls the word by making the first vowel long, cover up the ending and the 2nd consonant of the pair so that only the root word is visible. e.g. run[ning].
Say, **My turn.** Sound out, **rrruuunnn.**
Say that with me. Ready. Signal.
Student sounds out, *rrruuunnn* with you.
Your turn to sound out run. Ready.
Signal. Student sounds out, *rrruuunnn.*
Uncover the ending and the second consonant and say, **Now let's look at the whole word.**
My turn. Listen. rrruuunnnning.
Do that with me. Ready. Signal.

Your turn. Ready. Signal.
Say, **Now let's go back to the top of the list and start again.**

> ### TASK 4: READING SENTENCES

- Now you are going to read some sentences to practice some of these words.
- Turn to Lesson 35 on page 10 in your Reader.

- **Read the first sentence.**
- **Ready.** Signal.

- Repeat for each sentence in the exercise.

1. Quit hopping with that long stick.
2. When we go swimming we use flippers.
3. Justin is shopping. He is getting a kit to make a kite.
4. The tape shows that Dave is bigger than Tom.
5. He is setting up the dish before he serves the fish.
6. The cute cub was running down the slope of the hill.

✓ For errors made in words with double consonants, use the correction procedure in TASK 3.
For all other words use the model, lead, test correction procedure.

> ### TASK 5: SOUND FLUENCY CHECK 7

- The student has said 50+ sounds per minute in Sound Fluency Check 6 on page 1. Say, **Turn to page 11 in your Reader. There is a list of sounds from Lessons 1 to 35.**
- You are going to say these sounds as quickly as you can, remembering to

hold the sounds with the dots under them for one second.

- **Which way would you like to do this list?** Student chooses down or across.

- **Put your finger on the first sound.**
- **Ready. Please begin.** Time student for 30 seconds.
- Say, **Thank you.**

- Record sounds said correctly per minute in the Sounds Said Correctly column for Day 1 of Sound Fluency Check 7 on page 138 of the Workbook.
- Record number of errors and/or skipped sounds per minute in the Learning Opportunities column.

TASK 6: WORD FLUENCY CHECK 7

- The student has read 60+ words per minute in Word Fluency Check 6 on page 2. Say, **On page 12 there is a list of words from Lessons 1 to 35.**
- **You are going to read these words as quickly as you can. Which way would you like to read this list?** Student chooses down or across.

- **Put your finger on the first word.**
- **Ready. Please begin.** Time student for 30 seconds.
- Say, **Thank you.**

- Record words read correctly per minute in the Words Read Correctly column for Day 1 of Word Fluency Check 7 on page 139 of the Workbook.
- Record number of errors and/or skipped words per minute in the Learning Opportunities column.

TASK 7: STORY READING FLUENCY CHECK 6

- The student has reached fluency (200+ words/minute) in Story Reading Fluency Check 5. Say, **Now we are going to do a new Story Reading Fluency Check. Turn to page 13 in your Reader.**

- **Put your finger on the title. Get set to read the story.**
- **Ready. Please begin.** Time student for 1 minute.
- At the end of 1 minute say, **Thank you.**

- Record the number of words read correctly in the Words Read Correctly column for Day 1 of Story Reading Fluency Check 6 on page 140 of the Workbook.
- Record errors and/or skipped words in the Learning Opportunities column.

TASK 8: WORKBOOK EXERCISES

- Say, **Now we are going to do the Workbook part of the Lesson.**
- **Open your Workbook to Lesson 35 on page 18.**

Exercise 1: Practicing the Final e Rule

- **Find Exercise 1. In this exercise you are going to practice the Final e Rule.**
- **Read the list of words.**
- **Ready.** Signal.
- **Good. Now take your pencil and add an e to each word.**
- **Now read the words.**
- **Circle all the vowels that say their name.** Check.

Exercise 2: Printing Sounds

- **In Exercise 2 you are going to practice printing the letter for the sound zzz.**

- Have the student use the ball and arrows to trace all six of the sound zzz.

Exercise 3: Crossing Out Vowels that Say their Name

- **Now let's do Exercise 3. You are going to read each word and then cross out any vowel that says its name.**
- **What's the first word?**
- **Ready.** Signal. Student says, *pal.*
- **Is there a vowel that says its name in pal?**
- **Repeat for each word.**

*Exercise 4: Putting Story Events in Order

- **Let's do Exercise 4. You are going to review the story** A birthday for Jenny **by putting events from that story in the order that they happened. Open your Reader to page 8.**
- **Read the sentences in your Workbook. Number 1.**
- **Ready.** Signal. Student reads the first sentence.
- **Repeat for the rest of the sentences.**
- **Which one of these events came first?**
- **Ready.** Signal. Student says, *Today is Jenny's birthday.*
- **That's right. Put a number 1 on the line at the beginning of that sentence.**
- Have the student number the rest of the sentences from 2 to 6.

*Exercise 5: Practicing the Doubling Rule

- **Find Exercise 5. Read the list of words.**
- **Ready.** Signal. Student reads, *run, plan, shop, hop, set, swim and flip.*
- **Good reading! Now you are going to double the final consonant in each word.**
- **Look at the word run. What letter are you going to double?**
- **Ready.** Signal. Student says, *n.*

- **Yes, the n.**
- **In the first blank print an n.** Check. **Read that word.**
- **Now print an n in the second blank.** Check. **Read that word.**
- Repeat for the rest of the words.

Exercise 6: Crossword Puzzle

- **Exercise 6 is a crossword puzzle. There are pictures beside the puzzle to help you know what word to print in the boxes.**
- **Touch number 1. What is that a picture of?**
- **Ready.** Signal. Student says, *a glass.*
- **That's right. To help you spell that word there is a word list inside the frame under the birthday cake. Find the word glass. Now print the word glass in the boxes for number 1.** Check. **Put a check mark beside the word glass so that you know you have done it.**
- Repeat for the rest of the words.

Exercise 7: Using Instructions to Draw and Color a Picture

- **Now let's look at Exercise 7. You are going to draw a picture.**
- **Read the first sentence.**
- **Ready.** Signal. Student reads, *This man has a mask over his eyes.*
- **That's correct. Draw a mask on the man's face.**
- Have the student read each sentence and then draw each part of the picture.

Exercise 8: Answering a Riddle

- **Put your finger on Exercise 8. Read the riddle.**
- **Ready.** Signal. Student reads, *What thing has feet like flippers?*
- **To answer this riddle you are going to cross out all the zzz sounds. The letters**

that are left will be the answer.
- Take your pencil and cross out all the zzz's.
- Now print the letters that remain in the spaces below.
- What thing has feet like flippers?
- That's right, a frog.

Exercise 9: Vowel Power!

- Now let's look at Exercise 9. It's a Vowel Power! exercise. Read the question.
- **Ready.** Signal. Student reads, *What is another name for a diver?*
- You must fill in the blanks with two vowels to answer this question. What vowel will go in the first blank?
- **Ready.** Signal. Student answers, *an o.*
- Right. And in the second blank?
- **Ready.** Signal. Student answers, *an a.*
- Good. So what is another name for a diver?
- Yes, a frogman.

TASK 9:
AWARDING POINTS

- Record the total points for Lesson 35 on page 141 of the Workbook.

End of Lesson 35

LESSON 36

TASK 1:
PRACTICING SOUNDS

- Let's see if you can remember all of the sounds you have learned.
- Say the sound when I touch it. If you make a mistake, we will practice that sound and then do the row again.

- What's the first sound?
- **Ready.** Signal.

- Repeat for each sound in the list.

ck	ol	tch	ī	qu
n	sh	u	ing	b
ur	g	ō	y	ȳ
wh	o	ir	e	al
w	p	or	s	j
f	ē	r	x	k
a	z	th	u	ch
ā	d	t	l	er

i c m h ū

✓ If any error occurs, use correction procedure (my turn, do it with me, your turn) as in previous Lessons and repeat the row.

**TASK 2:
SOUNDING OUT WORDS**

- Now you are going to sound out some words. As I touch the sounds, you say them.

- First word.
- **Ready.** Signal. Student sounds out word.

- **Good work. What's that word?**
- **Ready.** Signal.

- Repeat for each word in the list.

c a tch

monster

mūsic

l a dd er

angry

swam

bottle

wrong

hungry

bottom

gather

happen

tunnel

himself

ship

problem

lesson

sank

 If any error occurs, use correction procedure (my turn, do it with me, your turn) as in previous Lessons.

TASK 3: READING WORDS

- Turn to TASK 2 in this Lesson. Say, **Now you are going to practice reading the words you sounded out.**

- **First word.**
- **Ready.** Signal. Student reads, *catch.*

- Repeat for each word in list.

 If necessary, use correction procedure (my turn, do it with me, your turn) as in previous Lessons.

TASK 4: READING RHYMING WORDS

- **Now you are going to read some words that rhyme with my.**
- Touch the dot in front of the word my. Slide your finger along the line and say **my.**

- **What's that word?**
- **Ready.** Signal.

- **All the words rhyme with my.**

- **Look at the next word.**
- **What's that word?**
- **Ready.** Signal.

- Repeat for each word in the list.

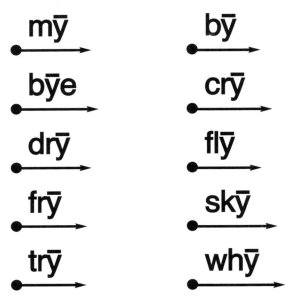

 Use correction procedure as in previous Lessons if necessary.

TASK 5: READING WORDS

- **Now you are going to practice reading some words you already know.**

- **First word.**
- **Ready.** Signal.

- Repeat for each word in list.

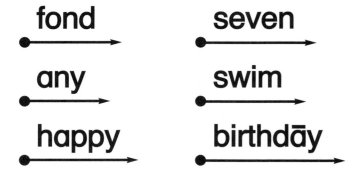

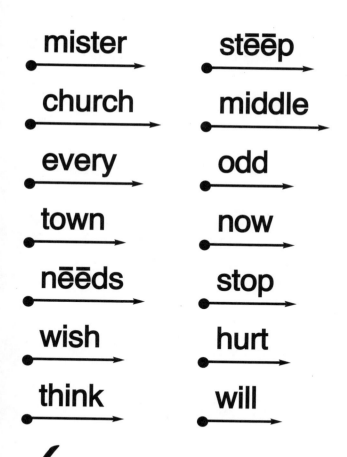

mister   stēēp

church   middle

every   odd

town   now

nēēds   stop

wish   hurt

think   will

✔ If necessary, use correction procedure (my turn, do it with me, your turn) as in previous Lessons.

TASK 6: SOUND FLUENCY CHECK 7

- Say, **Turn to page 11 in your Reader for a Sound Fluency Check.** Time student for 30 seconds.

- Record scores for Day 2 of Sound Fluency Check 7 on page 138 of the Workbook.

TASK 7: WORD FLUENCY CHECK 7

- **Now it's time for another Word Fluency Check. Turn to page 12 in your Reader.** Time student for 30 seconds.

- Record scores for Day 2 of Word Fluency Check 7 on page 139 of the Workbook.

TASK 8: STORY READING FLUENCY CHECK 6

- Say, **Now we are going to do a Story Reading Fluency Check. Turn to page 13 in your Reader.** Time student for 1 minute.

- Record scores for Day 2 of Story Reading Fluency Check 6 on page 140 of the Workbook.

TASK 9: WORKBOOK EXERCISES

- Say, **Now let's look at the Workbook Exercises.**
- **Open your Workbook to Lesson 36 on page 23.** Check.

Exercise 1: Crossing Out Short Sounds

- **Let's do Exercise 1. Some of the words that are printed here have short sounds. You must look at each word and cross out every short sound.**
- **Find the first word. What is that word?**
- **Ready.** Signal. Student says, *happen.*
- **Are there any short sounds in happen?**
- **Ready.** Signal. **Cross them out.**
- Repeat for each word.

Exercise 2: Drawing and Coloring Pictures

- **Now let's look at Exercise 2. Read the instructions.**
- **Ready.** Signal. Student reads, *Put the letter ȳ in the pan to make it fry.*
- **That's correct. Draw the letter ȳ in the pan.**
- Have the student read each sentence and then draw and color each picture. Be ready to make some suggestions if the student needs some help.

Exercise 3: Unscrambling Words

- Find Exercise 3. You are going to unscramble some letters to spell some words you know.
- Touch the first scrambled word. You must make a six-letter word with the sounds ooo, t, ooo, b, t and mmm. Can you find a six-letter word in the list that has those sounds?
- **Ready.** Signal. *Student answers, bottom.* **That's right, bottom.**
- **Print the word bottom in the blanks beside the first word. Put a check mark beside the word bottom in the word list so you know you have done it.**
- Repeat for each scrambled word.
- When the student has finished unscrambling all ten words, say, **Now print the circled letters in the blanks below to spell another word from Lesson 36. What's that word?**
- **Ready.** Signal. *Student says, tunnel.*

Exercise 4: Solving Codes to Answer a Riddle

- Let's look at Exercise 4. You are going to solve a code to answer the riddle, **What kind of music do mountains love?**
- **Let's figure out the sound that goes in each set of words.** Have the student read the words in each box, then print the missing sounds in each shape.
- **Good! You have figured out what each shape's sound is. Now solve the code to answer the riddle, What kind of music do mountains love?**
- **That's correct! Rock music.**

Exercise 5: Printing Words

- Now let's do Exercise 5. You are going to print some sound combinations in the blanks to make some words that you know.
- Look at the first picture. Tell me the sound combination that you must print in the blanks to make a word that matches that picture.
- **Ready.** Signal. *Student says, cooo.*
- **That's right. Print q-u in the blanks. What's that word?**
- **Ready.** Signal. *Student says, quiet.*
- Repeat for ring, sock, three, wheel and children.
- **Now print each of those sound combinations in the blanks below. Check. Read those sounds.**
- **Ready.** Signal. *Student reads, cooo, ing, ck, ththth, wooo and ch.*

Exercise 6: Printing Words

- In Exercise 6 you are going to practice printing some words that have sounds that you know.
- **Touch the first word. Tell me that word.**
- **Ready.** Signal. *Student says, buzz.*
- **Good reading! Follow the balls and arrows and print the sounds in the word buzz.**
- Repeat for fuzz.

```
TASK 10:
AWARDING POINTS
```

- Record the total points for Lesson 36 on page 141 of the Workbook.

End of Lesson 36

LESSON 37

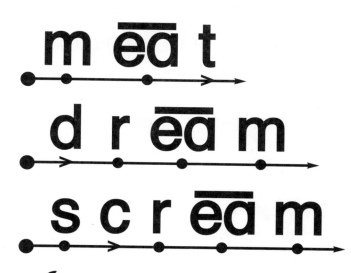

- When these two letters are together, they say the sound ēēē.
- **Listen.** Touch the dot under the ēā and say ēēē for one second. Lift your finger.
- **Listen again.** Repeat.

- **Say the sound with me. Keep on saying it as long as I touch it.**
- **Ready.** Signal.
- Repeat.

- **Your turn.**
- **Ready.** Signal.
- Repeat the task until the student does it as instructed.

✓ If any error occurs, use correction procedure (my turn, do it with me, your turn) as in previous Lessons.

- **Now you are going to sound out some words that have the sound combination you just learned. As I touch the sounds, you say them.**

- **First word.**
- **Ready.** Signal. Student sounds out word.
- **Good work.**

- **What's that word?**
- **Ready.** Signal.
- Repeat for each word in the list.

✓ If any error occurs, use correction procedure (my turn, do it with me, your turn) as in previous Lessons and begin the list again.

- When these two letters are together, they say the sound owww.
- **Listen.** Touch the dot under the ou and say **owww** for one second. Lift your finger.
- **Listen again.** Repeat.

- **Say the sound with me. Keep on saying it as long as I touch it.**
- **Ready.** Signal.
- Repeat.

- **Your turn.**
- **Ready.** Signal.
- Repeat the task until the student does it as instructed.

✓ If any error occurs, use correction procedure (my turn, do it with me, your turn) as in previous Lessons.

- Now you are going to sound out some words that have that sound combination. As I touch the sounds, you say them.

- **First word.**
- **Ready.** Signal.
- **Good work.**

- **What's that word?**
- **Ready.** Signal.

- Repeat for each word in the list.

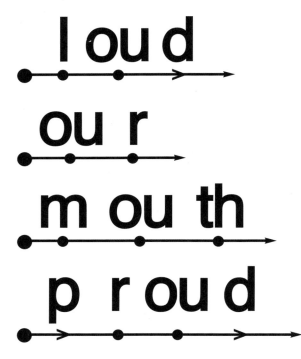

✔ If any error occurs, use correction procedure (my turn, do it with me, your turn) as in previous Lessons and begin the list again.

- When these two letters are together, they say the sound āāā.

- **Listen.** Touch the dot under the ai and say āāā for one second. Lift your finger.
- **Listen again.** Repeat.

- **Say the sound with me. Keep on saying it as long as I touch it.**
- **Ready.** Signal.
- Repeat.

- **Your turn.**
- **Ready.** Signal.
- Repeat the task until the student does it as instructed.

✔ If any error occurs, use correction procedure (my turn, do it with me, your turn) as in previous Lessons.

- Now let's practice some words that have that sound combination. As I touch the sounds, you say them.

- **First word.**
- **Ready.** Signal.

- **What's that word?**
- **Ready.** Signal.

- Repeat for each word in the list.

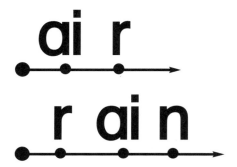

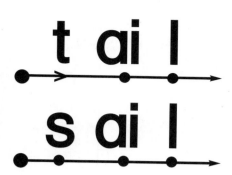

 If necessary, use correction procedure as in previous Lessons.

✓ If any error occurs, use correction procedure (my turn, do it with me, your turn) as in previous Lessons and begin the list again.

TASK 8: SOUNDING OUT WORDS

- Now you are going to sound out some words. As I touch the sounds, you say them.

- First word.
- **Ready.** Signal. Student sounds out word.

- **Good work. What's that word?**
- **Ready.** Signal.

- Repeat for each word in the list.

TASK 7: READING RHYMING WORDS

- **Now you are going to read some words that rhyme with out.**
- Touch the dot in front of the word **out.** Slide your finger along the line and say **out.**

- **What's that word?**
- **Ready.** Signal.

- **All the words rhyme with out.**

- **Look at the next word.**
- **What's that word?**
- **Ready.** Signal.

- Repeat for each word in the list.

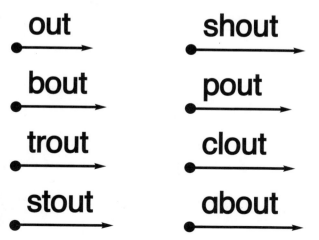

out   shout

bout   pout

trout   clout

stout   about

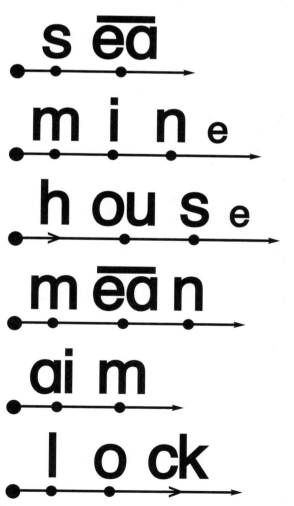

ēa t

s ou n d

a f r ai d

b ēa s t

g a t e

r ēa l

t r ai n

s t r ēa m

d i v e

TASK 9: SAYING THE UNDERLINED SOUNDS AND READING THE WORDS

- Now you are going to read some words with underlined sounds. Some of these words will follow the Final e Rule, some will not.
- First you will read the underlined sound, then you will read the word.

- Put your finger on the first word. Say, **What's the underlined sound?**
- **Ready.** Signal.

- **Good. Now read the word.**
- **Ready.** Signal.

- Repeat for each word in the list.

swam	white
bottom	town
catch	lake
more	monster
all	hide
teeth	any

TASK 10: STORY READING

- **Now it's time to read a story. Turn to Lesson 37 on page 15 in your Reader.**

<u>NOTE</u>: TASK 11 teaches the student about the word I. This TASK comes right after the sentence "I need some real meat to eat." Be sure to stop the student there and follow the instructions for TASK 11 below.

- **Put your finger on the title.**
- **Read the title please.**
- **Ready.** Signal.

- **Now read the story.**
- **Ready.** Signal.

<u>The big mean sea monster - part one</u>

A sea monster came up from the bottom of the sea.
The big beast said, "I will not eat fish any more.
I am not fond of trout.
I need some real meat to eat."

*TASK 11: TEACHING I AS A WORD

- Say to the student, **Let's stop here for a minute.** Touch the letter I and say, **This is the letter I. It is also the word I. When you talk about yourself, you sometimes say I. You might say, <u>I</u> went to school or <u>I</u> am going home.**
- Touch the word I. Say, **What is this word?**
- **Ready.** Signal. Student says, *I.*
- **That's right. I means that you or someone else is talking about themselves. What does I mean?**
- **Ready.** Signal. Student says, *That you or someone else is talking about themselves.*

- Good. Let's continue to read the story.

The sea monster has big white teeth.
He is green and brown and red.
He has a long tail.
The big beast swam up a stream to the gates of the town.
He said to himself, "I will try to catch some children when they come to swim in the stream.
I will eat them all up."
But the children can see the sea monster's long tail.
The children are afraid.
They shout, "Do not swim in the lake!
Run back to the gate.
Lock the big gate and hide in the house."
So the sea monster did not catch the children.
He made a loud sound and began to dive back into the sea.
He said, "I still need to eat. I will get some meat."

More to come

 If the student has a problem with any word, have him/her sound it out, say it and then start at the beginning of that sentence again. If the student makes 7 errors, reread the story from the beginning.

TASK 12: SOUND FLUENCY CHECK 7

- **Time for another Sound Fluency Check. Turn to page 11 in your Reader.** Time student for 30 seconds.

- Record scores for Day 3 of Sound Fluency Check 7 on page 138 of the Workbook.

TASK 13: WORD FLUENCY CHECK 7

- **Time for another Word Fluency Check. Turn to page 12.** Time student for 30 seconds.

- Record scores for Day 3 of Word Fluency Check 7 on page 139 of the Workbook.

TASK 14: STORY READING FLUENCY CHECK 6

- **Time for another Story Reading Fluency Check. Turn to page 13 in your Reader.** Time student for 1 minute.

- Record scores for Day 3 of Story Reading Fluency Check 6 on page 140 of the Workbook.

TASK 15: WORKBOOK EXERCISES

- Say, **Now we are going to do the Workbook part of the Lesson.**
- **Open your Workbook to Lesson 37 on page 28.** Check.

Exercise 1: Printing Sound Combinations

- **In Exercise 1 you are going to practice printing the sound combinations you learned in this Lesson.**
- Have student print five of the sound $\bar{e}\bar{e}\bar{e}$.
- Repeat for owww and $\bar{a}\bar{a}\bar{a}$.

Exercise 2: Printing Words in the Correct Sound Boxes

- **Find Exercise 2. Each of these words has the sound combination $\bar{e}\bar{e}\bar{e}$, owww or $\bar{a}\bar{a}\bar{a}$. You are going to print each word in the correct sound box** (point to

each box).
- **Read the first word.**
- **Ready.** Signal. Student reads, *loud.*
- **Which of these three sound combinations does the word loud have?**
- **Ready.** Signal. Student says, *owww.*
- **That's right. Print loud in the correct box.** Check.
- Repeat for each word in the list.

Exercise 3: Printing Sounds

- **In Exercise 3 you are going to practice printing the letter for the sound zzz.**
- Have the student use the ball and arrows to print six of the sound zzz.

Exercise 4: Circling the Correct Words from the Reader

- Find Exercise 4. Turn to Lesson 37 on page 15 in your Reader.
- In Exercise 4 there are sentences with blanks. Under each sentence are three choices. You are going to find the correct answer in your Reader and circle those words here.
- **Read the first sentence.**
- **Ready.** Signal.
- **Yes. There are three choices under the sentence. Read the three choices.**
- **Ready.** Signal.
- **Which answer goes in the blank?**
- **Ready.** Signal. Student answers, *the bottom of the sea.*
- **That's correct. Circle those words. Now read the sentence again.**
- **Ready.** Signal.
- Repeat for each sentence.

Exercise 5: Using Instructions to Draw and Color a Picture

- **Now let's look at Exercise 5. You are going to draw and color a picture of a sea monster. Read the first sentence.**

- **Ready.** Signal. Student reads, *The sea monster is red and brown.*
- **What colour will the sea monster be?**
- **Ready.** Signal. Student says, *red and brown.*
- **That's correct. Draw a sea monster and color it red and brown.** (If the student has a problem drawing the sea monster to start the picture, have him/her look at Exercise 6 for some help.)
- Have the student read each sentence and then draw or color each part of the picture.

Exercise 6: Answering a Riddle

- **Exercise 6 is a riddle. Read the riddle.**
- **Ready.** Signal. Student reads, *Where do sea monsters sleep?*
- **To answer the riddle you are going to print the alphabet letter that comes right before the letter below the line.**
- **What's the first letter below the line?**
- **Ready.** Signal. Student answers, *j.*
- **Yes, j. What letter in the alphabet comes right before the letter j?**
- **Ready.** Signal. Student says, *i.*
- **That's right, i. Print an i on the first line.**
- Repeat for the rest of the letters.
- **So where do sea monsters sleep?**
- **In water beds! Great work!**

TASK 15: AWARDING POINTS

- Record the total points for Lesson 37 on page 141 of the Workbook.

End of Lesson 37

LESSON 38

TASK 1: SOUNDING OUT WORDS

- **Now you are going to sound out some words. As I touch the sounds, you say them.**

- **First word.**
- **Ready.** Signal. Student sounds out word.

- **Good work. What's that word?**
- **Ready.** Signal.

- Repeat for each word in the list.

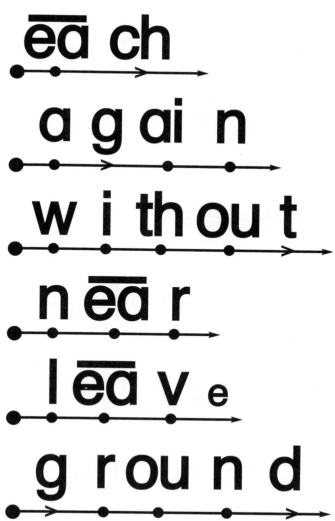

l e ss o n

a r o u n d

l u c k

s p ēā k

c o u n t

r ēā d

h u n g r y

f o u n d

h ēā r

a g a i n s t

r o u n d

w a i t

p a i n

r ēā ch

h a i r

y ēā r

a l o n e

w a v e

✓ If any error occurs, use correction procedure (my turn, do it with me, your turn) as in previous Lessons.

72

- Turn to TASK 1 in this Lesson. Say, **Now you are going to practice reading the words you sounded out.**
- **First word.**
- **Ready.** Signal. Student reads word.

- Repeat for each word in list.

✓ If necessary, use correction procedure (my turn, do it with me, your turn) as in previous Lessons.

- Touch the underlined sound in the first word. Say, **Tell me the underlined sound.**
- **Ready.** Signal.

- **Now tell me the word.**
- **Ready.** Signal.

- Repeat for each of the words in the list.

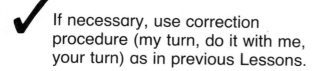

<u>w</u>ent	m<u>a</u>tes
afr<u>ai</u>d	h<u>i</u>de
h<u>i</u>d	r<u>ea</u>l
ab<u>ou</u>t	t<u>ai</u>l
s<u>ou</u>nd	str<u>ea</u>m
angr<u>y</u>	<u>ou</u>r
m<u>ea</u>n	m<u>u</u>d

✓ Use correction procedure (my turn, do it with me, your turn) as in previous Lessons if student makes an error.

- **Now we are going to read some words you have read before.**
- **First word.**
- **Ready.** Signal.

- Repeat for each set in the list.

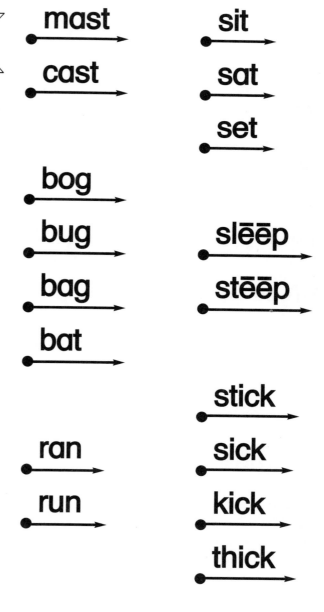

mast
cast

sit
sat
set

bog
bug
bag
bat

slēēp
stēēp

ran
run

stick
sick
kick
thick

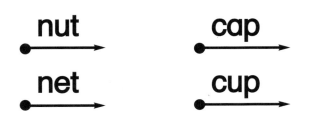

 If the student makes an error reading a word, use the correction procedure as in previous Lessons.

TASK 5: STORY READING

- **Now it's time to read a story. Turn to Lesson 38 on page 17 in your Reader.** Check.

- **Put your finger on the title.**
- **Read the title please.**
- **Ready.** Signal.

- **Now read the story.**
- **Ready.** Signal.

The big mean sea monster - part two

A sea monster came from the sea.
The sea monster has big white teeth and a long red tail.
The big beast swam up a stream to the gates of the little town.
He was trying to catch children who go to swim in the stream.
He is a real mean monster.
The children see the monster in the stream.
They are afraid.
They run from the stream to the town.
They lock the gate.
The monster does not catch the children.
The sea monster makes a loud sound and dives to the bottom of the sea.
He is hungry and angry.
He needs to find something to eat.

More to come

If the student has a problem with any word, have him/her sound it out, say it and then start at the beginning of that sentence again. If the student makes 7 errors, reread the story from the beginning.

TASK 6: SOUND FLUENCY CHECK 7

NOTE: If the student has said 50+ sounds correctly in 1 minute for three consecutive days, s/he may discontinue timings on Sound Fluency Check 7 if s/he so chooses.

- If not, say, **Time for a Sound Fluency Check. Turn to page 11 in your Reader.** Time student for 30 seconds.

- Record scores for Day 4 of Sound Fluency Check 7 on page 138 of the Workbook.

TASK 7: WORD FLUENCY CHECK 7

NOTE: If the student has read 60+ words correctly in 1 minute for three consecutive days, s/he may discontinue timings on Word Fluency Check 7 if s/he so chooses.

- If not, say, **Time for a Word Fluency Check. Turn to page 12.** Time student for 30 seconds.

- Record scores for Day 4 of Word Fluency Check 7 on page 139 of the Workbook.

TASK 8: STORY READING FLUENCY CHECK 6

NOTE: If the student has read 200+ words per minute in the story three consecutive times, s/he has reached fluency and does not need to try again on this Lesson unless s/he chooses to do so. Have the student choose another story from the Reader to be timed on.

- If the student has not yet reached fluency, say, **Time for another Story Reading Fluency Check. Turn to page 13 in your Reader.** Time student for one minute.

- Record scores for Day 4 of Story Reading Fluency Check 6 on page 140 of the Workbook.

TASK 9: WORKBOOK EXERCISES

- Say, **Now let's do the Workbook Exercises.**
- **Open your Workbook to Lesson 38 on page 33.** Check.

Exercise 1: Filling in the Blanks

- **You need your Reader for Exercise 1. Turn to Lesson 38 on page 17 of your Reader.**
- **You are going to fill in the blanks in Exercise 1 with the correct word from the story The big mean sea monster - part two.**
- **Read the first sentence.**
- **Ready.** Signal.
- **Find the correct words that complete that sentence and print those words in the blanks.** Check. **Now read the whole sentence.**
- Repeat for each sentence.

Exercise 2: Matching Rhyming Words

- **Find Exercise 2. It's a Rhyme Time! exercise. You are going to draw a line to match rhyming words.**
- **Read the first word.**
- **Ready.** Signal. Student reads, *sleep.*
- **Now touch the second group of words.**

Read the first word there.
- **Ready.** Signal. Student reads, *scream.*
- **Does sleep rhyme with scream?**
- Repeat until student finds the correct rhyming word, steep.
- **Good. Now draw a line to join the words sleep and steep.**
- Repeat for the rest of the words in the list.

Exercise 3: Printing Words

- **Look at Exercise 3. You have to print some words that have certain sound combinations. The missing letters for the words are inside the telephone bubble.**
- **Touch the first word you need to print. This word has three letters to be filled in. It begins with the sound combination ththth. Look in the list and find a blank with three letters after it. What letters did you find that would make a word starting with ththth?**
- **Ready.** Signal. Student says, *i-n-k.*
- **Right. Print i-n-k in the spaces for the first word. What's that word?**
- **Ready.** Signal. Student says, *think.*
- Repeat for each word.

Exercise 4: Printing Words in the Correct Sound Boxes

- **Find Exercise 4. Each of these words has the sound combination owww, $\bar{a}\bar{a}\bar{a}$ or $\bar{e}\bar{e}\bar{e}$. You are going to print each word in the correct sound box** (point to each box).
- **Read the first word.**
- **Ready.** Signal. Student reads, *each.*
- **Which of these three sound combinations does the word each have?**
- **Ready.** Signal. Student says, $\bar{e}\bar{e}\bar{e}$.
- **That's right. Print each in the correct box.** Check.
- Repeat for each word in the list.

Exercise 5: Putting Words in Alphabetical Order

- **Find Exercise 5. Read the words.**
- **Ready.** Signal. Student reads from ground to year.
- **In this exercise you are going to print these words in alphabetical order. You must look at the first letter in each word. What first letter in these words** (point to list) **comes first in the alphabet?**
- **Ready.** Signal. Student answers, *around.*
- **That's right! Print around in the blanks. Put a check mark beside around in the list.**
- **What is the word with a first letter that comes next in the alphabet?**
- **Ready.** Signal. Student says, *count.*
- **Well done. Print count in the second set of blanks.** Check.
- **Repeat for the rest of the words. When the student has finished doing all eight of them, say, Good work! You just put those eight words in alphabetical order.**
- **Now read the sentence below the word year.**
- **Ready.** Signal. Student reads, *The big mean sea monster is hungry and blank.*
- **Print the letters that are circled to find the answer. What's the word?**
- **That's right, angry.**

Exercise 6: Answering Riddles

- **Exercise 6 has some riddles. Read the first riddle.**
- **Ready.** Signal. Student reads, *What is a mouse's favorite game?*
- **Good reading! Any guesses?** Have student try to answer the riddle. If s/he is stumped, turn the Workbook over to read the answer.
- **Repeat for each of the three remaining riddles.**

- Record the total points for Lesson 38 on page 141 of the Workbook.

End of Lesson 38

LESSON 39

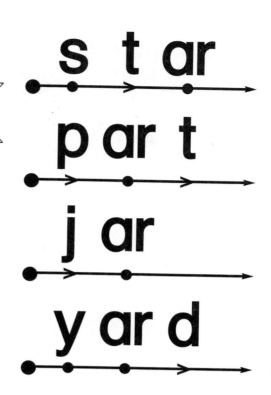

- When these two letters are together, they say the sound orrr.
- **Listen.** Touch the dot under the ar and say **orrr** for one second. Lift your finger.
- **Listen again.** Repeat.

- Say the sound with me. Keep on saying it as long as I touch it.
- **Ready.** Signal.
- Repeat.

- **Your turn.**
- **Ready.** Signal.
- Repeat the task until the student does it as instructed.

✓ If any error occurs, use correction procedure (my turn, do it with me, your turn) as in previous Lessons.

✓ If any error occurs, use correction procedure (my turn, do it with me, your turn) as in previous Lessons and begin the list again.

TASK 2: PRACTICING THE SOUND COMBINATION ar

- Now you are going to sound out some words that have the sound combination you just learned. As I touch the sounds, you say them.

- **First word.**
- **Ready.** Signal.

- **What's that word?**
- **Ready.** Signal.

- Repeat for each word in the list.

TASK 3: TEACHING THE SOUND COMBINATIONS oi as in oil and oy as in boy

- When these two letters are together, they say the sound ōyēēē.
- **Listen.** Touch the dots under the oi and oy and say **ōyēēē** for one second. Lift your finger.
- **Listen again.** Repeat.

- **Say the sound with me. Keep on saying it as long as I touch it.**
- **Ready.** Signal.
- Repeat.

- **Your turn.**
- **Ready.** Signal.
- Repeat the task until the student does it as instructed.

 If any error occurs, use correction procedure (my turn, do it with me, your turn) as in previous Lessons.

TASK 4: PRACTICING THE SOUND COMBINATIONS oi/oy

- Now you are going to sound out some words that have the sound combination ōyēēē. As I touch the sounds, you say them.

- **First word.**
- **Ready.** Signal.

- **What's that word?**
- **Ready.** Signal.

- Repeat for each word in the list.

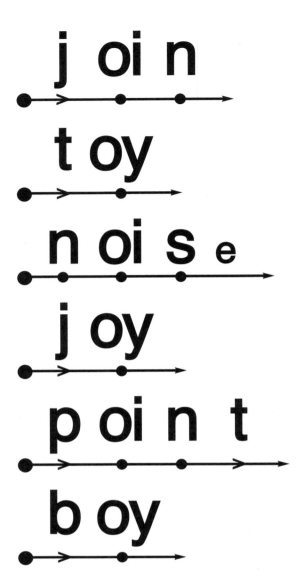

✓ If any error occurs, use correction procedure (my turn, do it with me, your turn) as in previous Lessons and begin the list again.

TASK 5: TEACHING THE SOUND COMBINATION oo as in cool

- When these two letters are together, they say the sound ooo.
- **Listen.** Touch the dot under the oo and say **ooo** for one second. Lift your finger.
- **Listen again.** Repeat.

- **Say the sound with me.**

- **Ready.** Signal.

- **Your turn.**
- **Ready.** Signal.
- Repeat the task until the student does it as instructed.

 If any error occurs, use correction procedure (my turn, do it with me, your turn) as in previous Lessons.

TASK 6: PRACTICING THE SOUND COMBINATION OO

- Now you are going to sound out some words that have the sound combination you just learned.

- **First word.**
- **Ready.** Signal.

- **What's that word?**
- **Ready.** Signal.

- Repeat for each word in the list.

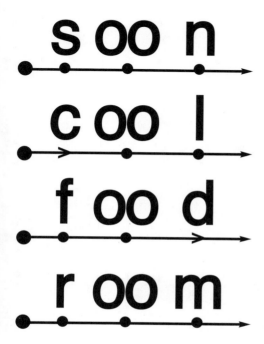

 If any error occurs, use correction procedure (my turn, do it with me, your turn) as in previous Lessons and begin the list again.

TASK 7: READING RHYMING WORDS

- Now you are going to read some words that rhyme with ear.
- Touch the dot in front of the word ear. Slide your finger along the line and say **ear**.

- **What's that word?**
- **Ready.** Signal.

- All the words rhyme with ear.

- **Look at the next word.**
- **What's that word?**
- **Ready.** Signal.

- Repeat for each word in the list.

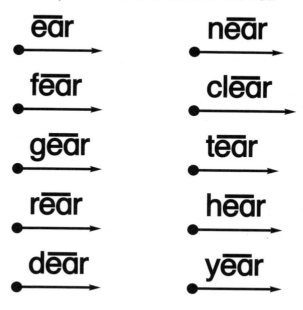

 If necessary, use correction procedure as in previous Lessons.

TASK 8: SOUNDING OUT WORDS

- Now you are going to sound out some words. As I touch the sounds, you say them.

- First word.
- **Ready.** Signal. Student sounds out word.

- **Good work. What's that word?**
- **Ready.** Signal.

- Repeat for each word in the list.

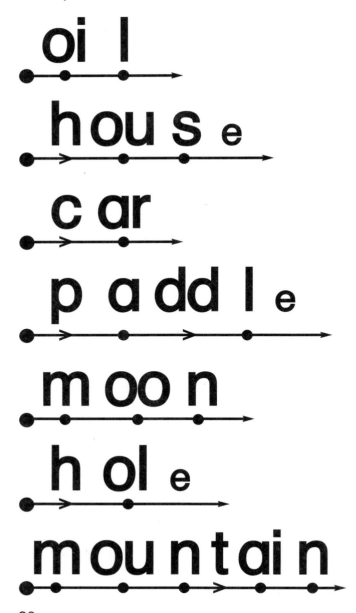

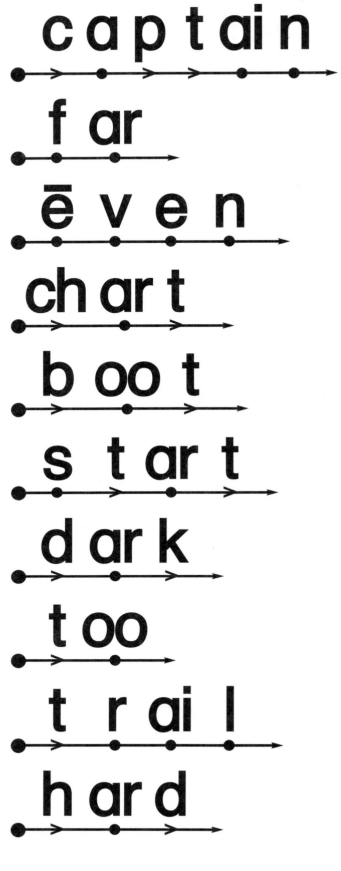

b r a v e

✓ If any error occurs, use correction procedure (my turn, do it with me, your turn) as in previous Lessons.

TASK 9: READING WORDS THAT BEGIN WITH SHORT SOUNDS

- Now you are going to read some words that begin with short sounds.

- **What's the first word?**
- **Ready.** Signal.

- Repeat for each of the words in the list.

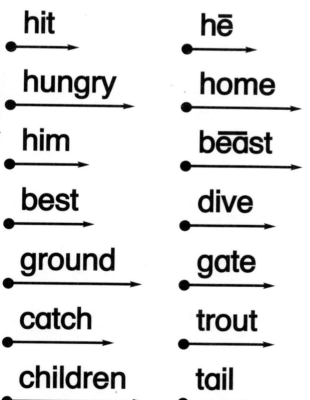

hit

hungry

him

best

ground

catch

children

hē

home

bēast

dive

gate

trout

tail

✓ If the student makes an error or stops between the sounds, use correction procedure (my turn, do it with me, your turn) as in previous Lessons and begin the list again.

TASK 10: STORY READING

- Now it's time to read a story. Turn to Lesson 39 on page 19 in your Reader. Check.

- **Put your finger on the title.**
- **Read the title please.**
- **Ready.** Signal.

- **Now read the story.**
- **Ready.** Signal.

The big mean sea monster - part three

The mean sea monster wants to eat the little children.
But the children see the monster and run home.
The sea monster dives into the sea.
He is hungry and angry.
He wants to eat meat not trout.
He sees a sailing ship and swims to get it.
When the ship's mates see the monster, they are afraid.
Now the captain of the ship is brave.
He hits the sea monster with a paddle.
But the sea monster makes a hole in the ship.
The ship is sinking.
And the monster is waiting.
        Still more to come

✓ If the student has a problem with any word, have him/her sound it out, say it and then start at the beginning of that sentence again. If the student makes 7 errors, reread the story from the beginning.

TASK 11: SOUND FLUENCY CHECK 7

REMINDER: If the student has said 50+ sounds correctly in 1 minute for any three days of the last four, s/he may discontinue timings on Sound Fluency Check 7 if s/he so chooses.

- If not, say, **Time for a Sound Fluency Check. Turn to page 11 in your Reader.** Time student for 30 seconds.

- Record scores for Day 5 of Sound Fluency Check 7 on page 138 of the Workbook.

REMINDER: If the student has been unable to say at least 50 sounds correctly per minute at least one time in Sound Fluency Check 7, finish and correct the Workbook Exercises for Lesson 39 but do not proceed to teach new material. Instead, reteach Lessons 35 through 39. Include daily practice and timings on Sound Fluency Check 7 on page 11. Circle and practice any sounds the student is having difficulty with. Record scores in the Additional Practice columns for Sound Fluency Check 7 on page 138 of the Student Workbook. Students should continue to be awarded points for working hard, paying attention, following instructions and doing well on fluency checks. When the student is able to say 50+ sounds from the list in 1 minute, begin Lesson 40.

TASK 12: WORD FLUENCY CHECK 7

REMINDER: If the student has read 60+ words correctly in 1 minute for any three days of the last four, s/he may discontinue timings on Word Fluency Check 7 if s/he so chooses.

- If not, say, **Time for a Word Fluency Check. Turn to page 12.** Time student for 30 seconds.

- Record scores for Day 5 of Word Fluency Check 7 on page 139 of the Workbook.

REMINDER: If the student has been unable to read at least 60 words correctly in 1 minute at least one time in Word Fluency Check 7, finish the Workbook Exercises for Lesson 39 but do not proceed with new material. Instead, redo Lessons 35 through 39. Include daily practice and timings on Word Fluency Check 7 on page 12. Circle and practice any words the student is having difficulty with. Students should continue to be awarded points for working hard, paying attention, following instructions and doing well on fluency checks. When the student is able to read 60+ words from the list in 1 minute, continue in the Reader with Lesson 40.

TASK 13: STORY READING FLUENCY CHECK 6

REMINDER: If the student has read 200+ words per minute in the story for three of the last four attempts, s/he has reached fluency and does not need to try again on this Lesson unless s/he chooses to do so. Have the student choose another story from the Reader to do a timing on.

- If the student has not yet reached fluency, say, **Time for another Story Reading Fluency Check. Turn to page 13 in your Reader.** Time student for one minute.

- Record scores for Day 5 of Story Reading Fluency Check 6 on page 140 of the Workbook.

NOTE: If the student has not yet reached fluency at 200+ words a minute in the same story on at least one timing, finish and correct the Workbook Exercises for Lesson 39, but do not proceed with new material. Instead, have the student practice reading the first half of the story until s/he can read it with fewer than 3 L.O.s in 30 seconds. Then practice the next half in the same manner. Combine the two sections and practice until the student can read them fluently in a minute. Record scores in the Additional Practice columns for Story Reading Fluency Check 6. Award points for working hard, paying attention, following instructions and doing well in fluency checks. When the student has reached fluency, begin Lesson 40.

TASK 14: WORKBOOK EXERCISES

- **Open your Workbook to Lesson 39 on page 38.** Check.

Exercise 1: Printing Sound Combinations

- **In Exercise 1 you are going to practice printing the sound combinations you learned in this Lesson.**
- Have student print five of the sound orrr.
- Repeat for ōyēēē, ōyēēē and ooo.

Exercise 2: Printing Words

- **Look at Exercise 2. You have print some words that have certain sound combinations. Read those sound combinations.**
- **Ready.** Signal. Student reads, ōyēēē, orrr, ooo, ēēē, āāā.
- **Touch the first word you need to print. It begins with the sound mmm and ends with nnn. What sound combination could you add to make a word you know?**

- **Ready.** Signal. Student says, ooo.
- **Right. Print ooo in the spaces for the first word. What's that word?**
- **Ready.** Signal. Student says, moon.
- **Good. Check off the word moon in the list.**
- Repeat for each word.

Exercise 3: Completing Various Tasks on Sentences from the Reader

- **In Exercise 3 you need your Reader. Find the story The big mean sea monster - part three in Lesson 39 on page 19.**
- **Look at the first sentence in your Workbook. You are going to fill in the missing vowels to complete the words. What is the missing vowel in the first word?**
- **Ready.** Signal.
- **Yes, e. Now find that sentence in the story and fill in the rest of the missing vowels.** Check.
- **Read sentence 2.**
- **Ready.** Signal. Student reads the sentence.
- **Cross out all the short sounds in this sentence.** Check.
- **Read sentence 3. Circle all the sound combinations in this sentence.** Check.
- **Read sentence 4. Circle the words that rhyme in each sentence.** Check.
- **Read sentence 5. Fill in the missing vowels to complete the words.** Check.
- **Read sentence 6. Cross out all the short sounds in this sentence.** Check.
- **Read sentence 7. Circle all the sound combinations in this sentence.** Check.

Exercise 4: Making New Words

- **In Exercise 4 you are going to make some new words from the letters in the word mountain.**
- **Can you see another word that you can make from some of the letters in**

mountain?
- Good! Print that word on the first line.
- Monitor the student as s/he prints new words. Be ready to make some suggestions.

Exercise 5: Solving a Code to Answer Some Riddles

- Let's look at Exercise 5. You are going to solve a code to answer four riddles.
- In the box, there are alphabet letters which have a number under them. To answer the riddles you must print the letter in the blanks above its number.
- Read the first riddle.
- **Ready.** Signal. Student reads, *Which sailor are most fish afraid of?*
- Good reading! Look in the box and find out what letter is number 8.
- **That's right, c. Print c in the first blank.**
- Repeat for each number.
- **Read what you have written to find out which sailor most fish are afraid of.**
- Yes! Captain Hook!
- Repeat for 2. (whales), 3. (starfish) and 4. (fish and ships).

TASK 15: AWARDING POINTS

- Record the total points for Lesson 39 on page 141 of the Workbook.

End of Lesson 39

LESSON 40

TASK 1: TEACHING THE SOUND COMBINATIONS au as in <u>au</u>to and aw as in s<u>aw</u>

- When these letters are together, they both say the sound ooo.
- **Listen.** Touch the dots under the au and aw and say **ooo** for one second. Lift your finger.
- **Listen again.** Repeat.

- Say the sound with me.
- **Ready.** Signal.
- Repeat.

- Your turn.
- **Ready.** Signal.
- Repeat the task until the student does it as instructed.

au aw

 If any error occurs, use correction procedure (my turn, do it with me, your turn) as in previous Lessons.

TASK 2: PRACTICING THE SOUND COMBINATIONS au and aw

- Now you are going to sound out some words that have the sound combinations you just learned. As I touch the sounds, you say them.

- First word.
- **Ready.** Signal.

- What's that word?
- **Ready.** Signal.

- Repeat for each word in the list.

s aw

b ē c au s e

f au l t

aw f u l

✓ If any error occurs, use correction procedure (my turn, do it with me, your turn) as in previous Lessons and begin the list again.

┌─────────────────────────────┐
│ TASK 3: TEACHING THE   │
│ SOUND COMBINATION   │
│ ould as in would   │
└─────────────────────────────┘

- When these two letters are together, they say the short sound ould.
- Listen. Tap the arrow under the ould and say ould.
- Listen again. Repeat.

- Say the sound with me.
- Ready. Signal.
- Repeat.

- Your turn.
- Ready. Signal.
- Repeat the task until the student does it as instructed.

ould

✓ If any error occurs, use correction procedure (my turn, do it with me, your turn) as in previous Lessons.

┌─────────────────────────────┐
│ TASK 4: PRACTICING THE   │
│ SOUND COMBINATION   │
│ ould   │
└─────────────────────────────┘

- Now you are going to sound out some words that have the short sound ould. As I touch the sounds, you say them.

- First word.
- Ready. Signal.

- What's that word?
- Ready. Signal.

- Repeat for each word in the list.

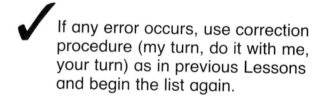

w ould

sh ould

c ould

✓ If any error occurs, use correction procedure (my turn, do it with me, your turn) as in previous Lessons and begin the list again.

- Let's read some words that rhyme with **saw**.
- Touch the dot in front of the word **saw**. Slide your finger along the line and say **saw**.

- **What's that word?**
- **Ready.** Signal.

- **All the words rhyme with saw.**

- **Look at the next word.**
- **What's that word?**
- **Ready.** Signal.

- Repeat for each word in the list.

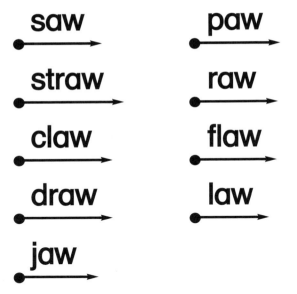

saw	paw
straw	raw
claw	flaw
draw	law
jaw	

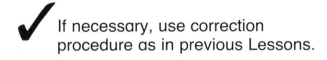

✔ If necessary, use correction procedure as in previous Lessons.

- **Now you are going to practice reading some words you already know. Be careful, some of the words may follow the Final e Rule.**

- First word.
- **Ready.** Signal.

- Repeat for each word in list.

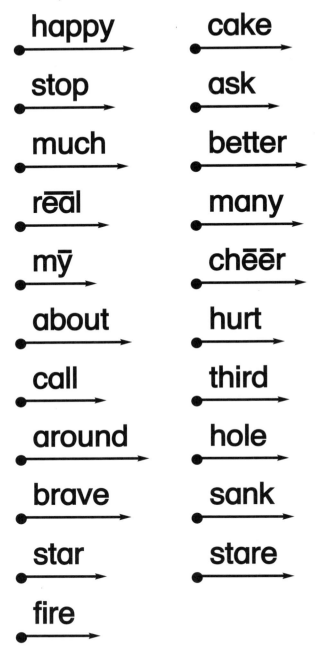

happy	cake
stop	ask
much	better
rēal	many
mȳ	chēēr
about	hurt
call	third
around	hole
brave	sank
star	stare
fire	

 If necessary, use correction procedure (my turn, do it with me, your turn) as in previous Lessons.

86

TASK 7: PRACTICING IRREGULAR WORDS

- You are going to read some irregular words you have already learned.

- Read the first word and spell it.
- **Ready.** Signal.

- Repeat for each word.

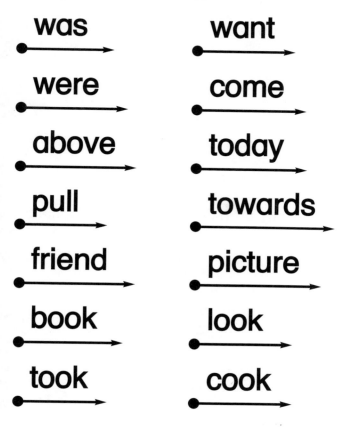

was

want

were

come

above

today

pull

towards

friend

picture

book

look

took

cook

✔ If necessary, use correction procedure from previous Lessons.

TASK 8: TEACHING IRREGULAR WORDS

- Say, **Here are some new irregular words. First I will read the word, then you will read the word and spell it.**

- **Listen. The first word is door.**
- **What word?**

- **Ready.** Signal.
- **Yes, door.**

- **Spell door.**
- **Ready.** Signal.

- Repeat for each word.

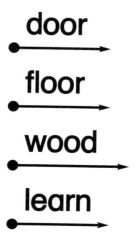

door

floor

wood

learn

✔ If necessary, use correction procedure from previous Lessons.

TASK 9: STORY READING

- Now it's time to read a story. Turn to Lesson 40 on page 20 in your Reader. Check.

- Put your finger on the title.
- **Read the title please.**
- **Ready.** Signal.

- **Now read the story.**
- **Ready.** Signal.

The big mean sea monster - part four

The mean sea monster makes a hole in the sailing ship.
And the ship is sinking.
A brave mate is in the sea.
The monster said to him, "Now I will eat you."
The mate said, "But if you eat me, I can not

87

get you any cake.
The monster stops.
"Do you have cake for me?" he asks.
"Yes," the mate said. "Would you like some?"
"Yes, very much!" the sea monster yells.
"I like cake a lot better than meat.
Get on my back and we will go and eat all of the cake."
And they did.
The monster is not mean now.
He has lots of cake and no fish.
Now he is a real happy sea monster.
　　The end of the story

✔ If the student has a problem with any word, have him/her sound it out, say it and then start at the beginning of that sentence again. If the student makes 7 errors, reread the story from the beginning.

TASK 10: SOUND FLUENCY CHECK 8

- The student has said 50+ sounds per minute in Sound Fluency Check 7 on page 11. Say, **Turn to page 22 in your Reader. There is a list of sounds from Lessons 1 to 40.**
- **You are going to say these sounds as quickly as you can, remembering to hold the sounds with the dots under them for one second.**
- **Which way would you like to do this list?** Student chooses down or across.

- **Put your finger on the first sound.**
- **Ready. Please begin.** Time student for 30 seconds.
- Say, **Thank you.**

- Record sounds said correctly per minute in the Sounds Said Correctly column for Day 1 of Sound Fluency Check 8 on page 138 of the Workbook.

- Record number of errors and/or skipped sounds per minute in the Learning Opportunities column.

TASK 11: WORD FLUENCY CHECK 8

- The student has read 60+ words per minute in Word Fluency Check 7 on page 12. Say, **On page 23 there is a list of words from Lessons 1 to 40.**
- **You are going to read these words as quickly as you can. Which way would you like to read this list?** Student chooses down or across.

- **Put your finger on the first word.**
- **Ready. Please begin.** Time student for 30 seconds.
- Say, **Thank you.**

- Record words read correctly per minute in the Words Read Correctly column for Day 1 of Word Fluency Check 8 on page 139 of the Workbook.
- Record number of errors and/or skipped words per minute in the Learning Opportunities column.

TASK 12: STORY READING FLUENCY CHECK 7

- The student has reached fluency (200+ words/minute) in Story Reading Fluency Check 6. Say, **Now we are going to do a new Story Reading Fluency Check. Turn to page 24 in your Reader.**

- **Put your finger on the title. Get set to read the story.**
- **Ready. Please begin.** Time student for 1 minute.
- At the end of 1 minute say, **Thank you.**

- Record the number of words read correctly in the Words Read Correctly column for Day 1 of Story Reading Fluency Check 7 on page 140 of the Workbook.

- Record errors and/or skipped words in the Learning Opportunities column.

TASK 13: WORKBOOK EXERCISES

- Say, **Now we are going to do the Workbook part of the Lesson.**
- **Open your Workbook to Lesson 40 on page 42.** Check.

Exercise 1: Answering Questions from the Reader

- **You need your Reader for Exercise 1. Turn to Lesson 40 on page 20 of your Reader.**
- **You are going to answer some questions from the story** <u>The big mean sea monster - part four</u>.
- **Read the first question.**
- **Ready.** Signal. Student reads, *What does the mean sea monster make in the sailing ship?*
- **Good. Now read the beginning of the answer.**
- **Ready.** Signal. Student reads, *The mean sea monster makes . . .*
- **Find the correct words that complete that sentence and print those words on the line.** Check. **Now read the whole sentence.**
- Repeat for each question.

Exercise 2: Circling the Word that Doesn't Belong

- **In Exercise 2 each line has a list of four words. Three of the words have something the same. One word does not. You are going to circle the word in each line that doesn't belong.**
- **Finger on number 1. Read each of those words.**

- **Ready.** Signal. Student reads, *star, part, ear, jar.*
- **Which of those words does not belong?**
- **Ready.** Signal. Student answers, *ear.*
- **That's right because all the other words have the sound combination orrr and ear has the sound combination ēēē.**
- Repeat for numbers 2 to 6.
- If the student is having difficulty, give him/her a hint or tell him/her the answer and ask for the reason that that word does not belong.

Exercise 3: Word Search Puzzle

- **Exercise 3 is a word search puzzle.**
- **In this puzzle words can go across, up and down or backwards.**
- **Read the first word in the list of the words that you will be looking for.**
- **Ready.** Signal. Student reads, *oil.*
- **The arrow beside the word tells you whether the word goes across, up, down or backwards. Look inside the puzzle. Go through each row until you find the letters o-i-l going up.**
- **That's right. Draw a circle around the word oil.**
- **Put a check mark beside the word oil in the list so that you know you have found it.**
- If the student is having problems finding the word, repeat steps above for each word in the list. If s/he can do the puzzle independently, allow him/her to do so.

Exercise 4: Printing Sound Combinations

- **In Exercise 4 you are going to practice printing the sound combinations you learned in this Lesson.**
- **Have student print four of the sound ooo.**
- Repeat for ooo and ould.

Exercise 5: Printing Words in the Correct Sound Boxes

- Find Exercise 5. Each of these words has the sound combination ooo, ooo or ould. You are going to print each word in the correct sound box (point to each box).
- **Read the first word.**
- **Ready.** Signal. Student reads, *food.*
- **Which of these three sound combinations does the word food have?**
- **Ready.** Signal. Student says, *ooo.*
- **That's right. Print food in the correct box.** Check.
- Repeat for each word in the list.

Exercise 6: Solving Codes to Answer a Riddle

- **Let's look at Exercise 6. You are going to solve a code to answer a riddle. Read the riddle.**
- **Ready.** Signal. Student reads, *When does Mrs. Claus mend Santa's socks?*
- **Let's figure out the sound that goes in each set of words.** Have the student read the words in each box, then print the missing sounds in each shape.
- **Good! You have figured out what each shape's sound is. Now solve the code to answer the riddle, When does Mrs. Claus mend Santa's socks?**
- **That's right! When they have ho-ho holes!**

TASK 14: AWARDING POINTS

- Record the total points for Lesson 40 on page 141 of the Workbook.

End of Lesson 40

LESSON 41

TASK 1: TEACHING THE SOUND COMBINATION igh as in hi**gh**

- **When these two letters are together, they say the sound īīī.**
- **Listen.** Touch the dot under the igh and say īīī for one second. Lift your finger.
- **Listen again.** Repeat.

- **Say the sound with me.**
- **Ready.** Signal.
- Repeat.

- **Your turn.**
- **Ready.** Signal.
- Repeat the task until the student does it as instructed.

 If any error occurs, use correction procedure (my turn, do it with me, your turn) as in previous Lessons.

TASK 2: PRACTICING THE SOUND COMBINATION igh

- Now you are going to sound out some words that have the sound combination you just learned. As I touch the sounds, you say them.

- **First word.**
- **Ready.** Signal.

- **What's that word?**
- **Ready.** Signal.

- Repeat for each word in the list.

h igh

f igh t

m igh t

✓ If any error occurs, use correction procedure (my turn, do it with me, your turn) as in previous Lessons and begin the list again.

TASK 3: TEACHING THE SOUND COMBINATION ea as in h<u>ea</u>d

- When these two letters are together, they say the sound eee.
- **Listen.** Touch the dot under the ea and say **eee** for one second. Lift your finger.
- **Listen again.** Repeat.

- **Say the sound with me.**
- **Ready.** Signal.
- Repeat.

- **Your turn.**
- **Ready.** Signal.
- Repeat the task until the student does it as instructed.

✓ If any error occurs, use correction procedure (my turn, do it with me, your turn) as in previous Lessons.

TASK 4: PRACTICING THE SOUND COMBINATION ea

- Now you are going to sound out some words that have the sound combination you just learned. As I touch the sounds, you say them.

- **First word.**
- **Ready.** Signal.
- **Good work.**

- **What's that word?**
- **Ready.** Signal.

- Repeat for each word in the list.

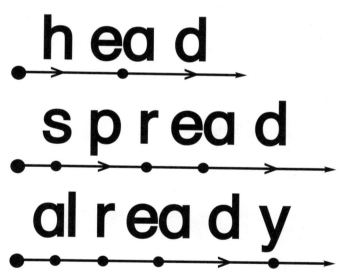

✓ If any error occurs, use correction procedure (my turn, do it with me, your turn) as in previous Lessons and begin the list again.

91

TASK 5: SOUNDING OUT WORDS

- **Now you are going to sound out some other words.**

- **First word.**
- **Ready.** Signal.

- **Good work. What's that word?**
- **Ready.** Signal.

- Repeat for each word in the list.

w ould

s aw

r ea d

ar m

s t ea d y

f au l t

c ould

b ē c au s e

f or e s t

sh ould

c a b i n

l o g

b ea r

aw f u l

m ou n t ai n

s i l v er

d ea d

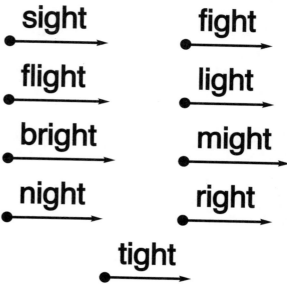

✔ If any error occurs, use correction procedure (my turn, do it with me, your turn) as in previous Lessons.

TASK 6: READING WORDS

- Turn to TASK 5 in this Lesson. Say, **Now you are going to practice reading the words you sounded out.**

- **First word.**
- **Ready.** Signal.

- Repeat for each word in list.

✔ If necessary, use correction procedure (my turn, do it with me, your turn) as in previous Lessons.

TASK 7: READING RHYMING WORDS

- **Now you are going to read some words that rhyme with sight.**
- Touch the dot in front of the word sight. Slide your finger along the line and say sight.

- **What's that word?**
- **Ready.** Signal.

- **All the words rhyme with sight.**

- **Look at the next word.**
- **What's that word?**
- **Ready.** Signal.

- Repeat for each word in the list.

✔ If necessary, use correction procedure as in previous Lessons.

TASK 8: SAYING THE UNDERLINED SOUNDS AND READING THE WORDS

- Touch the underlined sound in the first word.
- Say, **Tell me the underlined sound.**
- **Ready.** Signal.

- **Now tell me the word.**
- **Ready.** Signal.

- Repeat for each of the words in the list.

ab<u>ou</u>t	b<u>a</u>d	<u>c</u>are
<u>ai</u>d	d<u>ar</u>k	<u>ēar</u>
<u>h</u>air	f<u>ai</u>r	<u>i</u>ts
g<u>ar</u>den	<u>k</u>ill	y<u>ēar</u>
s<u>p</u>ell	p<u>aw</u>	<u>t</u>orn
s<u>er</u>ve	b<u>o</u>ld	<u>f</u>oll<u>ō</u>w

Use correction procedure (my turn, do it with me, your turn) as in previous Lessons if student makes an error.

┌─────────────────────────┐
│ TASK 9:   │
│ STORY READING   │
└─────────────────────────┘

- **Now it's time to read a new story. Turn to Lesson 41 on page 26 in your Reader.** Check.

- **Put your finger on the title.**
- **Read the title please.**
- **Ready.** Signal.

- **Now read the story.**
- **Ready.** Signal.

The boy who learns to read - part one

Jack lives in a cabin in the forest.
This forest has lots of pine trees.
It is on the side of a mountain.
Jack can not go to school.
It is too far away.
Each day Jack's father cuts logs and takes them to the saw mill.
Jack helps his father to cut down the trees and cut them into logs.
One day Jack found a bear cub that had hurt its paw.
He said to his dad, "What can we do with this hurt cub?"
His father said, "We will take him home.
Then we will look in our first-aid book to find out what to do."
They took the hurt bear cub home with them.
They got out the big book on first aid.
"What does it say?" his father said to Jack.
"I can't tell," said Jack, "because I can't read."
More to come

 If the student has a problem with any word, have him/her sound it out, say it and then start at the beginning of

that sentence again. If the student makes 7 errors, reread the story from the beginning.

┌─────────────────────────┐
│ TASK 10: SOUND FLUENCY │
│ CHECK 8   │
└─────────────────────────┘

- **Time for another Sound Fluency Check. Turn to page 22 in your Reader.** Time student for 30 seconds.

- Record scores for Day 2 of Sound Fluency Check 8 on page 138 of the Workbook.

┌─────────────────────────┐
│ TASK 11: WORD FLUENCY   │
│ CHECK 8   │
└─────────────────────────┘

- **Turn to page 23 for Word Fluency Check 8.** Time student for 30 seconds.

- Record scores for Day 2 of Word Fluency Check 8 on page 139 of the Workbook.

┌─────────────────────────┐
│ TASK 12: STORY READING │
│ FLUENCY CHECK 7   │
└─────────────────────────┘

- Say to the student, **We are now going to do our second Story Reading Fluency Check. Turn to page 24 in your Reader.** Time student for 1 minute.

- Record scores for Day 2 of Story Reading Fluency Check 7 on page 140 of the Workbook.

┌─────────────────────────┐
│ TASK 13:   │
│ WORKBOOK EXERCISES   │
└─────────────────────────┘

- **Open your Workbook to Lesson 41 on page 47.** Check.
- **Let's look at the Exercises.**

Exercise 1: Matching Words With the Same Sounds

- In Exercise 1 you are going to draw a line to match words that have the same sound or sound combination.
- Read the first word.
- **Ready.** Signal. Student reads, *start.*
- Now touch the second group of words. Read the first word there.
- **Ready.** Signal. Student reads, *about.*
- **Does start have the same sound or sound combination as about?**
- Repeat until student finds the correct word, *jar.*
- **Good. Now draw a line to join the words start and jar.**
- Repeat for the rest of the words in the list.

Exercise 2: Solving a Code

- Let's look at Exercise 2. You are going to use a code to print some sentences.
- Look in the box to find out what words certain letters or graphics represent. Have the student read each letter and word in the box.
- **Now let's look at sentence number 1. What word does the picture of the eye represent?**
- **Ready.** Signal. Student says, *I.*
- **Good. Print I on the line.**
- Repeat for each letter or graphic in the sentence. Then say, **Good printing. Now read that sentence.**
- **Ready.** Signal. Student reads, *I can see you.*
- Repeat for numbers 2 to 6.

Exercise 3: Printing Sound Combinations

- In Exercise 3 you are going to practice printing the letters for the sound combinations you learned in this Lesson.
- Have the student print four each of the sound combinations igh and ea.

Exercise 4: Filling in the Blanks

- You need your Reader for Exercise 4. Turn to Lesson 41 on page 26 of your Reader.
- You are going to fill in the blanks in Exercise 4 with the correct words from the story <u>The boy who learns to read - part one</u>.
- Read the first sentence.
- **Ready.** Signal.
- Find the correct words that complete that sentence and print those words in the blank. Check. **Now read the whole sentence.**
- Repeat for each sentence.

Exercise 5: Crossing Out Vowels that Say their Names

- Now let's do Exercise 5. You must read each word. Then you will cross out any vowel that says its name.
- What's the first word?
- **Ready.** Signal. Student says, *cabin.*
- Is there a vowel that says its name in cabin?
- Repeat for each word.

Exercise 6a: Making New Words

- In Exercise 6a you are going to make some new words from the letters in the word already.
- Can you see another word that you can make from some of the letters in already?
- **Good! Print that word on the first line.**
- Monitor the student as s/he prints new words. Be ready to make some suggestions.

Exercise 6b: Rhyme Time!

- Now you are going to print words from the letters in already that rhyme with the words in Exercise 6b.

- Read the first word.
- **Ready.** Signal. Student reads, *dear.*
- **Good. What is a word made from the letters in already that rhymes with dear?**
- **That's right, year. Print year in the blanks.** Check.
- Repeat for the rest of the words.

Exercise 7: Answering a Riddle

- **Exercise 7 is a riddle. Read the riddle.**
- **Ready.** Signal. Student reads, *What kind of animal can jump higher than a house?*
- **Good reading! Any guesses?** Have student try to answer the riddle. If s/he is stumped, turn the Workbook over to read the answer.

TASK 14: AWARDING POINTS

- Record the total points for Lesson 41 on page 141 of the Workbook.

End of Lesson 41

LESSON 42

TASK 1: PRACTICING SOUNDS

- **Let's do a quick review of all of the sounds you have learned.**
- **Say the sound when I touch it.**
- **Ready.** Signal.

m p c ol ck

er h ir u z

e x oy

✔ If any error occurs, use correction procedure (my turn, do it with me, your turn) as in previous Lessons and repeat the row.

· Now you are going to sound out some words made up of these sounds. As I touch the sounds, you say them.

· First word.
· **Ready.** Signal.

· **Good work. What's that word?**
· **Ready.** Signal.

· Repeat for each word in the list.

n o th ing

t ēā ch

s m o k e

p l ai n

t ēā m

f or g e t

f or g o t

c l ēā n

s t or m

d i nn er

s ou th

m or n ing

l ēā d er

97

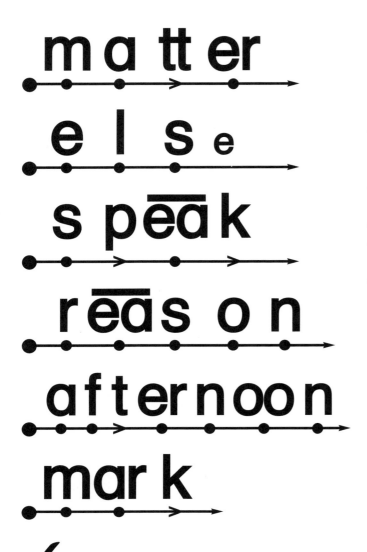

matter

else

speak

reason

afternoon

mark

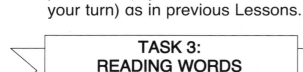 If any error occurs, use correction procedure (my turn, do it with me, your turn) as in previous Lessons.

TASK 3: READING WORDS

- Turn to TASK 2 in this Lesson. Say, **Now you are going to practice reading the words you sounded out.**

- **First word.**
- **Ready.** Signal. Student reads word.

- Repeat for each word in list.

 If necessary, use correction procedure (my turn, do it with me, your turn) as in previous Lessons.

TASK 4: SAYING THE UNDERLINED SOUNDS AND READING THE WORDS

- Touch the underlined sound in the first word. Say, **Tell me the underlined sound.**
- **Ready.** Signal.

- **Now tell me the word.**
- **Ready.** Signal.

- Repeat for each of the words in the list.

p<u>aw</u>	many	nor<u>th</u>
<u>qu</u>ick	rai<u>n</u>	<u>t</u>en
fi<u>x</u>	ga<u>v</u>e	d<u>ir</u>t
acr<u>o</u>ss	s<u>a</u>ve	st<u>ar</u>t
f<u>oo</u>d	s<u>ai</u>l	s<u>o</u>re
y<u>ar</u>d	br<u>igh</u>t	<u>ai</u>d

✓ Use correction procedure (my turn, do it with me, your turn) as in previous Lessons if student makes an error.

TASK 5: PRACTICING IRREGULAR WORDS

- **You are going to read some irregular words you have already learned.**

- **Read the first word and spell it.**
- **Ready.** Signal.

- Repeat for each word.

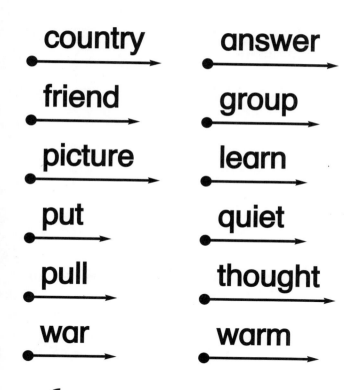

country   answer

friend   group

picture   learn

put   quiet

pull   thought

war   warm

✓ If necessary, use correction procedure from previous Lessons.

TASK 6: TEACHING IRREGULAR WORDS

- Say, **Here are some new irregular words. First I will read the word, then you will read the word and spell it.**

- **Listen. The first word is search.**
- **What word?**
- **Ready.** Signal.
- **Yes, search.**

- **Spell search.**
- **Ready.** Signal.

- Repeat for each word.

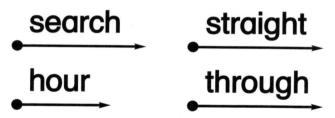

search   straight

hour   through

 ✓ If necessary, use correction procedure from previous Lessons.

TASK 7: STORY READING

- Now it's time to read the second part of the story you read the last time. Turn to Lesson 42 on page 28 in your Reader. Check.

- **Put your finger on the title.**
- **Read the title please.**
- **Ready.** Signal.

- **Now read the story.**
- **Ready.** Signal.

<u>The boy who learns to read - part two</u>

One bright morning Jack found a hurt cub in the pine forest.
He and his dad got it back to their warm cabin to fix its sore paw.
Jack went and got the first-aid book but he could not read it.
His dad said, "First I will use the book to help the bear cub.
Then I will start to teach you how to read."
His dad read the book and was able to fix the cub's paw.
Then he said to Jack, "Now you must learn to read.
We will work each night after dinner for one hour.
First I will teach you the sounds, then I will show you how to read words."
More to come

 ✓ If the student has a problem with any word, have him/her sound it out, say it and then start at the beginning of that sentence again. If the student makes 7 errors, reread the story from the beginning.

TASK 8: SOUND FLUENCY CHECK 8

- **Time for another Sound Fluency Check. Turn to page 22 in your Reader.** Time student for 30 seconds.

- Record scores for Day 3 of Sound Fluency Check 8 on page 138 of the Workbook.

TASK 9: WORD FLUENCY CHECK 8

- **Time for another Word Fluency Check. Turn to page 23.** Time student for 30 seconds.

- Record scores for Day 3 of Word Fluency Check 8 on page 139 of the Workbook.

TASK 10: STORY READING FLUENCY CHECK 7

- **Time for another Story Reading Fluency Check. Turn to page 24 in your Reader.** Time student for 1 minute.

- Record scores for Day 3 of Story Reading Fluency Check 7 on page 140 of the Workbook.

TASK 11: WORKBOOK EXERCISES

- Say, **Now we are going to do the Workbook part of the Lesson.**
- **Open your Workbook to Lesson 42 on page 53.** Check.

Exercise 1: Answering a Riddle

- **Exercise 1 is a riddle. Read the riddle.**
- **Ready.** Signal. Student reads, *What do little whales learn in school?*
- **To answer the riddle you are going to**

print the letter that is in one word but not in another.
- **Read number 1. What letter is in the word read but not in red?**
- **Ready.** Signal. Student answers, *a.*
- **Yes, a. Print an a in the first blank below.**
- Repeat for numbers 2 to 6.
- **So what do little whales learn in school?**
- **They learn their a, b, seas! Great work!**

*Exercise 2: True or False?

- **In Exercise 2 we are going to review the story <u>The boy who learns to read - part one</u> in your Reader. Open your Reader to page 26.**
- **You are going to read each sentence in your Workbook and decide whether it is true or false.**
- **Put your finger on number 1. Read that sentence.**
- **Ready.** Signal. Student reads sentence.
- **Good reading! Is that sentence true or false?**
- **Ready.** Signal. Student says, *false.*
- **Good. Print an F for False on the line beside the sentence.**
- Repeat for sentences 2 to 6.

Exercise 3: Filling in the Blanks

- **You also need your Reader for Exercise 3. Turn to Lesson 42 on page 28 of your Reader.**
- **You are going to fill in the blanks in Exercise 3 with the correct words from the story <u>The boy who learns to read - part two</u>.**
- **Read the first sentence.**
- **Ready.** Signal.
- **Find the correct words that complete that sentence and print those words in the blank.** Check. **Now read the whole sentence.**
- Repeat for each sentence.

Exercise 4: Making New Words

- In Exercise 4 you are going to make some new words from the letters in the word nothing.
- Can you see another word that you can make from some of the letters in nothing?
- Good! Print that word on the first line.
- Monitor the student as s/he prints new words. Be ready to make some suggestions.

Exercise 5: Rhyme Time!

- Find Exercise 5. There are some sounds written inside the light bulb. Read these sounds.
- You are going to print some words in the blanks that match the pictures. The words all rhyme with **tight**. You must add one of the sounds in the light bulb to the beginning of the word to make a rhyming word.
- What is the first picture?
- **Ready.** Signal. Student says, *birds flying.*
- Yes. What word can you print that rhymes with **tight** and begins with one of the sounds in the light bulb?
- **Ready.** Signal. Student says, *flight.*
- That's good, **flight**. Print **flight** in the blanks. Check.
- Repeat for each sound.

Exercise 6: Unscrambling Words

- Find Exercise 6. You are going to unscramble some letters to spell some words you know.
- Touch the first scrambled word. You must make a four-letter word with the sounds d, rrr, aaa and yēēē. Can you find a four-letter word in the grocery bag that has those sounds?
- **Ready.** Signal. Student answers, *yard.*

- That's right, **yard**. Print the word **yard** in the blanks beside the first word. Put a check mark beside the word **yard** in the word list so you know you have done it.
- Repeat for each scrambled word.
- Now print the circled letters in the blanks numbered 1 to 8. What are those words?
- **Ready.** Signal. Student says, *your name.*
- That's right. You are going to print your name in the book below. Check.

TASK 12: AWARDING POINTS

- Record the total points for Lesson 42 on page 141 of the Workbook.

End of Lesson 42

LESSON 43

- Now you are going to sound out some words. As I touch the sounds, you say them.

- **First word.**
- **Ready.** Signal.

- **What's that word?**
- **Ready.** Signal.

- Repeat for each word in the list.

tēa ch er

hundred

s ai l or

midnight

a s l ēē p

ēa s y

forget

c am p ing

r ēa d

read

s m e ll

a c r oss

jaw

e x a m p l e

c l ēa r

t r ai n

102

If any error occurs, use correction procedure (my turn, do it with me, your turn) as in previous Lessons.

TASK 2: READING RHYMING WORDS

- Now you are going to read some words that rhyme with **soon**.
- Touch the dot in front of the word **soon**. Slide your finger along the line and say **soon**.

- What's that word?
- **Ready.** Signal.

- All the words rhyme with **soon**.

- Look at the next word.
- What's that word?
- **Ready.** Signal.

- Repeat for each word in the list.

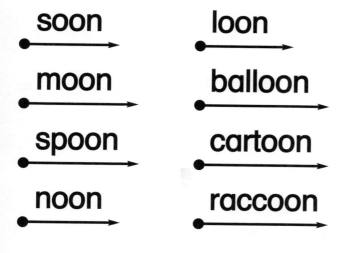

soon   loon

moon   balloon

spoon   cartoon

noon   raccoon

 Use correction procedure as in previous Lessons if necessary.

- Now you are going to read some words you already know.
- First word.
- **Ready.** Signal.

- Repeat for each word in the list.

bēcause   river

rich   splash

dāy   whip

must   could

right   study

lōw   store

wore   or

chore   bēfore

shore   tore

shōw   hard

sound   first

story   while

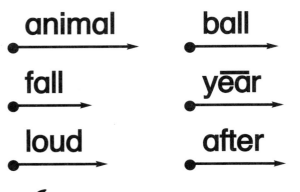

animal   ball

fall   yēar

loud   after

✓ If the student makes an error reading a word, use the correction procedure as in previous Lessons.

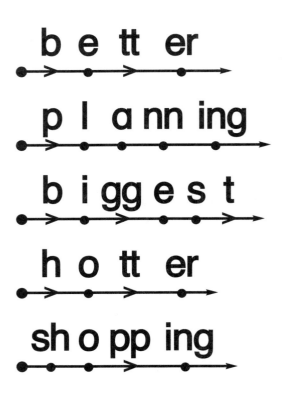

b e tt er

p l a nn ing

b i gg e s t

h o tt er

sh o pp ing

TASK 4: SOUNDING OUT WORDS WITH DOUBLE CONSONANTS

- **Now you are going to sound out some words. All of these words have double consonants before the ending.**

- Put your finger on the first word. Say, **Sound this word out.**
- **Ready.** Signal.

- **What's that word?**
- **Ready.** Signal.
- **Good!**

- Repeat for all of the words in the list.

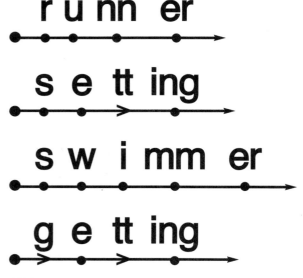

r u nn er

s e tt ing

s w i mm er

g e tt ing

 Use correction procedure in Lesson 35 if necessary.

TASK 5: PRACTICING IRREGULAR WORDS

- **You are going to read some irregular words you have already learned.**

- **Read the first word and spell it.**
- **Ready.** Signal.

- Repeat for each word.

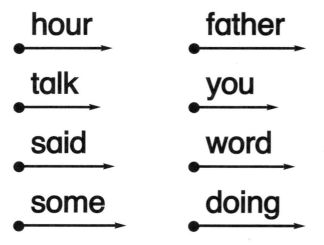

hour   father

talk   you

said   word

some   doing

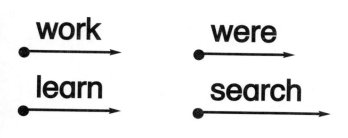

work

were

learn

search

 If necessary, use correction procedure from previous Lessons.

- Say, **Here are some new irregular words. First I will read the word, then you will read the word and spell it.**

- **Listen. The first word is worry.**
- **What word?**
- **Ready.** Signal.
- **Yes, worry.**

- **Spell worry.**
- **Ready.** Signal.

- Repeat for each word.

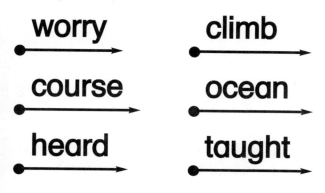

worry

climb

course

ocean

heard

taught

 If necessary, use correction procedure from previous Lessons.

TASK 7: STORY READING

- Now it's time to read the rest of the story about Jack learning to read. Turn to Lesson 43 on page 30 in your Reader. Check.

- **Put your finger on the title.**
- **Read the title please.**
- **Ready.** Signal.

- **Now read the story.**
- **Ready.** Signal.

<u>The boy who learns to read - part three</u>

Jack and his father were able to help the cub with the sore paw to get well.
As the cub got better, Jack's father began to teach Jack how to read.
First he taught him some letters and told him the sound that each letter makes.
Soon Jack began to sound out words.
Each day he sat learning with his father for an hour after dinner.
Soon Jack could read a short story.
But many words were still hard to read.
And he could not read fast.
His father said, "You are doing very well.
Work hard every day.
Soon you will be able to read out loud as fast as you can talk.
Then you will be a good reader."
His father was right.
In a little while Jack could read any book, even the big first-aid book.

The end of this story

 If the student has a problem with any word, have him/her sound it out, say it and then start at the beginning of that sentence again. If the student makes 7 errors, reread the story from the beginning.

TASK 8: SOUND FLUENCY CHECK 8

NOTE: If the student has said 50+ sounds correctly in 1 minute for three consecutive days, s/he may discontinue timings on Sound Fluency Check 8 if s/he so chooses.

- If not, say, **Time for a Sound Fluency Check. Turn to page 22 in your Reader.** Time student for 30 seconds.

- Record scores for Day 4 of Sound Fluency Check 8 on page 138 of the Workbook.

TASK 9: WORD FLUENCY CHECK 8

NOTE: If the student has read 60+ words correctly in 1 minute for three consecutive days, s/he may discontinue timings on Word Fluency Check 8 if s/he so chooses.

- If not, say, **Time for a Word Fluency Check. Turn to page 23.** Time student for 30 seconds.

- Record scores for Day 4 of Word Fluency Check 8 on page 139 of the Workbook.

TASK 10: STORY READING FLUENCY CHECK 7

NOTE: If the student has read 200+ words per minute in the story three consecutive times, s/he has reached fluency and does not need to try again on this Lesson unless s/he chooses to do so. Time student on another story of his/her choice in the Reader.

- If the student has not yet reached fluency, say, **Time for another Story Reading Fluency Check. Turn to page 24 in your Reader.** Time student for one minute.

- Record scores for Day 4 of Story Reading Fluency Check 7 on page 140 of the Workbook.

TASK 11: WORKBOOK EXERCISES

- Say, **Now you are going to do the Workbook Exercises.**
- **Open your Workbook to Lesson 43 on page 59.** Check.

Exercise 1: Practicing the Doubling Rule

- **Find Exercise 1. Read the list of words in Column A.**
- **Ready.** Signal. Student reads, *run, plan, hot, shop.*
- **Good reading! Now you are going to double the final consonant in each word and then add the ending e-r.**
- **Look at the word run. What letter are you going to double?**
- **Ready.** Signal.
- **Yes, the n.**
- **On the first line print n and add e-r.** Check.
- **What's that word?**
- **Ready.** Signal. Student says, *runner.*
- Repeat for the rest of the words in Column A.
- **Now read the list of words in Column B.**
- **Ready.** Signal. Student reads, *set, swim, get, run.*
- **Good. Now you are going to double the final consonant in each word and then add the ending i-n-g.**
- **Look at the word set. What letter are you going to double?**
- **Ready.** Signal.
- **Yes, the t.**
- **On the first line print t and add i-n-g.** Check.
- **What's that word?**
- **Ready.** Signal. Student says, *setting.*
- Repeat for the rest of the words in Column B.

Exercise 2: Printing the Correct Sound Combination

- Find Exercise 2. Read the two sound combinations.
- **Ready.** Signal. Student reads, $\bar{e}\bar{e}\bar{e}$, eee.
- **Good.** Now look at the three words in number 1. Which of those two sound combinations are in each of these three words?
- **Ready.** Signal. Student says, $\bar{e}\bar{e}\bar{e}$.
- **Good.** Print $\bar{e}\bar{e}\bar{e}$ on the line beside the words. Check.
- Repeat for 2, 3 and 4.

Exercise 3: Circling Vowels that Say their Names

- Now let's do Exercise 3. You must read each word and circle any vowel that says its name.
- **What's the first word?**
- **Ready.** Signal. Student says, *cabin.*
- **Is there a vowel that says its name in cabin?**
- Repeat for each word.

Exercise 4: Putting Story Events in Order

- Let's do Exercise 4. You are going to review the stories <u>The boy who learns to read - parts one and two</u> by putting events from those stories in order from 1 to 5. Open your Reader to page 26. Check.
- **Now read the sentences in your Workbook. Number 1.**
- **Ready.** Signal. Student reads the first sentence.
- Repeat for the rest of the sentences.
- **Which one of these events came first?**
- **Ready.** Signal. Student says, *One day in the forest Jack found a bear cub that had hurt its paw.*
- **That's right.** Put a number 1 on the line at the beginning of that sentence.

- Have the student number the rest of the sentences from 2 to 5.

Exercise 5: Filling in the Blanks

- You also need your Reader for Exercise 5. Turn to page 30.
- You are going to fill in the blanks in Exercise 5 with the correct word from the story <u>The boy who learns to read - part three</u>.
- **Read the first sentence.**
- **Ready.** Signal.
- Find the correct words that complete that sentence and print those words in the blanks. Now read the whole sentence.
- Repeat for each sentence.

Exercise 6: Answering a Riddle

- Put your finger on Exercise 6. Read the riddle.
- **Ready.** Signal. Student reads, *What does a bear get if he rubs his paws on a beach?*
- To answer this riddle you are going to cross out all the short sounds b, g, h, j and k. The letters that are left will be the answer.
- Take your pencil and cross out all the short sounds b, g, h, j and k.
- Now print the letters that remain in the spaces below.
- **What does a bear get if he rubs his paws on a beach?**
- **That's right, sandy claws!**

```
TASK 12:
AWARDING POINTS
```

- Record the total points for Lesson 43 on page 141 of the Workbook.

End of Lesson 43

LESSON 44

- When these two letters are together, they often say the sound wooo.
- **Listen.** Touch the dot under the wa and say **wooo** for one second. Lift your finger.
- **Listen again.** Repeat.

- **Say the sound with me. Keep on saying it as long as I touch it.**
- **Ready.** Signal.
- Repeat.

- **Your turn.**
- **Ready.** Signal.
- Repeat the task until the student does it as instructed.

wa

 If any error occurs, use correction procedure (my turn, do it with me, your turn) as in previous Lessons.

TASK 2: PRACTICING THE SOUND COMBINATION wa

- **Now you are going to sound out some words that have the sound combination you just learned. As I touch the sounds, you say them.**

- **First word.**
- **Ready.** Signal.

- **What's that word?**
- **Ready.** Signal.

- Repeat for each word in the list.

108

wa t er

wa sh

 If any error occurs, use correction procedure (my turn, do it with me, your turn) as in previous Lessons and begin the list again.

TASK 3: TEACHING THE SOUND g$_{i,e}$ as in ginger

- Point to the sound g$_{i,e}$ and say, **When this letter is followed by an i or an e, it often says a short soft sound.**

- **I am going to touch the sound and say it.**
- **Listen.** Tap the arrow under the g$_{i,e}$ and say **j**.
- **Listen again. j.**

- **Say the sound with me.**
- **Ready.** Signal.

- **Your turn.**
- **Ready.** Signal. Student says *j*.
- Repeat the task until the student does it as instructed.

g$_{i,e}$

 If necessary, use correction procedure (my turn, do it with me, your turn) as in previous lessons.

TASK 4: PRACTICING THE SOUND $g_{i,e}$

- Now you are going to sound out some words that have the short sound you just learned. Remember to put the sounds together without stopping.

- Sound out the first word.
- **Ready.** Signal.

- **Read that word.**
- **Ready.** Signal.

- Repeat for each of the words in the list.

g i n g er

l ar g e

ch ā n g e

✓ If the student makes an error or stops between the sounds, use correction procedure (my turn, do it with me, your turn) as in previous Lessons and begin the list again.

TASK 5: TEACHING THE SOUND $C_{i,e}$ as in i<u>c</u>e

- Point to the sound $c_{i,e}$ and say, **When this letter is followed by an i or an e, it says a soft sound.**

- **I am going to touch the sound and say it.**
- **Listen.** Touch the dot under the $c_{i,e}$ and say **sss** for one second.
- **Listen again. sss.**

- **Say the sound with me.**
- **Ready.** Signal.

- **Good job. Now it's your turn.**
- **Ready.** Touch the dot under the sound $c_{i,e}$ and listen to the student say the sound *sss*.
- Repeat the task until the student does it as instructed.

Ç$_{i,e}$

✓ If necessary, use correction procedure (my turn, do it with me, your turn) as in previous lessons.

TASK 6: PRACTICING THE SOUND $C_{i,e}$

- Now you are going to sound out some words that have the sound sss in them.

- **Sound out the first word.**
- **Ready.** Signal.

- **What's that word?**
- **Ready.** Signal.

- Repeat for each of the words in the list.

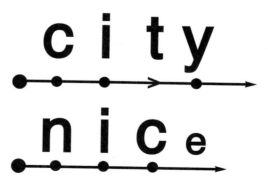

c i t y

n i c e

c er t ai n

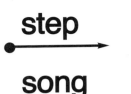
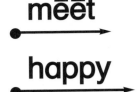

step

song

mēēt

happy

✓ If the student makes an error or stops between the sounds, use correction procedure (my turn, do it with me, your turn) as in previous Lessons and begin the list again.

✓ If necessary, use correction procedure (my turn, do it with me, your turn) as in previous Lessons.

TASK 7: READING WORDS

- Now you are going to practice reading some words you already know.

- First word.
- **Ready.** Signal.

- Repeat for each word in list.

TASK 8: SOUNDING OUT WORDS THAT BEGIN WITH SHORT SOUNDS

- Now you are going to sound out some words that begin with short sounds. Remember to put the sounds together without stopping.

- Sound out the first word.
- **Ready.** Signal.

- What's that word?
- **Ready.** Signal.

- Repeat for each of the words in the list.

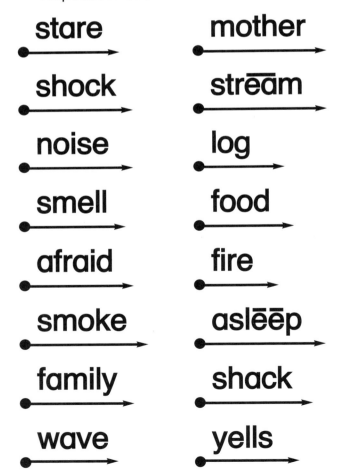

stare

shock

noise

smell

afraid

smoke

family

wave

mother

strēām

log

food

fire

aslēēp

shack

yells

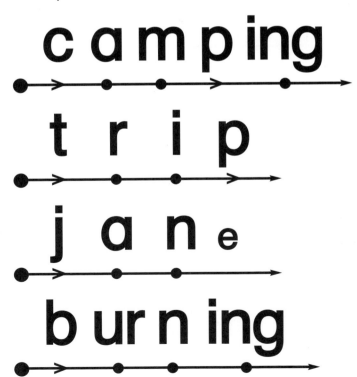

c a m p ing

t r i p

j a n e

b ur n ing

110

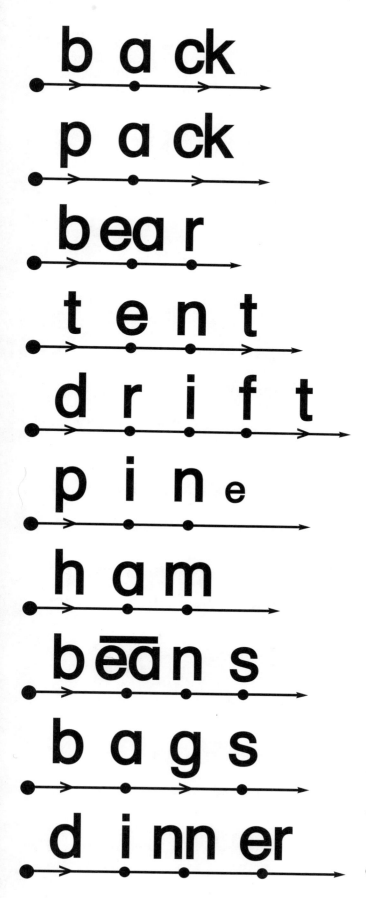

b a ck

p a ck

b ea r

t e n t

d r i f t

p i n e

h a m

b ēā n s

b a g s

d i nn er

g ō ing

c l aw

p ai n

g r ou n d

c ou n t

✓ If the student makes an error or stops between the sounds, use correction procedure (my turn, do it with me, your turn) as in previous Lessons and begin the list again.

TASK 9: PRACTICING IRREGULAR WORDS

- You are going to read some irregular words that you will see in this Lesson's story.

- Read the first word and spell it.
- **Ready.** Signal.

- Repeat for each word.

are   **their**

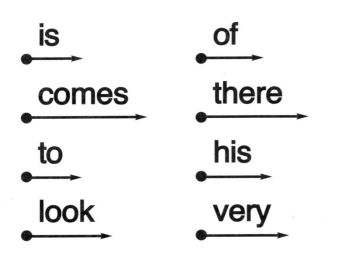

is →   of →

comes →   there →

to →   his →

look →   very →

 If necessary, use correction procedure from previous Lessons.

TASK 10: STORY READING

- **Now it's time to read a story. Turn to Lesson 44 on page 32 in your Reader.** Check.

- **Put your finger on the title.**
- **Read the title please.**
- **Ready.** Signal.

- **Now read the story.**
- **Ready.** Signal.

<u>Camping with a bear - part one</u>

Mark and Jane are happy.
They are going camping at the lake with their mother and father.
They all have back packs and sleeping bags and a tent.
They set up their tent near the water as the sun is setting.
They make a big dinner of beans and ham.
The fire burns low and the smoke drifts over the pines.
All of them curl up in their sleeping bags in the tent.
Soon they fall fast asleep.

A large brown bear smells the food from dinner.
He comes to see if there is any more to eat.
But the bear steps on a burning log and hurts his paw.
He makes a loud noise and wakes up the family.
They look out of the tent and see the bear.
They are very afraid.
The large brown bear stares at them from across the fire.
More to come

✓ If the student has a problem with any word, have him/her sound it out, say it and then start at the beginning of that sentence again. If the student makes 7 errors, reread the story from the beginning.

TASK 11: SOUND FLUENCY CHECK 8

<u>REMINDER</u>: If the student has said 50+ sounds correctly in 1 minute for any three days of the last four, s/he may discontinue timings on Sound Fluency Check 8 if s/he so chooses.

- If not, say, **Time for a Sound Fluency Check. Turn to page 22 in your Reader.** Time student for 30 seconds.

- Record scores for Day 5 of Sound Fluency Check 8 on page 138 of the Workbook.

<u>REMINDER</u>: If the student has been unable to say at least 50 sounds correctly per minute at least one time in Sound Fluency Check 8, finish and correct the Workbook Exercises for Lesson 44 but do not proceed to teach new material. Instead, reteach Lessons 40 through 44. Include daily practice and timings on Sound

Fluency Check 8 on page 22. Circle and practice any sounds the student is having difficulty with. Record scores in the Additional Practice columns for Sound Fluency Check 8 on page 138 of the Student Workbook. Students should continue to be awarded points for working hard, paying attention, following instructions and doing well on fluency checks. When the student is able to say 50+ sounds from the list in 1 minute, begin Lesson 45.

TASK 12: WORD FLUENCY CHECK 8

REMINDER: If the student has read 60+ words correctly in 1 minute for any three days of the last four, s/he may discontinue timings on Word Fluency Check 8 if s/he so chooses.

- If not, say, **Time for a Word Fluency Check. Turn to page 23.** Time student for 30 seconds.

- Record scores for Day 5 of Word Fluency Check 8 on page 139 of the Workbook.

REMINDER: If the student has been unable to read at least 60 words correctly in 1 minute at least one time in Word Fluency Check 8, finish the Workbook Exercises for Lesson 44 but do not proceed with new material. Instead, redo Lessons 40 through 44. Include daily practice and timings on Word Fluency Check 8 on page 23. Circle and practice any words the student is having difficulty with. Students should continue to be awarded points for working hard, paying attention, following instructions and doing well on fluency checks. When the student is able to read 60+ words from the list in 1 minute, continue in the Reader with Lesson 45.

TASK 13: STORY READING FLUENCY CHECK 7

REMINDER: If the student has read 200+ words per minute in the story for three of the last four attempts, s/he has reached fluency and does not need to try again on this Lesson unless s/he chooses to do so. Have the student choose another story from the Reader to do a timing on.

- If the student has not yet reached fluency, say, **Time for another Story Reading Fluency Check. Turn to page 24 in your Reader.** Time student for one minute.

- Record scores for Day 5 of Story Reading Fluency Check 7 on page 140 of the Workbook.

NOTE: If the student has not yet reached fluency at 200+ words a minute in the same story on at least one timing, finish and correct the Workbook Exercises for Lesson 44, but do not proceed with new material. Instead, have the student practice reading the first half of the story until s/he can read it with fewer than 3 L.O.s in 30 seconds. Then practice the next half in the same manner. Combine the two sections and practice until the student can read them fluently in a minute. Record scores in the Additional Practice columns for Story Reading Fluency Check 7. Award points for working hard, paying attention, following instructions and doing well in fluency checks. When the student has reached fluency, begin Lesson 45.

TASK 14: WORKBOOK EXERCISES

- **Open your Workbook to Lesson 44 on page 63.** Check.

Exercise 1: Crossword Puzzle

- Exercise 1 is a crossword puzzle. There are pictures to help you know what word to print in the boxes.
- Touch number 1. What is that a picture of?
- **Ready.** Signal. Student says, *a moon.*
- **That's right. To help you spell that word there is a word list inside the balloon. Find the word moon. Now print moon in the boxes for number 1.** Check.
- Repeat for each of the next five words.

Exercise 2: Printing Sounds

- In Exercise 2 you are going to practice printing the letters for the sounds you learned in this Lesson.
- Have the student print five of the sounds wooo, j and sss.

Exercise 3: Circling and Crossing out Sounds

- **In Exercise 3 you are going to circle all the sounds wooo, cross out all the sounds j and put a box around the sounds sss.**
- **Read the first word.**
- **Ready.** Signal. Student reads, *clean.*
- **Does the word clean have any of the sounds wooo, j or sss?**
- Repeat for each word. When student identifies a wooo, j or sss, have him/her circle it, cross it out or put a box around it.

Exercise 4: Solving a Code to Answer a Riddle

- **Let's look at Exercise 4. You are going to solve a code to answer two riddles. In the box certain symbols represent certain letters.**
- **Read the first riddle.**
- **Ready.** Signal. Student reads, *What is a cat's favorite dessert?*
- Yes. Figure out the letters that go in each blank.
- **Good! So what is a cat's favorite dessert?**
- **That's right, mice cream!**
- Repeat for second riddle, What is a cat's favorite drink? (Miced tea)

Exercise 5: Answering Questions from the Reader

- **You need your Reader for Exercise 5. Turn to page 32 of your Reader.** Check. **You are going to answer some questions from the story <u>Camping with a bear - part one</u>.**
- **Read the first question.**
- **Ready.** Signal. Student reads, *How do Mark and Jane feel?*
- **Good. Now read the beginning of the answer.**
- **Ready.** Signal. Student reads, *Mark and Jane . . .*
- **Find the correct words that complete that sentence and print those words on the line.** Check. **Now read the whole sentence.**
- Repeat for each question.

Exercise 6: Putting Words in Alphabetical Order

- **Find Exercise 6. Read the words.**
- **Ready.** Signal. Student reads from high to beans.
- **In this exercise you are going to print these words in alphabetical order. You must look at the first letter in each word. What first letter in these words** (point to list) **comes first in the alphabet?**
- **Ready.** Signal. Student answers, *act.*
- **That's right! Print act in the boxes. Put a check mark beside it.**
- **What is the word with a first letter that comes next in the alphabet?**
- **Ready.** Signal. Student says, *beans.*

- Well done. Print **beans** in the second set of boxes. Check.
- Repeat for the rest of the words. When the student has finished doing all seven of them, say, **Good work! You just put those seven words in alphabetical order.**
- Now print the letters that are circled in the blanks below to spell a favorite summertime activity. What is it?
- **That's right, camping.**

TASK 15:
AWARDING POINTS

- Record the total points for Lesson 44 on page 141 of the Workbook.

End of Lesson 44

TASK 1: PRACTICING
IRREGULAR WORDS

- You are going to read some irregular words you have already learned.

- **Read the first word and spell it.**
- **Ready.** Signal.

- Repeat for each word.

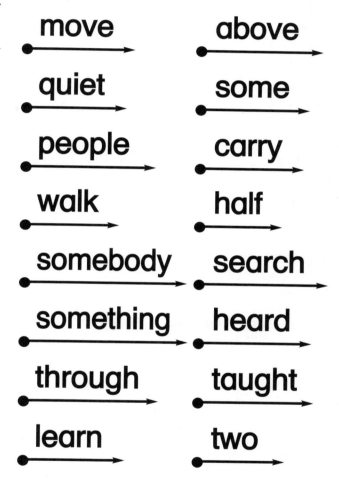

move above
quiet some
people carry
walk half
somebody search
something heard
through taught
learn two

 If necessary, use correction procedure from previous Lessons.

TASK 2: TEACHING IRREGULAR WORDS

- Say, **Here are some new irregular words. First I will read the word, then you will read the word and spell it.**

- **Listen. The first word is sure.**
- **What word?**
- **Ready.** Signal.
- **Yes, sure.**

- **Spell sure.**
- **Ready.** Signal.

- Repeat for each word.

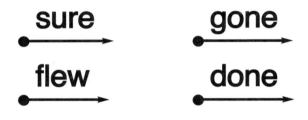

sure →   **gone** →

flew →   **done** →

 If necessary, use correction procedure from previous Lessons.

TASK 3: SAYING THE UNDERLINED SOUNDS AND READING THE WORDS

- Touch the underlined sound in the first word. Say, **Tell me the underlined sound.**
- **Ready.** Signal.

- **Now tell me the word.**
- **Ready.** Signal.

- Repeat for each of the words in the list.

a<u>c</u>ross   d<u>ea</u>d   h<u>e</u>re

l<u>ea</u>d   <u>ō</u>v<u>er</u>   r<u>ai</u>n

s<u>ou</u>th   r<u>ea</u>d   up<u>o</u>n

<u>e</u>very   <u>sh</u>out   ou<u>r</u>

<u>w</u>oke   s<u>ai</u>l   <u>al</u>w<u>ā</u>ys

d<u>ō</u>n't   <u>ēa</u>t   b<u>oy</u>

<u>n</u>ever   <u>ou</u>t   l<u>āy</u>

p<u>ar</u>t   <u>o</u>t<u>h</u>er   <u>th</u>r<u>ō</u>w

 Use correction procedure (my turn, do it with me, your turn) as in previous Lessons if student makes an error.

TASK 4: SOUNDING OUT WORDS

- Now you are going to sound out some new words. As I touch the sounds, you say them.

- **First word.**
- **Ready.** Signal.

- **Good. What's that word?**
- **Ready.** Signal.

- Repeat for each word in the list.

a pp ēa r →

f a n t a s t i c →

s k ȳ

m a tt er

ai r p or t

s a f e

f e l t

v oi c e

m e m b er

s al t

b r ēē z e

f or c e

a m ou n t

g l a ss

s i s t er

d ā n g er

s t u ff

h ēā l

r ē t urn

d a m a g e

✓ If any error occurs, use correction procedure (my turn, do it with me, your turn) as in previous Lessons.

117

- Say, **Now we are going to sound out some words that end in e-d.**
- **The ending e-d means something happened in the past.**
- **Usually e-d says the short sound d.**
- **Listen as I sound out the first word.** Sound out the word sniffed.

- **Say the sounds with me.**
- **Ready.** Signal.

- **Now do that all by yourself.**
- **Ready.** Signal.

- **That word is sniffed.**
- **What's that word?**
- **Ready.** Signal.

- Say, **Listen while I say the sounds for the next word.**

- Repeat Task for each word in the list.

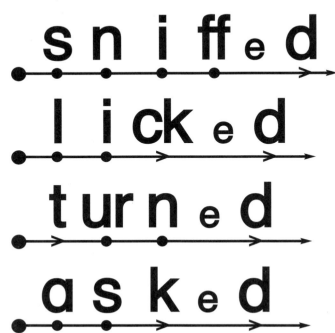

 If any error occurs, use correction procedure (my turn, do it with me, your turn) as in previous Lessons.

TASK 6: STORY READING

- Now it's time to read some more about the bear at the campsite. Turn to Lesson 45 on page 34 in your Reader. Check.

- **Put your finger on the title.**
- **Read the title please.**
- **Ready.** Signal.

- **Now read the story.**
- **Ready.** Signal.

<u>Camping with a bear - part two</u>

Mark, Jane and their mother and father were asleep when the bear came to their camp.
When they woke up and saw the bear they were very afraid.
"Don't move," father said in a quiet voice.
They all lay in their sleeping bags and were very, very quiet.
The bear sniffed the fire.
Then he licked his paw.
He came over to the tent and sniffed some more.
He did not smell food, but he did smell people.
He did not like that smell.
So he turned and went back into the woods.
The family lay still for a long time.
When they were sure the bear was gone, they went to their van.
After a while they fell asleep in the back.
They felt safe there.
The bear did not return.

The end of this story

✓ If the student has a problem with any word, have him/her sound it out, say it and then start at the beginning of that sentence again. If the student makes 7 errors, reread the story from the beginning.

TASK 7: SOUND FLUENCY CHECK 9

- The student has said 50+ sounds per minute in Sound Fluency Check 8 on page 22. Say, **Turn to page 36 in your Reader. There is a list of sounds from Lessons 1 to 45.**
- **You are going to say these sounds as quickly as you can, remembering to hold the sounds with the dots under them for one second.**
- **Which way would you like to do this list?** Student chooses down or across.

- **Put your finger on the first sound.**
- **Ready. Please begin.** Time student for 30 seconds.
- Say, **Thank you.**

- Record sounds said correctly per minute in the Sounds Said Correctly column for Day 1 of Sound Fluency Check 9 on page 138 of the Workbook.
- Record number of errors and/or skipped sounds per minute in the Learning Opportunities column.

TASK 8: WORD FLUENCY CHECK 9

- The student has read 60+ words per minute in Word Fluency Check 8 on page 23. Say, **On page 37 there is a list of words from Lessons 1 to 45.**
- **You are going to read these words as quickly as you can. Which way would you like to read this list?** Student chooses down or across.

- **Put your finger on the first word.**
- **Ready. Please begin.** Time student for 30 seconds.
- Say, **Thank you.**

- Record words read correctly per minute in the Words Read Correctly column for Day 1 of Word Fluency Check 9 on page 139 of the Workbook.
- Record number of errors and/or skipped words per minute in the Learning Opportunities column.

TASK 9: STORY READING FLUENCY CHECK 8

- The student has reached fluency (200+ words/minute) in Story Reading Fluency Check 7. Say, **Now we are going to do a new Story Reading Fluency Check. Turn to page 38 in your Reader.**

- **Put your finger on the title. Get set to read the story.**
- **Ready. Please begin.** Time student for 1 minute.
- At the end of 1 minute say, **Thank you.**

- Record the number of words read correctly in the Words Read Correctly column for Day 1 of Story Reading Fluency Check 8 on page 140 of the Workbook.
- Record errors and/or skipped words in the Learning Opportunities column.

TASK 10: WORKBOOK EXERCISES

- Say, **Now we are going to do the Workbook part of the Lesson.**
- **Open your Workbook to Lesson 45 on page 69.** Check.

Exercise 1: Crossword Puzzle

- Exercise 1 is a crossword puzzle.
- There are pictures beside the puzzle to help you know what word to print in the boxes.
- Touch number 1. What is that a picture of?
- **Ready.** Signal. Student says, *one hundred.*
- That's right. To help you spell that word there is a word list inside the cloud. Find the word **hundred.** Now print hundred in the boxes for number 1. Check.
- Repeat for the rest of the words.

Exercise 2: Filling in the Blanks

- You need your Reader for Exercise 2. Turn to Lesson 45 on page 34 of your Reader. Check.
- You are going to fill in the blanks in Exercise 2 with the correct word from the story <u>Camping with a bear - part two</u>.
- Read the first sentence.
- **Ready.** Signal.
- Find the correct words that complete that sentence and print those words in the blank. Check. **Now read the whole sentence.**
- Repeat for each sentence.

Exercise 3: Rhyme Time!

- Find Exercise 3. In this exercise you have to circle the pairs of words that rhyme.
- Read the first pair of words.
- **Ready.** Signal. Student reads, *sight, bright.*
- Yes. Do the words **sight** and **bright** rhyme?
- That's correct. They do rhyme. Draw a circle around them.
- Repeat for each pair of words.

Exercise 4: Solving a Code to Answer a Riddle

- Let's look at Exercise 4. You are going to solve a code to answer a riddle. Read the riddle.
- **Ready.** Signal. Student reads, *What did the teddy bear say when he was offered dessert?*
- **Let's figure out the sound that goes in each set of words.** Have the student read the words in each box, then print the missing sounds in each shape.
- Good! You have figured out what each shape's sound is. Now solve the code to answer the riddle, What did the teddy bear say when he was offered dessert?
- That's right! He said, "No thanks. I'm stuffed."

TASK 11: AWARDING POINTS

- Record the total points for Lesson 45 on page 141 of the Workbook.

End of Lesson 45

LESSON 46

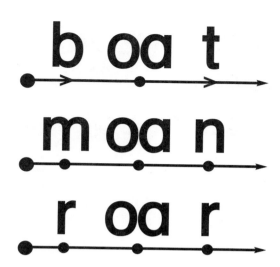

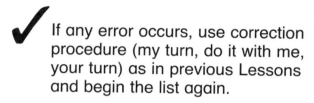

- When these two letters are together, they say the sound ōōō.
- **Listen.** Touch the dot under the oa and say ōōō for one second. Lift your finger.
- **Listen again.** Repeat.

- **Say the sound with me.**
- **Ready.** Signal.
- Repeat.

- **Your turn.**
- **Ready.** Signal.
- Repeat the task until the student does it as instructed.

✓ If any error occurs, use correction procedure (my turn, do it with me, your turn) as in previous Lessons.

- Now you are going to sound out some words that have the sound combination you just learned. As I touch the sounds, you say them.

- First word.
- **Ready.** Signal.

- What's that word?
- **Ready.** Signal.

- Repeat for each word in the list.

✓ If any error occurs, use correction procedure (my turn, do it with me, your turn) as in previous Lessons and begin the list again.

- Touch the underlined sound in the first word.
- Say, **Tell me the underlined sound.**
- **Ready.** Signal.

- Now tell me the word.
- **Ready.** Signal.

- Repeat for each of the words in the list.

sail<u>or</u>	al<u>o</u>ne
<u>c</u>ertain	<u>b</u>ēlōw
sou<u>th</u>	hi<u>gh</u>
br<u>a</u>ve	ōw<u>n</u>
<u>b</u>ored	damage
<u>h</u>uge	w<u>ō</u>n't

121

thank   wind

against   dear

reach   wait

 Use correction procedure (my turn, do it with me, your turn) as in previous Lessons if student makes an error.

TASK 4: READING RHYMING WORDS

- **Now you are going to read some words that rhyme with boat.**
- Touch the dot in front of the word boat. Slide your finger along the line and say boat.

- **What's that word?**
- **Ready.** Signal.

- **All the words rhyme with boat.**

- **Look at the next word.**
- **What's that word?**
- **Ready.** Signal.

- Repeat for each word in the list.

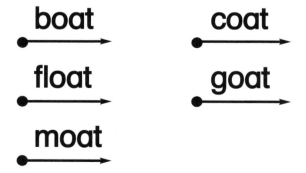

boat   coat

float   goat

moat

 Use correction procedure as in previous Lessons if necessary.

TASK 5: PRACTICING IRREGULAR WORDS

- **You are going to read some irregular words you have already learned.**

- **Read the first word and spell it.**
- **Ready.** Signal.

- Repeat for each word.

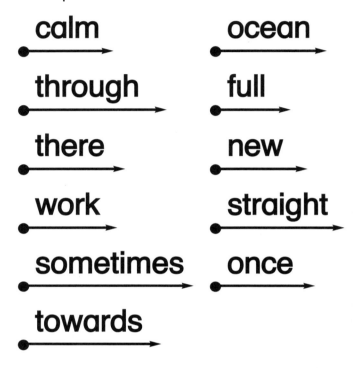

calm   ocean

through   full

there   new

work   straight

sometimes   once

towards

 If necessary, use correction procedure from previous Lessons.

TASK 6: TEACHING IRREGULAR WORDS

- Say, **Here are some new irregular words. First I will read the word, then you will read the word and spell it.**

- **Listen. The first word is island.**
- **What word?**
- **Ready.** Signal.
- **Yes, island.**

- **Spell island.**

- **Ready.** Signal.

- Repeat for each word.

island

Hawaii

shipwreck

true

blue

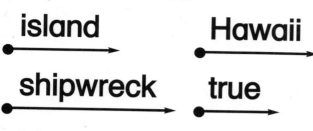

✓ If necessary, use correction procedure from previous Lessons.

TASK 7: SOUNDING OUT WORDS

- Now you are going to sound out some words. As I touch the sounds, you say them.

- **First word.**
- **Ready.** Signal.

- **Good. What's that word?**
- **Ready.** Signal.

- Repeat for each word in the list.

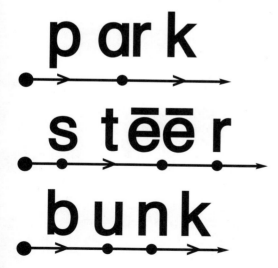

p ar k

s tēē r

b u n k

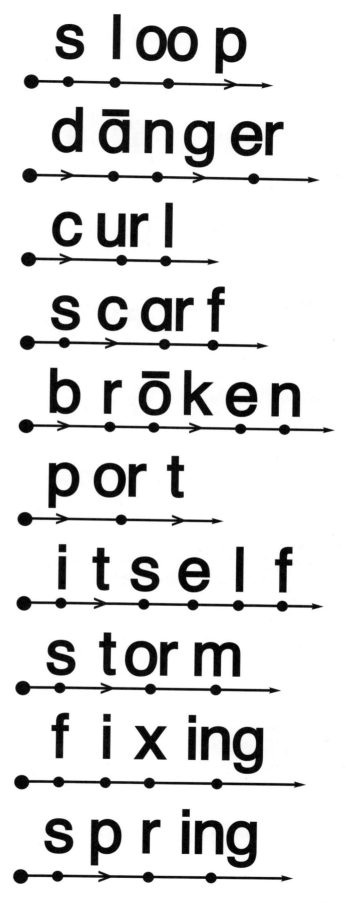

s l oo p

d ā n g er

c ur l

s c ar f

b r ō k e n

p or t

i t s e l f

s t or m

f i x ing

s p r ing

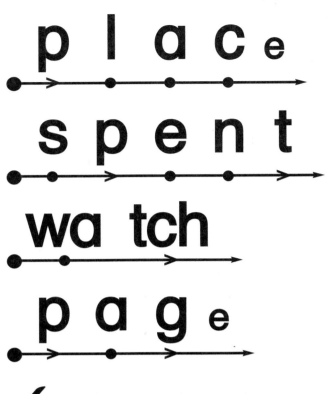

p l a c e

s p e n t

wa tch

p a g e

 If any error occurs, use correction procedure (my turn, do it with me, your turn) as in previous Lessons.

TASK 8:
READING WORDS

- Turn to TASK 7 in this Lesson. Say, **Now you are going to practice reading the words you just sounded out.**

- **First word.**
- **Ready.** Signal.

- Repeat for each word in list.

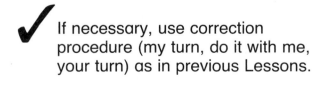 If necessary, use correction procedure (my turn, do it with me, your turn) as in previous Lessons.

TASK 9:
STORY READING

- **Now it's time to read a story. Turn to Lesson 46 on page 40 in your Reader.** Check.

- **Put your finger on the title.**
- **Read the title please.**
- **Ready.** Signal.

- **Now read the story.**
- **Ready.** Signal.

The shipwreck - part one

Carla is a sailor.
She sails her boat alone across huge oceans.
She sails all day and all night, through calm seas and through storms.
The boat steers itself when she is asleep or is eating or working below.
She is sometimes very brave and sometimes very bored.
Sometimes when there is no wind, she floats for a long time in the middle of the ocean.
Once the mast of her boat was broken by a great wave in an awful storm.
Her sloop got into port but she spent a month fixing the damage.
After this she set sail for the islands of New Zealand.
On the way she stopped in Hawaii and in Bora Bora.
Now she is sailing southwest under a full moon.
She curls up in her bunk and falls asleep.
Soon she would be in great danger.

More to come

If the student has a problem with any word, have him/her sound it out, say it and then start at the beginning of that sentence again. If the student makes 7 errors, reread the story from the beginning.

TASK 10: SOUND FLUENCY CHECK 9

- Time for another Sound Fluency Check. **Turn to page 36 in your Reader.** Time student for 30 seconds.

- Record scores for Day 2 of Sound Fluency Check 9 on page 138 of the Workbook.

TASK 11: WORD FLUENCY CHECK 9

- Time for another Word Fluency Check. **Turn to page 37.** Time student for 30 seconds.

- Record scores for Day 2 of Word Fluency Check 9 on page 139 of the Workbook.

TASK 12: STORY READING FLUENCY CHECK 8

- Say to the student, **We are now going to do our second Story Reading Fluency Check. Turn to page 38 in your Reader.** Time student for 1 minute.

- Record scores for Day 2 of Story Reading Fluency Check 8 on page 140 of the Workbook.

TASK 13: WORKBOOK EXERCISES

- Say, **Now we are going to do the Workbook part of the Lesson.**
- **Open your Workbook to Lesson 46 on page 74.** Check.

Exercise 1: Filling in the Blanks

- **You need your Reader for Exercise 1. Turn to Lesson 46 on page 40 of your Reader.**
- **You are going to fill in the blanks in Exercise 1 with the correct word from the story The shipwreck - part one.**
- **Read the first sentence.**
- **Ready.** Signal.
- **Find the correct word that completes that sentence and print that word in the blank.** Check. **Now read the whole sentence.**
- Repeat for each sentence.

Exercise 2: Crossing Out Short Sounds

- **Now let's do Exercise 2. Some of the words that are printed here have short sounds or short sound combinations. You must look at each word and cross out every short sound or short sound combination.**
- **What's the first word?**
- **Ready.** Signal. Student says, *certain.*
- **Are there any short sounds in certain?**
- **Ready.** Signal. **Cross it out.**
- Repeat for each word.

Exercise 3: Printing Sounds

- **In Exercise 3 you are going to practice printing the letters for the sound combination ōōō.**
- Have the student print five of the sound combination ōōō.

Exercise 4: Word Search Puzzle

- **Find Exercise 4. It's a word search puzzle.**
- **Read the first word in the list of words that you will be looking for.**
- **Ready.** Signal. Student reads, *roar.*
- **The arrow beside the word tells you whether the word goes across, up, down or backwards. Look in the puzzle. Go through each row until you find the letters r-o-a-r.**

- That's right. Draw a circle around the word roar.
- Put a check mark beside the word roar in the list so that you know you have found it.
- If the student is having problems finding the word, repeat steps above for each word in the list. If s/he can do the puzzle independently, allow him/her to do so.

Exercise 5: Following a Maze to Answer a Riddle

- Find Exercise 5. In this exercise you are going to go through the water maze to collect some letters to answer a riddle. Read the riddle.
- **Ready.** Signal. Student reads, *What is the world's slowest boat?*
- **Put your pencil on the arrow at the top of the maze.** Check. **Now start through the maze. When you get to a letter, print it in the blanks. If you hit a wave start over again.** Check that the student is following the correct path.
- When the student has successfully gone through the maze and has printed the five letters in the blanks, say, **So what is the world's slowest boat? That's right! A snail boat!**
- Repeat for the riddle, How do you mail a boat? (You ship it!)

```
TASK 14:
AWARDING POINTS
```

- Record the total points for Lesson 46 on page 141 of the Workbook.

End of Lesson 46

LESSON 47

```
TASK 1: TEACHING THE
SOUND COMBINATION
kn as in knee
```

- When these two letters are together, they say the sound **nnn**.
- **Listen.** Touch the dot under the kn and say **nnn** for one second. Lift your finger.
- **Listen again.** Repeat.

- Say the sound with me. Keep on saying it as long as I touch it.
- **Ready.** Signal.
- Repeat.

- Your turn.
- **Ready.** Signal.
- Repeat the task until the student does it as instructed.

 If any error occurs, use correction procedure (my turn, do it with me, your turn) as in previous Lessons.

```
TASK 2: PRACTICING THE
SOUND COMBINATION kn
```

- Now you are going to sound out some words that have the sound combination you just learned. As I touch the sounds, you say them.

- First word.
- **Ready.** Signal.

- What's that word?
- **Ready.** Signal.

- Repeat for each word in the list.

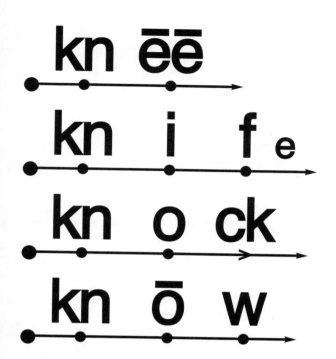

✓ If any error occurs, use correction procedure (my turn, do it with me, your turn) as in previous Lessons and begin the list again.

TASK 3: TEACHING THE SOUND COMBINATION ly as in quickly

- When these two letters are together, they say the sound lēēē.
- **Listen.** Touch the dot under the ly and say lēēē for one second. Lift your finger.
- **Listen again.** Repeat.

- **Say the sound with me.**
- **Ready.** Signal.
- Repeat.

- **Your turn.**
- **Ready.** Signal.
- Repeat the task until the student does it as instructed.

✓ If any error occurs, use correction procedure (my turn, do it with me, your turn) as in previous Lessons.

TASK 4: PRACTICING THE SOUND COMBINATION ly

- Now you are going to sound out some words that have the sound combination you just learned. As I touch the sounds, you say them.

- **First word.**
- **Ready.** Signal.

- **What's that word?**
- **Ready.** Signal.

- Repeat for each word in the list.

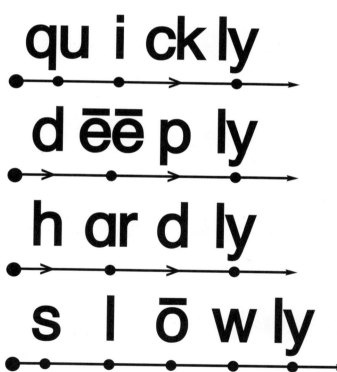

✓ If any error occurs, use correction procedure (my turn, do it with me, your turn) as in previous Lessons and begin the list again.

TASK 5: SAYING THE UNDERLINED SOUNDS AND READING THE WORDS

- Touch the underlined sound in the first word. Say, **Tell me the underlined sound.**
- **Ready.** Signal.

- **Now tell me the word.**
- **Ready.** Signal.

- Repeat for each of the words in the list.

b<u>oa</u>t   <u>wa</u>ter

sin<u>k</u>   <u>c</u>abin

<u>a</u>lmost   bē<u>ing</u>

dānger   <u>w</u>aves

r<u>igh</u>t   st<u>ea</u>dy

bē<u>g</u>an   s<u>a</u>lt

<u>fi</u>lled   <u>b</u>unk

<u>g</u>ash   f<u>ar</u>

just   sl<u>oo</u>p

bā<u>y</u>   m<u>oo</u>n

l<u>ar</u>ge   <u>f</u>resh

<u>h</u>elp   fr<u>ēē</u>

 Use correction procedure (my turn, do it with me, your turn) as in previous Lessons if student makes an error.

TASK 6: PRACTICING IRREGULAR WORDS

- You are going to read some irregular words you have already learned.

- **Read the first word and spell it.**
- **Ready.** Signal.

- Repeat for each word.

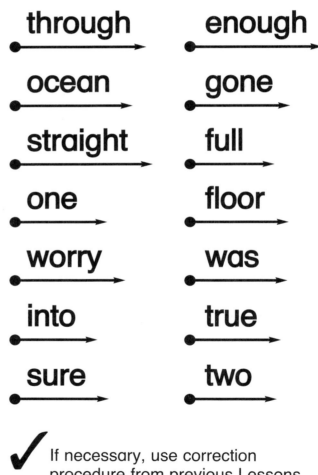

through   enough

ocean   gone

straight   full

one   floor

worry   was

into   true

sure   two

 If necessary, use correction procedure from previous Lessons.

- Say, **Here are two new irregular words.
First I will read the word, then you will
read the word and spell it.**

- Listen. **The first word is pour.**
- **What word?**
- **Ready.** Signal.
- **Yes, pour.**

- **Spell pour.**
- **Ready.** Signal.

- Repeat for early.

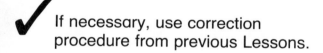

✓ If necessary, use correction
procedure from previous Lessons.

- Now you are going to sound out some
words. As I touch the sounds, you say
them.

- **First word.**
- **Ready.** Signal.

- **Good. What's that word?**
- **Ready.** Signal.

- Repeat for each word in the list.

129

steady

dropped

space

thrōwn

pīlot

kept

fair

prōpane

 If any error occurs, use correction procedure (my turn, do it with me, your turn) as in previous Lessons.

TASK 9: STORY READING

- Now it's time to read more about Carla the sailor. Turn to Lesson 47 on page 42 in your Reader. Check.

- Put your finger on the title.
- Read the title please.
- Ready. Signal.

- Now read the story.
- Ready. Signal.

The shipwreck - part two

Carla was asleep in the cabin of her sloop.
She did not know that she was sailing into danger.
The boat was sailing itself.
It was going fast and straight.
The moon was shining on the waves.
There was a steady fresh breeze.
Not far ahead a large container was floating in the water.
It had been on a container ship.
But it had broken free in a storm and had dropped into the ocean.
It was full of propane bottles and salt water.
It was right in the path of Carla's sloop.
Carla slept on.
Just after midnight Carla was thrown out of her bunk when the large container hit the sloop.
Water poured into the cabin through a huge gash in the side of the boat.
Carla lay on the floor, knocked out by the crash.
As the water poured in, the sloop slowly began to sink.
Carla was far out at sea with no one to help.
Still more to come

 If the student has a problem with any word, have him/her sound it out, say it and then start at the beginning of that sentence again. If the student makes 7 errors, reread the story from the beginning.

TASK 10: SOUND FLUENCY CHECK 9

- **Time for another Sound Fluency Check. Turn to page 36 in your Reader.** Time student for 30 seconds.

- Record scores for Day 3 of Sound Fluency Check 9 on page 138 of the Workbook.

TASK 11: WORD FLUENCY CHECK 9

- **Time for another Word Fluency Check. Turn to page 37.** Time student for 30 seconds.

- Record scores for Day 3 of Word Fluency Check 9 on page 139 of the Workbook.

TASK 12: STORY READING FLUENCY CHECK 8

- **Time for another Story Reading Fluency Check. Turn to page 38 in your Reader.** Time student for 1 minute.

- Record scores for Day 3 of Story Reading Fluency Check 8 on page 140 of the Workbook.

TASK 13: WORKBOOK EXERCISES

- Say, **Now it's time to do the Workbook Exercises.**
- **Open your Workbook to Lesson 47 on page 78.** Check.

Exercise 1: Printing Words and Sounds

- **In Exercise 1 you are going to practice printing the word knee.**
- Have the student print three of the word knee.
- When the student has completed the three of them, have them identify and print five of the sound combination ly.

Exercise 2: Matching Rhyming Words

- **Find Exercise 2 on your worksheet. It's a Rhyme Time! exercise. You are going to draw a line to match rhyming words.**
- **Read the first word.**
- **Ready.** Signal. Student reads, *care.*
- **Now touch the second group of words. Read the first word there.**
- **Ready.** Signal. Student reads, *blue.*
- **Does care rhyme with blue?**
- Repeat until student finds the correct rhyming word, stare.
- **Good. Now draw a line to join the words care and stare.**
- Repeat for the rest of the words in the list.

Exercise 3: Filling in the Blanks

- **You need your Reader for Exercise 3. Turn to Lesson 47 on page 42 of your Reader.** Check.
- **You are going to fill in the blanks in Exercise 3 with the correct words from the story The shipwreck - part two.**
- **Read the first sentence.**
- **Ready.** Signal.
- **Find the correct words that complete that sentence and print those words in the blank.** Check. **Now read the whole sentence.**
- Repeat for each sentence.

Exercise 4: Using Instructions to Draw and Color a Picture

- Now let's look at Exercise 4. What is this a picture of?
- **Ready.** Signal. Student says, *a sailboat.*
- **That's right. Read the first sentence.**
- **Ready.** Signal. Student reads, *Carla's sloop is blue.*
- **What colour will the sailboat be?**
- **Ready.** Signal. Student says, *blue.*
- **That's correct. Color the sailboat blue.**
- Have the student read each sentence and then draw or color each part of the picture.

Exercise 5: Answering a Riddle

- **Put your finger on Exercise 5. Read the riddle.**
- **Ready.** Signal. Student reads, *What do you call a fish with two legs?*
- **To answer this riddle you are going to cross out all the lēēē sounds. The letters that are left will be the answer.**
- **Take your pencil and cross out all the lēēē's.**
- **Now print the letters that remain in the spaces below.**
- **What do you call a fish with two legs?**
- **That's right, a two-knee fish!**

```
            TASK 14:
        AWARDING POINTS
```

- Record the total points for Lesson 47 on page 141 of the Workbook.

End of Lesson 47

LESSON 48

```
        TASK 1: SOUNDING
           OUT WORDS
```

- Now you are going to sound out some words. As I touch the sounds, you say them.

- **First word.**
- **Ready.** Signal.

- **What's that word?**
- **Ready.** Signal.

- Repeat for each word in the list.

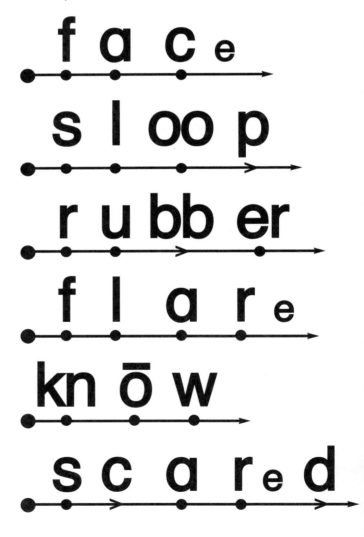

s u n k

w i d e

s l i p

ō n ly

m ou th

✓ If any error occurs, use correction
procedure (my turn, do it with me,
your turn) as in previous Lessons.

**TASK 2: SOUNDING OUT
WORDS THAT BEGIN WITH
SHORT SOUNDS**

- Now you are going to sound out some
  words that begin with short sounds.
  Remember to put the sounds together
  without stopping.

- Sound out the first word.
- **Ready.** Signal.

- What's that word?
- **Ready.** Signal.

- Repeat for each of the words in the list.

g r a bb e d

b o bb ing

b i no c ū l ars

ch ar t

p l a c e

c oo l

p l ā y

c on t ai n

d r o pp e d

p r ō p a n e

133

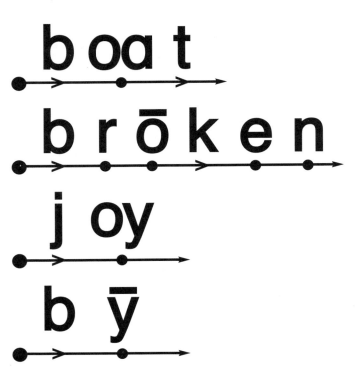

b oa t

b r ō k e n

j oy

b ȳ

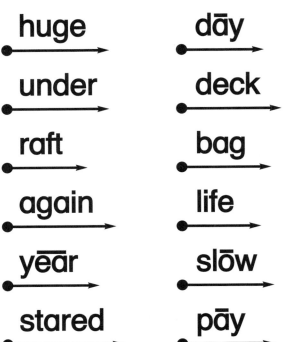

huge

under

raft

again

yēar

stared

dāy

deck

bag

life

slōw

pāy

✓ If necessary, use correction procedure (my turn, do it with me, your turn) as in previous Lessons.

TASK 3: READING WORDS

- Now you are going to practice reading some words you already know.

- First word.
- **Ready.** Signal.

- Repeat for each word in list.

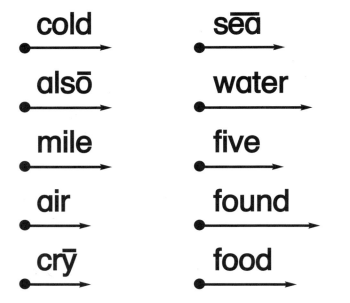

cold

alsō

mile

air

crȳ

sēā

water

five

found

food

TASK 4: STORY READING

- Now it's time to read more about Carla and her sloop. **Turn to Lesson 48 on page 44 in your Reader.** Check.

- Put your finger on the title.
- Read the title please.
- **Ready.** Signal.

- Now read the story.
- **Ready.** Signal.

The shipwreck - part three

Carla woke up when the cold water hit her face.
She was in shock and scared.
But she was also smart and brave.
She grabbed the bag that had food and water for a time just like this.

She also grabbed charts, binoculars, her sleeping bag and her flares.
Then she went on deck and got the rubber life raft into the water.
The sloop began to slip under the water.
Carla climbed into the raft and cut it free from the boat.
Then she sat there, bobbing about in a huge ocean.
Carla stared at the place where her sloop had sunk.
And she began to cry.

One more to come

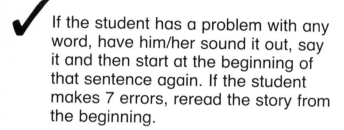 If the student has a problem with any word, have him/her sound it out, say it and then start at the beginning of that sentence again. If the student makes 7 errors, reread the story from the beginning.

TASK 5: SOUND FLUENCY CHECK 9

NOTE: If the student has said 50+ sounds correctly in 1 minute for three consecutive days, s/he may discontinue timings on Sound Fluency Check 9 if s/he so chooses.

- If not, say, **Time for a Sound Fluency Check. Turn to page 36 in your Reader.** Time student for 30 seconds.

- Record scores for Day 4 of Sound Fluency Check 9 on page 138 of the Workbook.

TASK 6: WORD FLUENCY CHECK 9

NOTE: If the student has read 60+ words correctly in 1 minute for three consecutive days, s/he may discontinue timings on Word Fluency Check 9 if s/he so chooses.

- If not, say, **Time for a Word Fluency Check. Turn to page 37.** Time student for 30 seconds.

- Record scores for Day 4 of Word Fluency Check 9 on page 139 of the Workbook.

TASK 7: STORY READING FLUENCY CHECK 8

NOTE: If the student has read 200+ words per minute in the story three consecutive times, s/he has reached fluency and does not need to try again on this Lesson unless s/he chooses to do so. Have the student choose another story from the Reader to be timed on.

- If the student has not yet reached fluency, say, **Time for another Story Reading Fluency Check. Turn to page 38 in your Reader.** Time student for one minute.

- Record scores for Day 4 of Story Reading Fluency Check 8 on page 140 of the Workbook.

TASK 8: WORKBOOK EXERCISES

- **Open your Workbook to Lesson 48 on page 82.** Check.

Exercise 1: Practicing the Doubling Rule

- **Find Exercise 1. Read the list of words.**
- **Ready.** Signal. Student reads, *shop, shut, fit, spot, plan.*
- **Good reading! Now you are going to double the final consonant in each word and then add the ending e-r.**
- **Look at the word shop. What letter are you going to double?**
- **Ready.** Signal.
- **Yes, the p.**
- **On the first line print s-h-o-p-p and add**

135

e-r. Check.

- **What's that word?**
- **Ready.** Signal. Student says, *shopper.*
- **Good. Now you are going to double the final consonant and add the ending i-n-g.**
- **What letter are you going to double in shop?**
- **Ready.** Signal.
- **Yes, the p.**
- **On the first line print s-h-o-p-p and add i-n-g.** Check.
- **What's that word?**
- **Ready.** Signal. Student says, *shopping.*
- Repeat for the rest of the words.

Exercise 2: Making New Words

- **In Exercise 2 you are going to make some new words from the letters in the word binoculars.**
- **The words you make are going to rhyme with the words that are printed below.**
- **Can you find a word from the letters in binoculars that rhymes with bar?**
- **Good! Print car on the first line.**
- Monitor the student as s/he prints new words. Be ready to make some suggestions.

Exercise 3: Reading the Sound and Saying the Words

- **Look at Exercise 3.** Point to kn. **Say this sound.**
- **Ready.** Signal. Student says, *nnn.*
- **Good. Now read the words below.**
- Repeat for ly.

Exercise 4: Printing Words in the Correct Boxes

- **Find Exercise 4. Some of these words have vowels that say their names. You are going to print those words in this box.** (Point to left-hand box.) **Some of**

the words have vowels that don't say their names. You are going to print those words in this box.** (Point to right-hand box.)
- **Read the first word.**
- **Ready.** Signal. Student reads, *under.*
- **Does under have a vowel that says its name?**
- **That's right, it doesn't. Print under in the correct box.** Check.
- Repeat for each word in the list.

Exercise 5: Putting Story Events in Order

- **Let's do Exercise 5. You are going to review the stories The shipwreck - parts one and two by putting events from those stories in order from 1 to 6. Open your Reader to page 40.**
- **Now read the sentences in your Workbook. Number 1.**
- **Ready.** Signal. Student reads the first sentence.
- Repeat for the rest of the sentences.
- **Which one of these events came first?**
- **Ready.** Signal. Student says, *Carla is a sailor.*
- **That's right. Put a number 1 on the line at the beginning of that sentence.**
- Have the student number the rest of the sentences from 2 to 6.

Exercise 6: Completing Various Tasks on Sentences from the Reader

- **In Exercise 6 you also need your Reader. Find Part Three of The shipwreck on page 44.** Check.
- **Read the first question in your Workbook. Find the answer to that question and print it on the line.** Check.
- **Read number 2. List those five things.** Check.
- **Read number three. Find the answer to that question and print it on the lines.** Check.
- **Read sentence 4. Cross out all the**

short sounds in this sentence. Check.
- Read sentence 5. Circle all the vowels. Check.
- Read the sentences in number 6. Circle the words in which a final e makes the vowel say its name. Check.
- Read number 7. Follow those instructions. Check.

TASK 9: AWARDING POINTS

- Record the total points for Lesson 48 on page 141 of the Workbook.

End of Lesson 48

LESSON 49

TASK 1: TEACHING THE SOUND COMBINATION ph as in phone

- When these two letters are together, they say the sound fff.
- **Listen.** Touch the dot under the ph and say **fff** for one second. Lift your finger.
- **Listen again.** Repeat.

- **Say the sound with me.**
- **Ready.** Signal.
- Repeat.

- **Your turn.**
- **Ready.** Signal.
- Repeat the task until the student does it as instructed.

 If any error occurs, use correction procedure (my turn, do it with me, your turn) as in previous Lessons.

- Now you are going to sound out some words that have the sound combination **fff**. As I touch the sounds, you say them.

- **First word.**
- **Ready.** Signal.

- **What's that word?**
- **Ready.** Signal.

- Repeat for each word in the list.

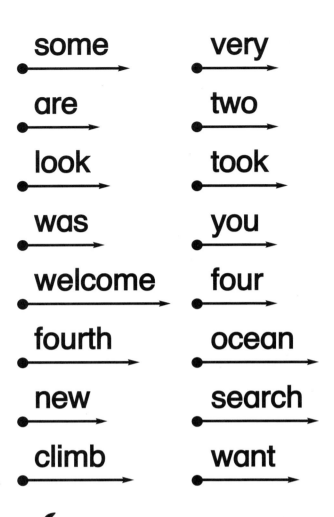

ph o n e

d o l ph i n

phōtōgraph

✓ If any error occurs, use correction procedure (my turn, do it with me, your turn) as in previous Lessons and begin the list again.

- You are going to practice some irregular words that you will be reading in this Lesson's story.

- **Read the first word and spell it.**
- **Ready.** Signal.

- Repeat for each word.

some
are
look
was
welcome
fourth
new
climb

very
two
took
you
four
ocean
search
want

✓ If necessary, use correction procedure from previous Lessons.

- Say, **Here are some new irregular words you will see in the story. First I will read the word, then you will read the word and spell it.**

- **Listen. The first word is radio.**
- **What word?**
- **Ready.** Signal.
- **Yes, radio.**

- **Spell radio.**
- **Ready.** Signal.

- Repeat for each word.

radio →

knew →

crew →

special →

✓ If necessary, use correction procedure from previous Lessons.

TASK 5: SOUNDING OUT WORDS

- Now you are going to sound out some words. As I touch the sounds, you say them.

- First word.
- **Ready.** Signal.

- **Good work. What's that word?**
- **Ready.** Signal.

- Repeat for each word in the list.

a pp ēa r →

r o p e →

n o th ing →

e m p t y →

s c a nn e d →

l a dd er →

p r o b l e m →

e d g e →

d r ȳ →

b o th er →

c a p t ai n →

bē c a m e →

a b oa r d →

b a s e →

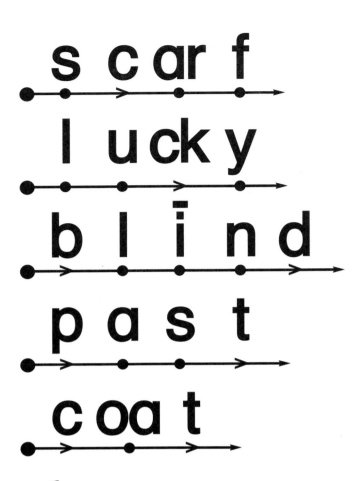

scarf

lucky

blind

past

coat

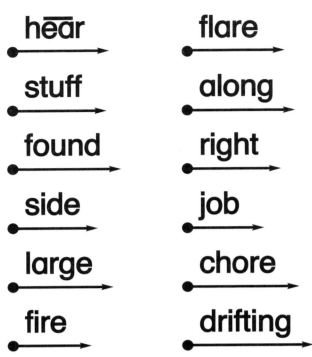

hēar

stuff

found

side

large

fire

flare

along

right

job

chore

drifting

✓ If necessary, use correction procedure (my turn, do it with me, your turn) as in previous Lessons.

TASK 7: STORY READING

- Now it's time to read about what happens to Carla the sailor. Turn to Lesson 49 on page 45 in your Reader. Check.

- Put your finger on the title.
- Read the title please.
- **Ready.** Signal.

- Now read the story.
- **Ready.** Signal.

The shipwreck - part four

The sun came up and the day became very hot.
Carla woke up and looked over the edge of her life raft.
She could see only miles and miles of empty ocean.

✓ If any error occurs, use correction procedure (my turn, do it with me, your turn) as in previous Lessons.

TASK 6: READING WORDS

- Now you are going to practice reading some words you already know.

- First word.
- **Ready.** Signal.

- Repeat for each word in list.

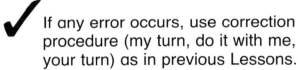

steady

airplane

watch

soon

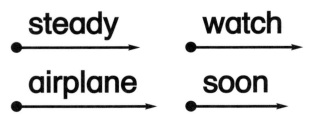

Then some dolphins swam around the raft.
They jumped out of the water and seemed to want to play.
That made Carla feel better.
She took her binoculars and scanned the ocean.
Nothing.
Carla sat drifting for three days and three nights.
On the fourth day a large ship appeared.
It came right at her.
She fired a flare.
The ship slowed down and came alongside the raft.
The crew yelled down to her.
They dropped a rope ladder for her to climb up.
Carla found out that they had been looking for her for two days.
"You did not radio your base for two days, so we knew there was a problem," the captain said.
"An airplane saw some stuff floating near where you might have been, so we began a search.
Welcome aboard. Are you all right?"
Carla was tired but happy.
Soon she was back on dry land.
And soon she had a new sloop.
The end

✔ If the student has a problem with any word, have him/her sound it out, say it and then start at the beginning of that sentence again. If the student makes 7 errors, reread the story from the beginning.

TASK 8: SOUND FLUENCY CHECK 9

REMINDER: If the student has said 50+ sounds correctly in 1 minute for any three days of the last four, s/he may discontinue timings on Sound Fluency Check 9 if s/he so chooses.

- If not, say, **Time for a Sound Fluency Check. Turn to page 36 in your Reader.** Time student for 30 seconds.

- Record scores for Day 5 of Sound Fluency Check 9 on page 138 of the Workbook.

REMINDER: If the student has been unable to say at least 50 sounds correctly per minute at least one time in Sound Fluency Check 9, finish and correct the Workbook Exercises for Lesson 49 but do not proceed to teach new material. Instead, reteach Lessons 45 through 49. Include daily practice and timings on Sound Fluency Check 9 on page 36. Circle and practice any sounds the student is having difficulty with. Record scores in the Additional Practice columns for Sound Fluency Check 9 on page 138 of the Student Workbook. Students should continue to be awarded points for working hard, paying attention, following instructions and doing well on fluency checks. When the student is able to say 50+ sounds from the list in 1 minute, begin Lesson 50.

TASK 9: WORD FLUENCY CHECK 9

REMINDER: If the student has read 60+ words correctly in 1 minute for any three days of the last four, s/he may discontinue timings on Word Fluency Check 9 if s/he so chooses.

- If not, say, **Time for a Word Fluency Check. Turn to page 37.** Time student for 30 seconds.

- Record scores for Day 5 of Word Fluency Check 9 on page 139 of the Workbook.

REMINDER: If the student has been unable to read at least 60 words correctly in 1 minute at least one time in Word Fluency Check 9, finish the Workbook Exercises for Lesson 49 but do not proceed with new material. Instead, redo Lessons 45 through 49. Include daily practice and timings on Word Fluency Check 9 on page 37. Circle and practice any words the student is having difficulty with. Students should continue to be awarded points for working hard, paying attention, following instructions and doing well on fluency checks. When the student is able to read 60+ words from the list in 1 minute, continue in the Reader with Lesson 50.

TASK 10: STORY READING FLUENCY CHECK 8

REMINDER: If the student has read 200+ words per minute in the story for three of the last four attempts, s/he has reached fluency and does not need to try again on this Lesson unless s/he chooses to do so. Do a timing on another story of the student's choice.

- If the student has not yet reached fluency, say, **Time for another Story Reading Fluency Check. Turn to page 38 in your Reader.** Time student for one minute.

- Record scores for Day 5 of Story Reading Fluency Check 8 on page 140 of the Workbook.

NOTE: If the student has not yet reached fluency at 200+ words a minute in the same story on at least one timing, finish and correct the Workbook Exercises for Lesson 49, but do not proceed with new material. Instead, have the student practice reading the first half of the story until s/he can read it with fewer than 3 L.O.s in 30 seconds. Then practice the next half in the same manner. Combine the two sections and practice until the student can read them fluently in a minute. Record scores in

the Additional Practice columns for Story Reading Fluency Check 8. Award points for working hard, paying attention, following instructions and doing well in fluency checks. When the student has reached fluency, begin Lesson 50.

TASK 11: WORKBOOK EXERCISES

- **Open your Workbook to Lesson 49 on page 87.** Check.

Exercise 1: Unscrambling Words to Fill in the Blanks

- **You need your Reader for Exercise 1. Turn to page 45 of your Reader. You are going to fill in the blanks in Exercise 1 with the correct word from the story <u>The shipwreck - part four</u>. The words are scrambled.**
- **Read the first sentence.**
- **Ready.** Signal.
- **Look at the scrambled letters. Figure out the correct word that completes that sentence. Print that word in the blank.** Check. **Now read the whole sentence.**
- **Repeat for each sentence.**

Exercise 2: Solving a Code

- **This Exercise is called Fun with Words. Read the question.**
- **Ready.** Signal. Student reads, *What is this word?*
- **Can you think of the word that those two letters represent?**
- **Good! Now complete that word by filling in the blanks.** Check.

Exercise 3: Making New Words

- **In Exercise 3 you are going to make some new words from the letters in the word photograph.**
- **Can you see another word that you can**

make?
- Good! Print that word on the first line.
- Monitor the student as s/he prints new words. Be ready to make some suggestions.

Exercise 4: Printing Words

- In Exercise 4 you are going to practice printing the word **photograph**.
- Monitor the student as s/he prints the word four times.

Exercise 5: Answering a Riddle

- **Exercise 5 is a riddle. Read the riddle.**
- **Ready.** Signal. Student reads, *How are cars and elephants alike?*
- **To answer the riddle you are going to print the letter that is in one word but not in another.**
- **Read number 1. What letter is in the word tent but not in ten?**
- **Ready.** Signal. Student answers, *t.*
- **Yes, t. Print a t in the first blank below.**
- Repeat for numbers 2 to 6.
- **So how are cars and elephants alike?**
- **They both have trunks! Great work!**

**TASK 12:
AWARDING POINTS**

- Record the total points for Lesson 49 on page 141 of the Workbook.

End of Lesson 49

LESSON 50

**TASK 1: PRACTICING
IRREGULAR WORDS**

- You are going to read some irregular words you have already learned.

- Read the first word and spell it.
- **Ready.** Signal.

- Repeat for each word.

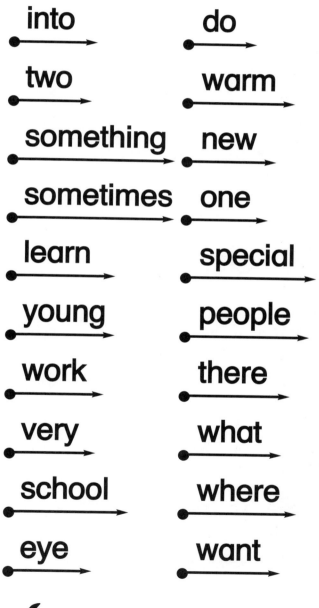

into	do
two	warm
something	new
sometimes	one
learn	special
young	people
work	there
very	what
school	where
eye	want

 If necessary, use correction procedure from previous Lessons.

143

TASK 2: SOUNDING OUT WORDS

- Now you are going to sound out some words. As I touch the sounds, you say them.

- First word.
- **Ready.** Signal.

- **Good! What's that word?**
- **Ready.** Signal.

- Repeat for each word in the list.

p ī l o t

ē̄a ch

r oa m

m ā y b ē

w i th ou t

g r a v i t y

b o ther

j oi n

pr ō g r a m

m or n ing

t ē̄a m

f or c e

s p a c e

l ā t er

m e m b er

✓ If any error occurs, use correction procedure (my turn, do it with me, your turn) as in previous Lessons.

144

- Now you are going to sound out some words that begin with short sounds. Remember to put the sounds together without stopping.

- Sound out the first word.
- **Ready.** Signal.

- **What's that word?**
- **Ready.** Signal.

- Repeat for each of the words in the list.

h ea d

c al l

b ē cau s e

d i ff e r e n t

d r ēā m

h ar d

b r igh t

p l a c e

t o l d

j o b

b l ī n d

p a n t s

g a p e

d r ȳ

h ō b ō

p a tch e s

t r i p

If the student makes an error or stops between the sounds, use correction procedure (my turn, do it with me, your turn) as in previous Lessons and begin the list again.

TASK 4: SAYING THE UNDERLINED SOUNDS AND READING THE WORDS

- Touch the underlined sound in the first word.
- Say, **Tell me the underlined sound.**
- **Ready.** Signal.

- **Now tell me the word.**
- **Ready.** Signal.

- Repeat for each of the words in the list.

ne<u>ck</u>	fl<u>oa</u>t
y<u>ēa</u>r	mu<u>ch</u>
fl<u>ȳ</u>	w<u>ou</u>ld
n<u>igh</u>t	st<u>ar</u>
st<u>a</u>re	<u>ai</u>rplane
s<u>oo</u>n	n<u>a</u>me
fl<u>igh</u>t	<u>al</u>w<u>āy</u>s
wr<u>o</u>ng	tr<u>ai</u>n

 Use correction procedure (my turn, do it with me, your turn) as in previous Lessons if student makes an error.

TASK 5: STORY READING

- Now it's time to read a story. Turn to **Lesson 50 on page 47 in your Reader.** Check.

- **Put your finger on the title.**
- **Read the title please.**
- **Ready.** Signal.

- **Now read the story.**
- **Ready.** Signal.

<u>The space trip - part one</u>

Tom always dreamed of going into space.
Often at night he would stare at the stars and wish to go there.
He learned to fly an airplane when he was still very young.
After school he joined the Air Force and became a pilot.
Two years later he was asked to join the space team.
He trained very, very hard.
There was much to learn and a lot to do.
He soon learned to float without gravity.
He learned to fly the space ship.
He learned what to do if something went wrong.
He learned to do the job of each of the members of his team.
Then one bright morning he got a call from the head of the space program.
"We want you to go on a very special space flight," he told Tom.

More to come

 If the student has a problem with any word, have him/her sound it out, say it and then start at the beginning of that sentence again. If the student makes 7 errors, reread the story from the beginning.

TASK 6: SOUND FLUENCY CHECK 10

- The student has said 50+ sounds per minute in Sound Fluency Check 9 on page 36. Say, **Turn to page 49 in your Reader. There is a list of sounds from Lessons 1 to 50.**
- **You are going to say these sounds as quickly as you can, remembering to hold the sounds with the dots under them for one second.**
- **Which way would you like to do this list?** Student chooses down or across.

- **Put your finger on the first sound.**
- **Ready. Please begin.** Time student for 30 seconds.
- Say, **Thank you.**

- Record sounds said correctly per minute in the Sounds Said Correctly column for Day 1 of Sound Fluency Check 10 on page 138 of the Workbook.
- Record number of errors and/or skipped sounds per minute in the Learning Opportunities column.

TASK 7: WORD FLUENCY CHECK 10A

- The student has read 60+ words per minute in Word Fluency Check 9 on page 37. Say, **On page 50 there is a list of words from Lessons 1 to 50.**
- **You are going to read these words as quickly as you can. Which way would you like to read this list?** Student chooses down or across.

- **Put your finger on the first word.**
- **Ready. Please begin.** Time student for 30 seconds.
- Say, **Thank you.**

- Record words read correctly per minute in the Words Read Correctly column for Day 1 of Word Fluency Check 10A on page 139 of the Workbook.
- Record number of errors and/or skipped words per minute in the Learning Opportunities column.

TASK 8: STORY READING FLUENCY CHECK 9

- The student has reached fluency (200+ words/minute) in Story Reading Fluency Check 8. Say, **Now we are going to do a new Story Reading Fluency Check. Turn to page 52 in your Reader.**

- **Put your finger on the title. Get set to read the story.**
- **Ready. Please begin.** Time student for 1 minute.
- At the end of 1 minute say, **Thank you.**

- Record the number of words read correctly in the Words Read Correctly column for Day 1 of Story Reading Fluency Check 9 on page 140 of the Workbook.
- Record errors and/or skipped words in the Learning Opportunities column.

TASK 9: WORKBOOK EXERCISES

- Say, **Now we are going to do the Workbook part of the Lesson.**
- **Open your Workbook to Lesson 50 on page 91.** Check.

Exercise 1: Circling Short Sounds

- **In Exercise 1 you must look at each word and circle every short sound or short sound combination.**
- **Read the first word.**
- **Ready.** Signal. Student reads, *do.*
- **Are there any short sounds in do?**

- **Ready.** Signal. **Circle it.**
- Repeat for each word in the list.

Exercise 2: Answering Questions

- **Find Exercise 2. You are going to answer some questions from the story** <u>The space trip - part one</u>**. Open your Reader to page 47.**
- **Now read the first question in your Workbook.**
- **Ready.** Signal. Student reads question.
- **Part of the answer is done for you. Read that part now please.**
- **Ready.** Signal.
- **Find those words in your Reader and fill in the rest of the sentence to answer the question.** Check.
- **So where had Tom always dreamed of going?**
- **Ready.** Signal. Student reads the whole answer to this question.
- Repeat for questions 2 to 4.

Exercise 3: Putting Words in Alphabetical Order

- **Read the words in Exercise 3.**
- **Ready.** Signal. Student reads from sight to teeth.
- **In this exercise you are going to print these words in alphabetical order. You must look at the first letter in each word. What first letter in these words comes first in the alphabet?**
- **Ready.** Signal. Student answers, *always.*
- **That's right! Print always in the blanks. Put a check mark beside it.**
- **What is the word with a first letter that comes next in the alphabet?**
- **Ready.** Signal. Student says, *example.*
- **Well done. Print example on the second set of blanks.** Check.
- Repeat for the rest of the words. When the student has finished doing all nine

of them, say, **Good work! You just put those nine words in alphabetical order.**

Exercise 4: Answering a Riddle

- **Exercise 4 is a riddle. Read the riddle.**
- **Ready.** Signal. Student reads, *How would lambs travel into space?*
- **Good reading! To answer this riddle you have to print the letters that are circled in Exercise 3 in the blanks below.** Check.
- **So how would lambs travel into space?**
- **That's right, in a space sheep!**

Exercise 5: Crossing Out the Word that Doesn't Belong

- **In Exercise 5 each line has a list of four words. Three of the words have something the same. One word does not. You are going to cross out the word in each line that doesn't belong.**
- **Finger on number 1. Read each of those words.**
- **Ready.** Signal. Student reads, *knee, knife, kept, know.*
- **Which of those words does not belong?**
- **Ready.** Signal. Student answers, *kept.*
- **That's right, because all the other words have the sound combination k-n and kept only has the sound k.**
- Repeat for numbers 2 to 10.
- If the student is having difficulty, give him/her a hint or tell him/her the answer and ask for the reason that that word does not belong.

> **TASK 10:**
> **AWARDING POINTS**

- Record the total points for Lesson 50 on page 141 of theWorkbook.

End of Lesson 50

LESSON 51

TASK 1: TEACHING THE
SOUND COMBINATIONS
tion as in mo<u>tion</u> and
sion as in ten<u>sion</u>

- When these letters are together, they say the short sound **shun**.
- **Listen.** Tap the arrows under the tion and the sion and say **shun**. Lift your finger.
- **Listen again.** Repeat.

- **Say the sound with me.**
- **Ready.** Signal.
- Repeat.

- **Your turn.**
- **Ready.** Signal.
- Repeat the task until the student does it as instructed.

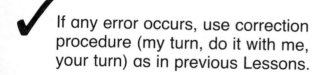

✔ If any error occurs, use correction procedure (my turn, do it with me, your turn) as in previous Lessons.

TASK 2: PRACTICING THE
SOUND COMBINATIONS
tion and **sion**

- Now you are going to sound out some words that have the sound combinations you just learned. As I touch the sounds, you say them.

- **First word.**
- **Ready.** Signal.

- **What's that word?**
- **Ready.** Signal.

- Repeat for each word in the list.

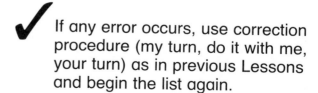

✔ If any error occurs, use correction procedure (my turn, do it with me, your turn) as in previous Lessons and begin the list again.

- Now you are going to sound out some words. As I touch the sounds, you say them.

- First word.
- **Ready.** Signal.

- Good work. What's that word?
- **Ready.** Signal.

- Repeat for each word in the list.

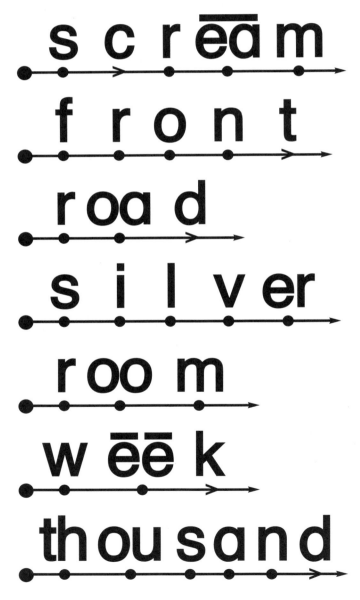

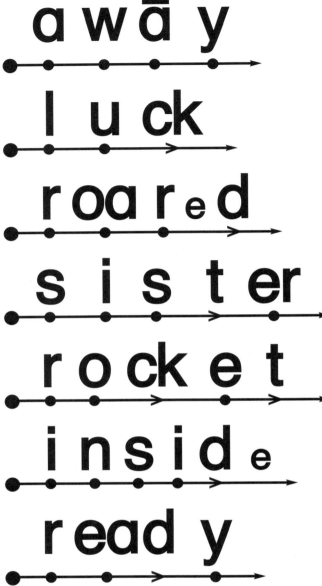

✓ If any error occurs, use correction procedure (my turn, do it with me, your turn) as in previous Lessons.

- Turn to TASK 3 in this Lesson. Say, **Now you are going to practice reading the words you sounded out.**

- First word.
- **Ready.** Signal.

- Repeat for each word in list.

✓ If necessary, use correction procedure (my turn, do it with me, your turn) as in previous Lessons.

TASK 5: SOUNDING OUT WORDS THAT BEGIN WITH SHORT SOUNDS

- Now you are going to sound out some words that begin with short sounds. Remember to put the sounds together without stopping.

- Sound out the first word.
- **Ready.** Signal.

- What's that word?
- **Ready.** Signal.

- Repeat for each of the words in the list.

c a r e f u l

b ē h ī n d

p o w e r

g r ō u n d

b ē l o n g

p oi n t

d ir t y

t ēa m

b ē f or e

h u n d r e d

ch ar t

b ur n ing

p r ō g r a m

b oo t

d a n c e

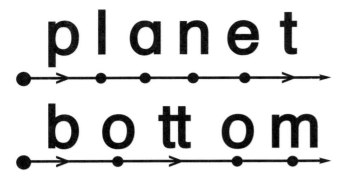

✓ If the student makes an error or stops between the sounds, use correction procedure (my turn, do it with me, your turn) as in previous Lessons and begin the list again.

look   sure
good   half
true   blue
towards   is

✓ If necessary, use correction procedure from previous Lessons.

TASK 6: PRACTICING IRREGULAR WORDS

- You are going to read some irregular words you have already learned.

- **Read the first word and spell it.**
- **Ready.** Signal.

- Repeat for each word.

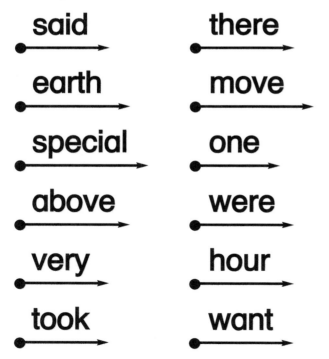

said   there
earth   move
special   one
above   were
very   hour
took   want

TASK 7: TEACHING IRREGULAR WORDS

- Say, **Here are some new irregular words. First I will read the word, then you will read the word and spell it.**

- **Listen. The first word is although.**
- **What word?**
- **Ready.** Signal.
- **Yes, although.**

- **Spell although.**
- **Ready.** Signal.

- Repeat for each word.

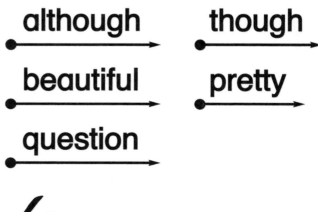

although   though
beautiful   pretty
question

✓ If necessary, use correction procedure from previous Lessons.

TASK 8: STORY READING

- **Now it's time to read another story about Tom the astronaut. Turn to Lesson 51 on page 54 in your Reader.** Check.

- **Put your finger on the title.**
- **Read the title please.**
- **Ready.** Signal.

- **Now read the story.**
- **Ready.** Signal.

<u>The space trip - part two</u>

"We want you to go on a special mission," the head man said to Tom.
He showed Tom a chart.
"We think that there is life on this planet.
And we want you and your team to go there to find out for sure.
Good luck!"
The silver space ship was all ready.
Even though it was as big as a train, there was not much room to move around inside.
On take off, the rockets had so much power that they made the space ship go over one thousand miles an hour.
In no time, the space ship was more than one hundred miles above the earth.
Then the rockets stopped burning and dropped off the bottom of the space ship.
They burned up before they were half way to the ground.
The silver ship roared towards the planet.
But it was still miles and miles away.
Tom looked back towards home.
The earth was blue and white and beautiful.
But it too was very, very far away.

There is still more to this story

 If the student has a problem with any word, have him/her sound it out, say it and then start at the beginning of that sentence again. If the student makes 7 errors, reread the story from the beginning.

TASK 9: SOUND FLUENCY CHECK 10

- **Time for another Sound Fluency Check. Turn to page 49 in your Reader.** Time student for 30 seconds.

- Record scores for Day 2 of Sound Fluency Check 10 on page 138 of the Workbook.

TASK 10: WORD FLUENCY CHECK 10A

- **Time for another Word Fluency Check. Turn to page 50.** Time student for 30 seconds.

- Record scores for Day 2 of Word Fluency Check 10A on page 139 of the Workbook.

TASK 11: STORY READING FLUENCY CHECK 9

- Say to the student, **We are now going to do our second Story Reading Fluency Check. Turn to page 52 in your Reader.** Time student for 1 minute.

- Record scores for Day 2 of Story Reading Fluency Check 9 on page 140 of the Workbook.

TASK 12: WORKBOOK EXERCISES

- Say, **Now we are going to do the Workbook Exercises.**

- **Open your Workbook to Lesson 51 on page 95.** Check.

Exercise 1: Printing Sounds

- **In Exercise 1 you are going to practice printing the letters for the sound combinations shun.**
- Have the student print three each of the sound combinations shun.

Exercise 2: Word Search Puzzle

- **Exercise 2 is a word search puzzle. Read the first word in the list of words that you will be looking for.**
- **Ready.** Signal. Student reads, *mission.*
- **The arrow beside the word tells you whether the word goes across, up, down or backwards. Look in the puzzle. Go through each row until you find the letters m-i-s-s-i-o-n.**
- **That's right. Draw a circle around the word mission.**
- **Put a check mark beside the word in the list so that you know you have found it.**
- If the student is having problems finding the word, repeat steps above for each word in the list. If s/he can do the puzzle independently, allow him/her to do so.

Exercise 3: Unscrambling Words to Fill in the Blanks

- **You need your Reader for Exercise 3. Turn to page 54 of your Reader. You are going to fill in the blanks in Exercise 3 with the correct word from the story The space trip - part two. The words are scrambled.**
- **Read the first sentence.**
- **Ready.** Signal.
- **Look at the scrambled letters. Figure out the correct word that completes that**

sentence. **Print that word in the blanks.** Check. **Now read the whole sentence.**
- Repeat for each sentence.

Exercise 4: Using Instructions to Draw and Color a Picture

- **Now let's look at Exercise 4. Read the first sentence.**
- **Ready.** Signal. Student reads, *This is a planet.*
- Have the student read each sentence and then draw or color each part of the picture.

Exercise 5: Following a Maze to Answer a Question

- **Find Exercise 5. In this exercise you are going to go through the star maze to collect the letters to answer the question, What does every astronaut love to hear?**
- **Put your pencil on the arrow at the top of the star.** Check. **Now start through the maze. When you get to a letter, print it in the blanks below. If you hit a wall start over again.** Check that the student is following the correct path.
- When the student has successfully gone through the maze and has printed the eight letters in the blanks, say, **So, what does every astronaut love to hear?**
- **That's right! Blast off!**

```
TASK 13:
AWARDING POINTS
```

- Record the total points for Lesson 51 on page 141 of the Workbook.

End of Lesson 51

LESSON 52

- Now you are going to practice reading some words you already know.

- First word.
- Ready. Signal.

- Repeat for each word in list.

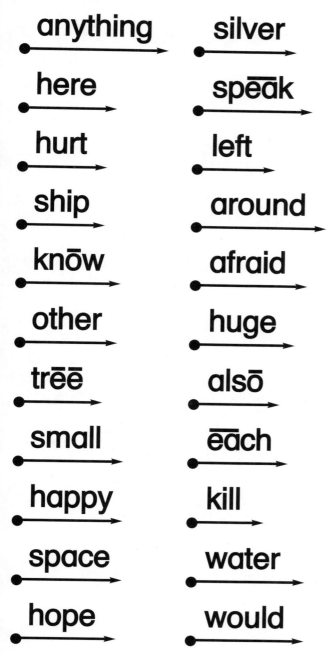

anything	silver
here	spēak
hurt	left
ship	around
knōw	afraid
other	huge
trēē	alsō
small	ēach
happy	kill
space	water
hope	would

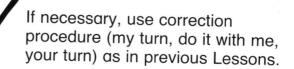

✓ If necessary, use correction procedure (my turn, do it with me, your turn) as in previous Lessons.

TASK 2: SOUNDING OUT WORDS

- Now you are going to sound out some words. As I touch the sounds, you say them.

- First word.
- Ready. Signal.

- Good work. What's that word?
- Ready. Signal.

- Repeat for each word in the list.

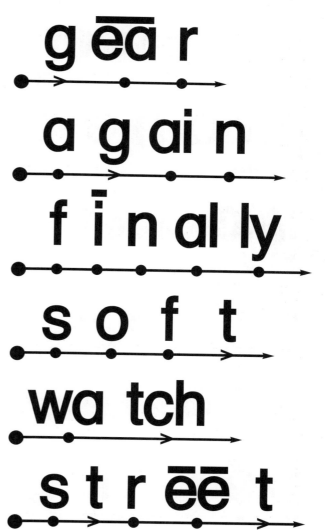

g ēa r

a g ai n

f ī n al ly

s o f t

wa tch

s t r ēē t

155

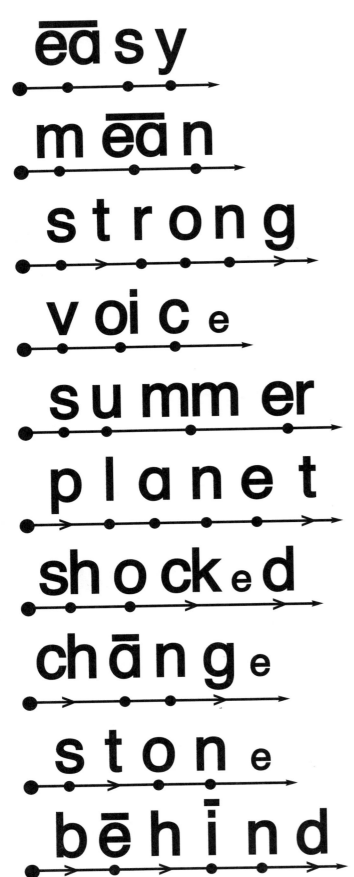

ēa s y

m **ēa** n

s t r o n g

v oi c **e**

s u mm er

p l **a** n e t

sh o ck **e** d

ch **ā** n g **e**

s t o n **e**

b **ē** h **ī** n d

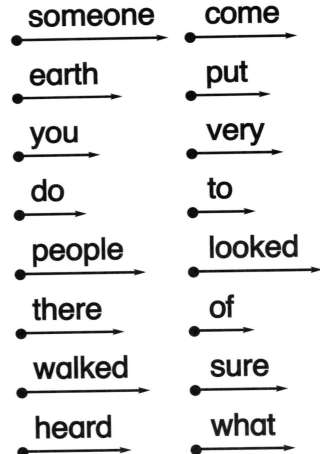

s n a k **e**

✓ If any error occurs, use correction procedure (my turn, do it with me, your turn) as in previous Lessons.

- You are going to read some irregular words you have already learned.

- Read the first word and spell it.
- **Ready.** Signal.

- Repeat for each word.

someone	come
earth	put
you	very
do	to
people	looked
there	of
walked	sure
heard	what

talking → **want** →

 If necessary, use correction procedure from previous Lessons.

```
TASK 4: TEACHING
IRREGULAR WORDS
```

- Say, **Here are some new irregular words. First I will read the word, then you will read the word and spell it.**

- **Listen. The first word is sign.**
- **What word?**
- **Ready.** Signal.
- **Yes, sign.**

- **Spell sign.**
- **Ready.** Signal.

- Repeat for each word.

sign →

become →

anyone →

 If necessary, use correction procedure from previous Lessons.

```
TASK 5:
STORY READING
```

- Now it's time to read more about Tom and his trip into outer space. Turn to Lesson 52 on page 56 in your Reader. Check.

- • Put your finger on the title.
- • Read the title please.
- • **Ready.** Signal.

- • **Now read the story.**
- • **Ready.** Signal.

The space trip - part three

After a long time in space, Tom and his team were happy to finally land on the small planet. They all looked out of the space ship but they did not see anyone or anything.
Tom put on his space gear and left the silver ship.
Then he walked around looking for signs of life.
He heard a voice behind him.
He turned but there was no one there.
The voice came from a tree.
"What do you want?" the voice asked.
Tom was shocked.
"Are you talking or is there someone behind the tree?"
"I am speaking to you," the tree said.
"What do you want?" it asked again.
"I am looking for life on this planet," Tom said.
"I know that," said the tree.
"And I also know that you are from earth.
You people on earth kill each other."
"I did not come here to hurt you," Tom told the tree.
"I hope not," the tree said.
"If you did want to hurt me, I would become a stone or water."
Again Tom was shocked.
"Do you mean that you can change into other things?" he asked.
"Sure. Watch!"
And with that the tree turned into a huge snake.
Tom was very afraid.
    There is still more to this story

If the student has a problem with any word, have him/her sound it out, say it and then start at the beginning of that sentence again. If the student makes 7 errors, reread the story from the beginning.

TASK 6: SOUND FLUENCY CHECK 10

- **Time for another Sound Fluency Check. Turn to page 49 in your Reader.** Time student for 30 seconds.

- Record scores for Day 3 of Sound Fluency Check 10 on page 138 of the Workbook.

TASK 7: WORD FLUENCY CHECK 10A

- **Time for another Word Fluency Check. Turn to page 50.** Time student for 30 seconds.

- Record scores for Day 3 of Word Fluency Check 10A on page 139 of the Workbook.

TASK 8: STORY READING FLUENCY CHECK 9

- **Time for another Story Reading Fluency Check. Turn to page 52 in your Reader.** Time student for 1 minute.

- Record scores for Day 3 of Story Reading Fluency Check 9 on page 140 of the Workbook.

TASK 9: WORKBOOK EXERCISES

- **Open your Workbook to Lesson 52 on page 99.** Check.

Exercise 1: Solving a Code to Answer a Riddle

- **Let's look at Exercise 1. You are going to solve a code to answer a riddle. Read the riddle.**
- **Ready.** Signal. Student reads, *How are dogs and trees alike?*
- **Each alphabet letter is represented by a number. Fill in the blanks with the correct letter.** Check.
- **Good! How are dogs and trees alike?**
- **That's right. They both have barks!**

Exercise 2: Vowel Power!

- **Exercise 2 is a Vowel Power! exercise. You must fill in the blanks with vowels to make words that you know. The words are in the list.** (Point to list of words to the left of the rocket.)
- **Touch the first word. What vowels go in those blanks?**
- **Ready.** Signal. Student answers, *e, a, u, i, u.*
- **Print those vowels in the blanks.** Check.
- **Now read that word.**
- **Ready.** Signal. Student reads, *beautiful.*
- **Repeat for each word.**

Exercise 3: Printing Words to Match their Meaning

- **Now let's look at Exercise 3. In this exercise you are going to print words to look like their meaning. One word is done for you. Read that word.**
- **Ready.** Signal. Student reads, *sign.*
- **Read the other words.**
- **Ready.** Signal.
- **Take your pencil and print those words as best you can to match their meaning.**
- Be ready to make some suggestions if the student is having difficulty with any of the words.

Exercise 4: Answering Questions from the Reader

- You need your Reader for Exercise 4. Turn to Lesson 52 on page 56 of your Reader.
- You are going to answer some questions from the story <u>The space trip - part three</u>.
- Read the first question.
- **Ready.** Signal. Student reads, *When they all looked out of the space ship what did they see?*
- **Good. Now read the beginning of the answer.**
- **Ready.** Signal. Student reads, *They . . .*
- **Find the correct words that complete that sentence and print those words on the line.** Check. **Now read the whole sentence.**
- Repeat for each question.

Exercise 5: Filling in the Blanks

- Now you are going to fill in the blanks in Exercise 5 with the correct word from the story. Read the first sentence.
- **Ready.** Signal.
- **Find the correct word that completes that sentence and print that word in the blank.** Check. **Now read the whole sentence.**
- Repeat for each sentence.

Exercise 6: Crossword Puzzle

- Exercise 6 is a crossword puzzle. The words in the puzzle are the words that you just filled in the blanks in Exercise 5.
- Some of the words go down; some of them go across.
- Look at number 1 in Exercise 5. What word did you fill in that blank?
- Yes, signs. Print the word signs in the boxes for number 1 down in the

crossword puzzle. Check.
- Repeat for the rest of the words.

TASK 10: AWARDING POINTS

- Record the total points for Lesson 52 on page 141 of the Workbook.

End of Lesson 52

LESSON 53

- You are going to read some irregular words you already know.

- Read the first word and spell it.
- **Ready.** Signal.

- Repeat for each word.

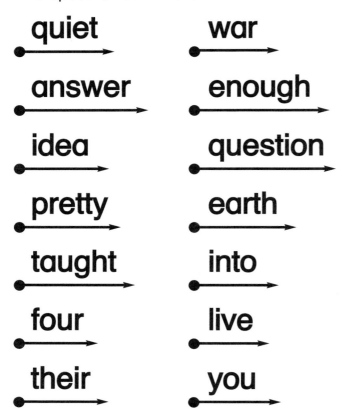

quiet

answer

idea

pretty

taught

four

their

war

enough

question

earth

into

live

you

✓ If necessary, use correction procedure from previous Lessons.

- Say, **Here are a four new irregular words. First I will read the word, then you will read the word and spell it.**

- **Listen. The first word is receive.**

- **What word?**
- **Ready.** Signal.
- **Yes, receive.**

- **Spell receive.**
- **Ready.** Signal.

- Repeat for each word.

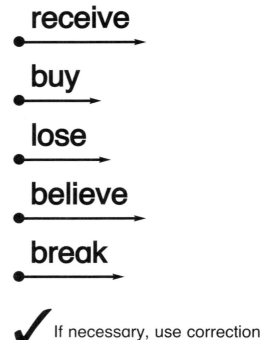

receive

buy

lose

believe

break

✓ If necessary, use correction procedure from previous Lessons.

- Now you are going to sound out some words. As I touch the sounds, you say them.

- **First word.**
- **Ready.** Signal.

- **Good work. What's that word?**
- **Ready.** Signal.

- Repeat for each word in the list.

power

snake

hardly

ready

gīant

enter

ahead

chip

straw

strānge

lēave

edge

rēturn

māybē

kept

page

disappēar

mēēt

pēace

✓ If any error occurs, use correction procedure (my turn, do it with me, your turn) as in previous Lessons.

161

TASK 4: READING WORDS

- Turn to TASK 3 in this Lesson. Say, **Now you are going to practice reading the words you sounded out.**

- **First word.**
- **Ready.** Signal.

- Repeat for each word in list.

✓ If necessary, use correction procedure (my turn, do it with me, your turn) as in previous Lessons.

TASK 5: SAYING THE UNDERLINED SOUNDS AND READING THE WORDS

- Touch the underlined sound in the first word. Say, **Tell me the underlined sound.**
- **Ready.** Signal.

- **Now tell me the word.**
- **Ready.** Signal.

- Repeat for each of the words in the list.

t<u>ur</u>n	f<u>ou</u>nd
t<u>a</u>ll	si<u>x</u>
bett<u>er</u>	pla<u>c</u>e
t<u>ēa</u><u>ch</u>	pu<u>zz</u>le
w<u>ai</u>t	stop
c<u>ou</u>ld	<u>ch</u>ān̄ge

told   long

ne<u>v</u>er   k<u>i</u>ll

tr<u>ȳ</u>   <u>p</u>lanet

<u>f</u>īnd   <u>kn</u>ōw

✓ Use correction procedure (my turn, do it with me, your turn) as in previous Lessons if student makes an error.

TASK 6: STORY READING

- **Now it's time to read more about Tom the astronaut. Turn to Lesson 53 on page 58 in your Reader.** Check.

- **Put your finger on the title.**
- **Read the title please.**
- **Ready.** Signal.

- **Now read the story.**
- **Ready.** Signal.

<u>The space trip - part four</u>

The tree had turned into a giant snake.
Then it turned into a tall man.
"If you want to know about our planet, I will help you," the tall man said.
"But if you try to kill us like you do on earth, I will disappear.
You will never find me again."
Tom and the man talked for a long, long time.
The tall man told Tom about his special power to change so that nothing could hurt him.
He also told Tom about how they lived in peace on that small planet.
He said, "Tell your people that if they stop their wars, we will teach them our powers."

After a long time, Tom and his team finally got back on the space ship.

They were sad to leave the small planet.

But they also could hardly wait to get home to tell the others what they had found.

When they did, the others made plans to return to that planet to meet the strange beings.

Maybe their powers could make earth a better place to live.

There is no more to this story

 If the student has a problem with any word, have him/her sound it out, say it and then start at the beginning of that sentence again. If the student makes 7 errors, reread the story from the beginning.

TASK 7: SOUND FLUENCY CHECK 10

NOTE: If the student has said 50+ sounds correctly in 1 minute for three consecutive days, s/he may discontinue timings on Sound Fluency Check 10 if s/he so chooses.

- If not, say, **Time for a Sound Fluency Check. Turn to page 49 in your Reader.** Time student for 30 seconds.

- Record scores for Day 4 of Sound Fluency Check 10 on page 138 of the Workbook.

TASK 8: WORD FLUENCY CHECK 10A

NOTE: If the student has read 60+ words correctly in 1 minute for three consecutive days in Word Fluency Check 10A, s/he should continue timings on Word Fluency Check 10B on page 51.

- If not, say, **Time for a Word Fluency Check. Turn to page 50.** Time student for 30 seconds.

- Record scores for Day 4 of Word Fluency Check 10A on page 139 of the Workbook.

TASK 9: STORY READING FLUENCY CHECK 9

NOTE: If the student has read 200+ words per minute in the story three consecutive times, s/he has reached fluency and does not need to try again on this Lesson unless s/he chooses to do so. Have the student choose another story from the Reader to be timed on.

- If the student has not yet reached fluency, say, **Time for another Story Reading Fluency Check. Turn to page 52 in your Reader.** Time student for one minute.

- Record scores for Day 4 of Story Reading Fluency Check 9 on page 140 of the Workbook.

TASK 10: WORKBOOK EXERCISES

- Say, **Now we are going to do the Workbook part of the Lesson.**
- **Open your Workbook to Lesson 53 on page 104.** Check.

Exercise 1: Printing Words

- **In Exercise 1 you are going to print some words in boxes that make a square frame. There are pictures as clues and the words you will use are in the frame that the pilot is holding.** (Point to words.) **Read those words.**
- **Ready.** Signal. Student reads the 8 words inside the frame.

- Now look at the first picture. What is it?
- **Ready.** Signal. Student says, *a straw.*
- **Good. Find the word straw in the list and print it in the boxes going down.** Check.
- Repeat for each picture.

Exercise 2: Matching Rhyming Words

- **Find Exercise 2 on your worksheet. It's a Rhyme Time! exercise. You are going to draw a line to match rhyming words.**
- **Read the first word.**
- **Ready.** Signal. Student reads, *buy.*
- **Now touch the second group of words. Read the first word there.**
- **Ready.** Signal. Student reads, *air.*
- **Does buy rhyme with air?**
- Repeat until student finds the correct rhyming word, why.
- **Good. Now draw a line to join the words buy and why.**
- Repeat for the rest of the words in the list.

Exercise 3: True or False?

- **Find Exercise 3. In this exercise we are going to review Parts 1 to 3 of The space trip in your Reader.**
- **You are going to read each sentence in your Workbook and decide whether it is true or false.**
- **Put your finger on number 1. Read that sentence.**
- **Ready.** Signal. Student reads sentence.
- **Good reading! Is that sentence true or false?**
- **Ready.** Signal. Student says, *true.*
- **Good. Print a T for True on the line beside the sentence.**
- Repeat for sentences 2 to 8.

Exercise 4: Answering Questions from the Reader

- **You need your Reader for Exercise 4. Turn to Lesson 53 on page 58 of your Reader.**
- **You are going to answer some questions from the story The space trip - part four.**
- **Read the first question.**
- **Ready.** Signal. Student reads, *What did the giant snake turn into?*
- **Good. Now read the beginning of the answer.**
- **Ready.** Signal. Student reads, *The giant snake turned into. . .*
- **Find the correct words that complete that sentence and print those words on the line.** Check. **Now read the whole sentence.**
- Repeat for each question.

Exercise 5: Making New Words

- **In Exercise 5 you are going to make some new words from the letters in the word disappear.**
- **Can you see another word that you can make from some of the letters in disappear?**
- **Good! Print that word on the first line.**
- Monitor the student as s/he prints new words. Be ready to make some suggestions.

TASK 11: AWARDING POINTS

- Record the total points for Lesson 53 on page 141 of the Workbook.

End of Lesson 53

LESSON 54

TASK 1: SAYING THE UNDERLINED SOUNDS AND READING THE WORDS

- Let's practice saying some sounds in words that you know.
- Tell me the underlined sound in the first word.
- **Ready.** Signal.

- **Now tell me the word.**
- **Ready.** Signal.

- Repeat for each of the words in the list.

Use correction procedure (my turn, do it with me, your turn) as in previous Lessons if student makes an error.

TASK 2: PRACTICING SOUNDS

- Now let's run through all of the sounds you have learned.
- Say the sound when I touch it. If you make a mistake, we will practice that sound and then do the row again.

- What's the first sound?
- **Ready.** Signal.

- Repeat for each sound in the list.

ph<u>o</u>t<u>o</u>graph   kn<u>ee</u>

binoc<u>u</u>lars   <u>a</u>lready

ma<u>tch</u>   m<u>ou</u>th

aftern<u>oo</u>n   k<u>ee</u>p

large   <u>ai</u>m

r<u>aw</u>   <u>w</u>ithout

<u>h</u>ouse   i<u>n</u>side

ro<u>ck</u>et   sh<u>ould</u>

bu<u>zz</u>   sp<u>ea</u>k

f<u>ir</u>st   rubb<u>er</u>

per<u>ch</u>   <u>qu</u>ite

ould	z	t	sh	w
a	i	oa	ck	g
wh	er	b	ē	n
x	ly	f	l	ph
m	r	d	ea	ou
tch	ȳ	ir	ing	oi
oo	ā	k	v	igh

165

g~i,e~ aw or ch p

y kn e th ar

ēa w ur a s

o c~i,e~ au j u

sion h ai qu c

tion i ō al ol

ū oy

b**o**ld	t**oy**
b**ēhī**nd	**s**poon
b**ē**c**au**se	finall**y**
h**igh**	r**oa**d
sk**ȳ**	mis**sion**
sl**ēē**p**ing**	b**ē**side
airp**or**t	**wh**ich
gather	**t**ension
load	c**u**tting
sh**e**lf	**f**ēēl
mile	fantasti**c**

✓ If any error occurs, use correction procedure (my turn, do it with me, your turn) as in previous Lessons and repeat the row.

TASK 3: SAYING MORE UNDERLINED SOUNDS AND READING THE WORDS

- **Let's practice saying some more of these sounds in words that you know.**
- **Tell me the underlined sound in the first word.**
- **Ready.** Signal.

- **Now tell me the word.**
- **Ready.** Signal.

- Repeat for each of the words in the list.

✓ Use correction procedure (my turn, do it with me, your turn) as in previous Lessons if student makes an error.

TASK 4: PRACTICING IRREGULAR WORDS

- **Now you are going to read some irregular words you have already learned.**

- **Read the first word and spell it.**
- **Ready.** Signal.

- Repeat for each word.

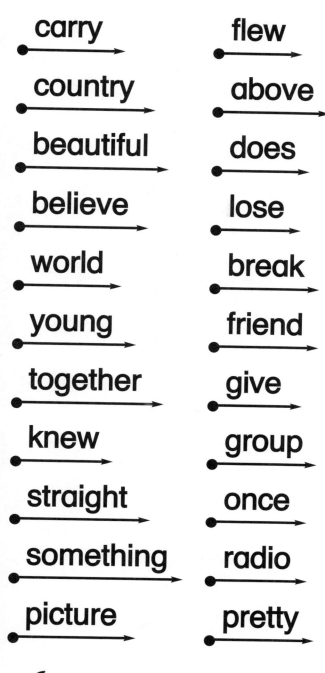

carry   flew

country   above

beautiful   does

believe   lose

world   break

young   friend

together   give

knew   group

straight   once

something   radio

picture   pretty

- What word?
- Ready. Signal.
- Yes, die.

- Spell die.
- Ready. Signal.

- Repeat for each word.

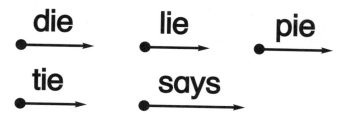

die   lie   pie

tie   says

✓ If necessary, use correction procedure from previous Lessons.

TASK 6: SAYING MORE UNDERLINED SOUNDS AND READING THE WORDS

- You're going to practice saying more sounds in words that you know.
- Tell me the underlined sound in the first word.
- Ready. Signal.

- Now tell me the word.
- Ready. Signal.

- Repeat for each of the words in the list.

m<u>o</u>st   c<u>ar</u>

<u>v</u>ase   <u>a</u>mong

e<u>x</u>tension   <u>c</u>ertain

<u>th</u>ousand   luck<u>y</u>

<u>ea</u>t   <u>sh</u>out

✓ If necessary, use correction procedure from previous Lessons.

TASK 5: TEACHING IRREGULAR WORDS

- Say, **Here are some new irregular words. The first four rhyme. I will read the word, then you will read the word and spell it.**
- **Listen. The first word is die.**

w̲ē   d̲ēēply

b̲unk   jaw

r̲ēal   n̲oise

rētu̲rn   bo̲dy

attentio̲n   ta̲ke

lik̲e   ri̲ver

 Use correction procedure (my turn, do it with me, your turn) as in previous Lessons if student makes an error.

TASK 7: SOUND FLUENCY CHECK 10

REMINDER: If the student has said 50+ sounds correctly in 1 minute for any three days of the last four, s/he may discontinue timings on Sound Fluency Check 10 if s/he so chooses.

- If not, say, **Time for a Sound Fluency Check. Turn to page 49 in your Reader.** Time student for 30 seconds.

- Record scores for Day 5 of Sound Fluency Check 10 on page 138 of the Workbook.

REMINDER: If the student has been unable to say at least 50 sounds correctly per minute at least one time in Sound Fluency Check 10, finish and correct the Workbook Exercises for Lesson 54 but do not proceed to teach new material. Instead, reteach Lessons 50 through 54 with particular emphasis on the sounds. Include

168

daily practice and timings on Sound Fluency Check 10 on page 49. Circle and practice any sounds the student is having difficulty with. Record scores in the Additional Practice columns for Sound Fluency Check 10 on page 138 of the Student Workbook. Students should continue to be awarded points for working hard, paying attention, following instructions and doing well on fluency checks. When the student is able to say 50+ sounds from the list in 1 minute, begin Lesson 55.

TASK 8: WORD FLUENCY CHECK 10A

REMINDER: If the student has read 60+ words correctly in 1 minute for any three days of the last four in Word Fluency Check 10A, s/he should continue timings on Word Fluency Check 10B.

- If not, say, **Time for a Word Fluency Check. Turn to page 50.** Time student for 30 seconds.

- Record scores for Day 5 of Word Fluency Check 10A on page 139 of the Workbook.

REMINDER: If the student has been unable to read at least 60 words correctly in 1 minute at least one time in Word Fluency Check 10A, finish the Workbook Exercises for Lesson 54 but do not proceed with new material. Instead, redo Lessons 50 through 54. Include daily practice and timings on Word Fluency Check 10A on page 50. Circle and practice any words the student is having difficulty with. Students should continue to be awarded points for working hard, paying attention, following instructions and doing well on fluency checks. When the student is able to read 60+ words from the list in 1 minute, continue in the Reader with Lesson 55.

TASK 9: STORY READING FLUENCY CHECK 9

REMINDER: If the student has read 200+ words per minute in the story for three of the last four attempts, s/he has reached fluency and does not need to try again on this Lesson unless s/he chooses to do so. Do a timing on another story of the student's choice.

- If the student has not yet reached fluency, say, **Time for another Story Reading Fluency Check. Turn to page 52 in your Reader.** Time student for one minute.

- Record scores for Day 5 of Story Reading Fluency Check 9 on page 140 of the Workbook.

NOTE: If the student has not yet reached fluency at 200+ words a minute in the same story on at least one timing, finish and correct the Workbook Exercises for Lesson 54, but do not proceed with new material. Instead, have the student practice reading the first half of the story until s/he can read it with fewer than 3 L.O.s in 30 seconds. Then practice the next half in the same manner. Combine the two sections and practice until the student can read them fluently in a minute. Record scores in the Additional Practice columns for Story Reading Fluency Check 9. Award points for working hard, paying attention, following instructions and doing well in fluency checks. When the student has reached fluency, begin Lesson 55.

TASK 10: WORKBOOK EXERCISES

- Say, **Now we are going to do some exercises in your Workbook.**
- **Open your Workbook to Lesson 54 on page 108.** Check.

Exercise 1: Putting Words in Alphabetical Order

- Find Exercise 1. Read the words.
- **Ready.** Signal. Student reads from giant to lose.
- In this exercise you are going to print these words in alphabetical order. You must look at the first letter in each word. What first letter in these words comes first in the alphabet?
- **Ready.** Signal. Student answers, *action*.
- That's right! Print action in the blanks. Put a check mark beside it.
- What is the word with a first letter that comes next in the alphabet?
- **Ready.** Signal. Student says, *beautiful*.
- **Well done. Print beautiful on the second set of blanks.** Check.
- Repeat for the rest of the words. When the student has finished doing all ten of them, say, **Good work! You just put those ten words in alphabetical order.**
- **Now print the letters that are circled in the blanks below to spell another word that you know. What's that word?**
- That's right, attention.

Exercise 2: Circling Vowels that Say their Names and Crossing Out Short Sounds

- Now let's do Exercise 2. You must read each word. Then you will circle any vowel that says its name and cross out every short sound or short sound combination.
- **What's the first word?**
- **Ready.** Signal. Student says, *one*.
- Is there a vowel that says its name in one? Are there any short sounds in one?
- Repeat for each sound in each word.

Exercise 3: Putting Story Events in Order

- In Exercise 3 you are going to review Parts 1 to 4 of the story <u>The space trip</u> by putting events in order from 1 to 6.
- Read the sentences in your Workbook. Number 1.
- **Ready.** Signal. Student reads the first sentence.
- Repeat for the rest of the sentences.
- **Which one of these events came first?**
- **Ready.** Signal. Student says, *Tom dreams of space.*
- **That's right. Put a number 1 on the line at the beginning of that sentence.**
- Have the student number the rest of the sentences from 2 to 6.

Exercise 4: Circling the Correct Sound Combinations

- **Now let's do Exercise 4. Look at each picture. You are going to circle the sound combination that completes the word for that picture.**
- **What's the first picture?**
- **Ready.** Signal. Student says, *a fish.*
- **The last two letters are missing. Is the correct sound combination shshsh or ch?**
- **That's right, shshsh. Circle shshsh. Print shshsh in the blanks.**
- Repeat for each word.

Exercise 5: Answering a Riddle

- Exercise 5 is a riddle. The riddle asks, What bird never uses a comb?
- To answer the riddle you are going to print the alphabet letter that comes right before the letter below the line.
- **What's the first letter below the line?**
- **Ready.** Signal. Student answers, *u.*
- **Yes, u. What letter in the alphabet comes right before the letter u?**
- **Ready.** Signal. Student says, *t.*
- **That's right, t. Print a t on the first line.**
- Repeat for the rest of the letters.
- **So what bird never uses a comb?**
- **The bald eagle! Great work!**

Exercise 6: Printing Words to Match their Meaning

- **Now let's look at Exercise 6. Read the instructions.**
- **Ready.** Signal.
- **Yes, you are going to print words to look like their meaning.**
- **Read the words.**
- **Ready.** Signal. Student reads, *giant, pie, river, high.*
- **Take your pencil and print those words as best you can to match their meaning.**
- Be ready to make some suggestions if the student is having difficulty with any of the words.

TASK 10: AWARDING POINTS

- Record the total points for Lesson 54 on page 141 of the Workbook.

End of Lesson 54

LESSON 55

- Now you are going to sound out some words. As I touch the sounds, you say them.

- First word.
- Ready. Signal.

- Good work. What's that word?
- Ready. Signal.

- Repeat for each word in the list.

shaft

wa sh

min e

suddenly

ōpening

spac e

māybē

forget

silly

Phil

awful

startl e

rēally

skill

explor e

scrēam

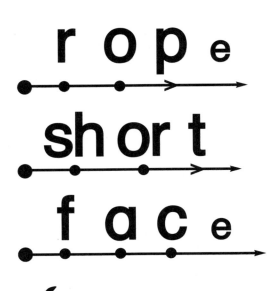

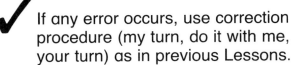

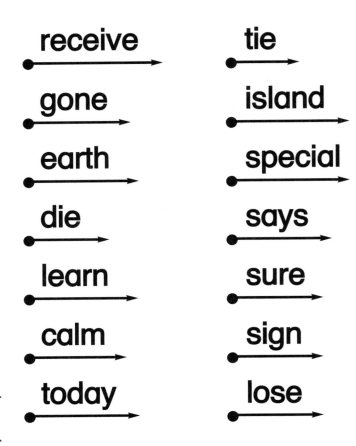

✓ If any error occurs, use correction procedure (my turn, do it with me, your turn) as in previous Lessons.

TASK 2: PRACTICING IRREGULAR WORDS

- You are going to read some irregular words you have already learned.

- Read the first word and spell it.
- Ready. Signal.

- Repeat for each word.

question   done

welcome   look

heard   believe

somewhere   worry

wood   early

✓ If necessary, use correction procedure from previous Lessons.

TASK 3: SOUNDING OUT WORDS THAT BEGIN WITH SHORT SOUNDS

- Now you are going to sound out some words that begin with short sounds. Remember to put the sounds together without stopping.

- Sound out the first word.
- Ready. Signal.

- What's that word?
- Ready. Signal.

- Repeat for each of the words in the list.

gold

damp

clēan

tīny

hol e

jump

cav e

head

tunnel

hik e

crāzy

crawl

bottom

too

disappēar

bēgan

check

hockē y

pocke t

✓ If necessary, use correction procedure in previous Lessons and begin the list again.

TASK 4: STORY READING

- **Now it's time to read a new story. Turn to Lesson 55 on page 60 in your Reader.** Check.

- **Put your finger on the title.**
- **Read the title please.**
- **Ready.** Signal.

- **Now read the story.**
- **Ready.** Signal.

The cave-in - part one

One day Cathy and Phil began to explore a cave that they found while they were hiking.
"This looks like an old mine," Phil said.
Cathy said, "Maybe we will find some gold!"
They tied a rope to a tree near the opening of the cave.
Then they began to go down the mine shaft.
Soon they reached the bottom of the shaft.
There was a tunnel that went down to the right.
It was dark and really damp.
Suddenly Cathy screamed.
A large bat flew past her face and out of the tunnel.
It startled her.
More bats left the cave, making the two explorers jump each time.
Then Cathy saw a small opening.
"I would like to check that out," she said.
"It's too small a space for me," Phil said.
"Maybe you should forget about going in there, Cathy.
It could fall in on you."
"Don't worry, Phil. I'll be all right," Cathy said.
"Wait here. I'll be back soon."
She crawled into the tiny hole and out of sight.
A short while later Phil heard a loud crash and a scream.
Then nothing.
The tunnel had caved in.

And Cathy was somewhere inside it.
There is more to come

 If the student has a problem with any word, have him/her sound it out, say it and then start at the beginning of that sentence again. If the student makes 7 errors, reread the story from the beginning.

TASK 5: SOUND FLUENCY CHECK 11

- The student has said 50+ sounds per minute in Sound Fluency Check 10 on page 49. Say, **Turn to page 62 in your Reader. There is a list of sounds from Lessons 1 to 55.**
- **You are going to say these sounds as quickly as you can, remembering to hold the sounds with the dots under them for one second.**
- **Which way would you like to do this list?** Student chooses down or across.

- **Put your finger on the first sound.**
- **Ready. Please begin.** Time student for 30 seconds.
- Say, **Thank you.**

- Record sounds said correctly per minute in the Sounds Said Correctly column for Day 1 of Sound Fluency Check 11 on page 138 of the Workbook.
- Record number of errors and/or skipped sounds per minute in the Learning Opportunities column.

TASK 6: WORD FLUENCY CHECK 11A

- The student has read 60+ words per minute in Word Fluency Check 10A on page 50. Say, **On page 63 there is a list of words from Lessons 1 to 55.**
- **You are going to read these words as quickly as you can. Which way would you like to read this list?** Student chooses down or across.

- **Put your finger on the first word.**
- **Ready. Please begin.** Time student for 30 seconds.
- Say, **Thank you.**

- Record words read correctly per minute in the Words Read Correctly column for Day 1 of Word Fluency Check 11A on page 139 of the Workbook.
- Record number of errors and/or skipped words per minute in the Learning Opportunities column.

TASK 7: STORY READING FLUENCY CHECK 10

- The student has reached fluency (200+ words/minute) in Story Reading Fluency Check 9. Say, **Now we are going to do a new Story Reading Fluency Check. Turn to page 65 in your Reader.**

- **Put your finger on the title. Get set to read the story.**
- **Ready. Please begin.** Time student for 1 minute.
- At the end of 1 minute say, **Thank you.**

- Record the number of words read correctly in the Words Read Correctly column for Day 1 of Story Reading Fluency Check 10 on page 140 of the Workbook.
- Record errors and/or skipped words in the Learning Opportunities column.

TASK 8: WORKBOOK EXERCISES

- It's time to do some Workbook Exercises.
- Open your Workbook to Lesson 55 on page 112. Check.

Exercise 1: Answering Questions from the Reader

- You need your Reader for Exercise 1. Turn to Lesson 55 on page 60. Check. You are going to answer some questions from the story The cave-in - part one.
- **Read the first question.**
- **Ready.** Signal. Student reads, *What were Cathy and Phil doing when they found the cave?*
- **Good. Now read the beginning of the answer.**
- **Ready.** Signal. Student reads, *They found the cave while . . .*
- **Find the correct words that complete that sentence and print those words on the line.** Check. **Now read the whole sentence.**
- Repeat for each question.

Exercise 2: Solving a Code to Answer a Riddle

- **Let's look at Exercise 2. You are going to solve a code to answer a riddle. Read the riddle.**
- **Ready.** Signal. Student reads, *What kind of bat doesn't have wings?*
- **Let's figure out the sound that goes in each set of words.** Have the student read the words in each box, then print the missing sounds in each shape.
- **Good! You have figured out what each shape's sound is. Now solve the code to answer the riddle.**
- **So what kind of bat doesn't have wings?**
- Yes, a baseball bat!

Exercise 3: Circling the Word that Doesn't Belong

- In Exercise 3 each line has a list of four words. Three of the words have something the same. One word does not. You are going to circle the word in each line that doesn't belong.
- Finger on number 1. Read each of those words.
- **Ready.** Signal. Student reads, *opening, bottom, phone, rope.*
- **Which of those words does not belong?**
- **Ready.** Signal. Student answers, *bottom.*
- **That's right because in all the other words the vowel o says its name.**
- Repeat for numbers 2 to 6.
- If the student is having difficulty, give him/her a hint or tell him/her the answer and ask for the reason that that word does not belong.

Exercise 4: Word Search Puzzle

- Exercise 4 is a word search puzzle. Read the first word in the list of the words that you will be looking for.
- **Ready.** Signal. Student reads, *cave.*
- **The arrow beside the word tells you whether the word goes across, up, down or backwards. Look in the puzzle. Go through each row until you find the letters c-a-v-e going down.**
- **That's right. Draw a circle around the word cave.**
- **Put a check mark beside the word cave in the list so that you know you have found it.**
- If the student is having problems finding the word, repeat steps above for each word in the list. If s/he can do the puzzle independently, allow him/her to do so.

- Record the total points for Lesson 55 on page 141 of the Workbook.

End of Lesson 55

LESSON 56

- You are going to review some irregular words you have already learned.

- Read the first word and spell it.
- Ready. Signal.

- Repeat for each word.

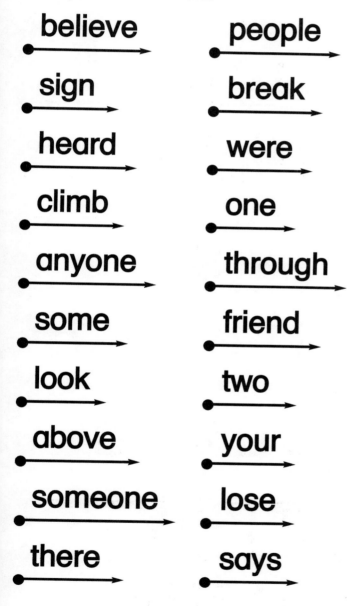

believe

people

sign

break

heard

were

climb

one

anyone

through

some

friend

look

two

above

your

someone

lose

there

says

✓ If necessary, use correction procedure from previous Lessons.

TASK 2: TEACHING IRREGULAR WORDS

- Say, **Here are some new irregular words. First I will read the word, then you will read the word and spell it.**

- Listen. The first word is **laugh.**
- **What word?**
- Ready. Signal.
- **Yes, laugh.**

- Spell **laugh.**
- Ready. Signal.

- Repeat for each word in the list.

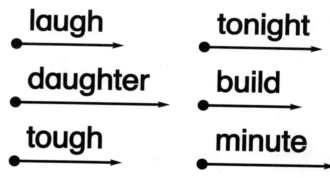

laugh

tonight

daughter

build

tough

minute

✓ If necessary, use correction procedure from previous Lessons.

TASK 3: SOUNDING OUT WORDS

- Now you are going to sound out some words. As I touch the sounds, you say them.

- **First word.**
- **Ready.** Signal.

- **Good work. What's that word?**
- **Ready.** Signal.

- Repeat for each word in the list.

b ēa m

ph o n e

r o p e

f i r e figh t er

w ē' r e

c a r e f u l

s a f e

t r ai l

s aw

p ar k ing

p a s t

kn o ck e d

m igh t

l e g

t r a pp e d

c a v e d

a l i v e

p l ēa s e

b rō k e̦ n

✔ If any error occurs, use correction procedure (my turn, do it with me, your turn) as in previous Lessons.

**TASK 4:
READING WORDS**

- Now you are going to practice reading some words you will see in this Lesson's story.

- First word.
- **Ready.** Signal.

- Repeat for each word in list.

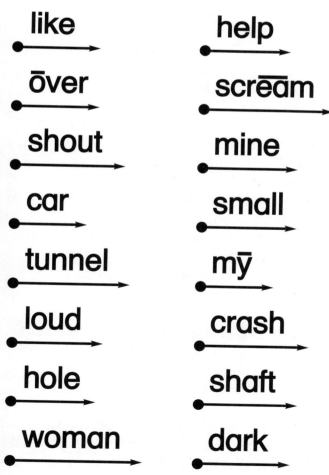

like	help
ōver	scrēam
shout	mine
car	small
tunnel	mȳ
loud	crash
hole	shaft
woman	dark

sound

called

quite

think

across

ōpening

✔ If necessary, use correction procedure (my turn, do it with me, your turn) as in previous Lessons.

**TASK 5:
STORY READING**

- Now it's time to join Phil and Cathy in the old mine. Turn to Lesson 56 on page 67 in your Reader. **Check.**

- Put your finger on the title.
- Read the title please.
- **Ready.** Signal.

- Now read the story.
- **Ready.** Signal.

The cave-in - part two

Phil heard the crash and the scream.
He ran over to the small opening.
He called to Cathy but did not hear a sound.
Phil climbed up the rope and ran down the trail to the parking lot.
Some people were in the lot.
He said to them, "Help me, please!
The tunnel caved in.
My friend is trapped!"
One man said, "I have a car phone.
I will call for help."
The others went back with Phil to the mine.
When they got down into the shaft, they looked into the small tunnel.
A woman said, "I am quite small.
I can get in there."

179

Phil said, "It is not safe down there.
If you go, be very careful."
The woman went past him and into the dark hole.
After a few minutes she called out, "Your friend is alive, but she has been knocked out.
There is an old beam across her leg.
I think her leg might be broken."
Just then there was a loud shout from above.
"We're coming down!" someone said.
Two firefighters came down the rope.
They looked into the smaller tunnel.
They did not like what they saw.

                There is more to come

 If the student has a problem with any word, have him/her sound it out, say it and then start at the beginning of that sentence again. If the student makes 7 errors, reread the story from the beginning.

TASK 6: SOUND FLUENCY CHECK 11

- **Time for another Sound Fluency Check. Turn to page 62 in your Reader.** Time student for 30 seconds.

- Record scores for Day 2 of Sound Fluency Check 11 on page 138 of the Workbook.

TASK 7: WORD FLUENCY CHECK 11A

- **Time for another Word Fluency Check. Turn to page 63.** Time student for 30 seconds.

- Record scores for Day 2 of Word Fluency Check 11A on page 139 of the Workbook.

TASK 8: STORY READING FLUENCY CHECK 10

- Say to the student, **We are now going to do our second Story Reading Fluency Check. Turn to page 65 in your Reader.** Time student for 1 minute.

- Record scores for Day 2 of Story Reading Fluency Check 10 on page 140 of the Workbook.

TASK 9: WORKBOOK EXERCISES

- Say, **Now we are going to do the Workbook part of the Lesson.**
- **Open your Workbook to Lesson 56 on page 116.** Check.

Exercise 1: Matching Rhyming Words

- **Find Exercise 1 on your worksheet. It's a Rhyme Time! exercise. You are going to draw a line to match rhyming words.**
- **Read the first word.**
- **Ready.** Signal. Student reads, *car.*
- **Now touch the second group of words. Read the first word there.**
- **Ready.** Signal. Student reads, *come.*
- **Does car rhyme with come?**
- Repeat until student finds the correct rhyming word, are.
- **Good. Now draw a line to join the words car and are.**
- Repeat for the rest of the words in the list.

Exercise 2: Circling the Vowel a that Says its Name and Crossing Out the Vowel a that doesn't Say its Name

- **Now let's do Exercise 2. You are going to read a short paragraph. Then you will circle any a that says its name and cross out any a that doesn't say its**

name. Read the paragraph.
- **Ready.** Signal. Student reads the whole paragraph.
- **Now look at the first word with an underlined vowel. What's that word?**
- **Ready.** Signal. Student says, *what.*
- **Does the underlined vowel say its name or not?**
- **That's correct, it doesn't say its name. Cross it out.**
- Repeat for each underlined vowel a.

Exercise 3: Putting Story Events in Order

- **Let's do Exercise 3. You are going to review the story** <u>The cave-in - part one</u> **by putting events from that story in order from 1 to 6. Open your Reader to page 60.** Check.
- **Now read the sentences in your Workbook. Number 1.**
- **Ready.** Signal. Student reads the first sentence.
- Repeat for the rest of the sentences.
- **Which one of these events came first?**
- **Ready.** Signal. Student says, *Cathy and Phil go hiking and find a cave.*
- **That's right. Put a number 1 on the line at the beginning of that sentence.**
- Have the student number the rest of the sentences from 2 to 6.

Exercise 4: Answering Questions from the Reader

- You also need your Reader for Exercise 4. Turn to Lesson 56 on page 67 of your Reader. You are going to answer some questions from the story <u>The cave-in - part two</u>.
- **Read the first question.**
- **Ready.** Signal. Student reads, *List four things Phil did after he heard the crash and the scream.*
- **Find the first thing that he did. Print those words on the line.** Check. Repeat

for the three other things. **Now read the four sentences.**
- Repeat for each question.

Exercise 5: Solving a Code to Answer a Riddle

- Let's look at Exercise 5. You are going to solve a code to answer a riddle. Read the riddle.
- **Ready.** Signal. Student reads, *How did the firefighter feel when all his friends forgot his birthday?*
- **Good reading! Each letter is represented by a shape with a dot. Fill in the blanks below with the correct letter.** Check.
- **Good! You have figured out what each shape's letter is. So how did the firefighter feel when all his friends forgot his birthday?**
- **He was burned up!**

Exercise 6: Crossword Puzzle

- Go to Exercise 6 on the next page. It's a crossword puzzle.
- There are pictures as clues and the words for the pictures are printed beside the phone.
- **Touch number 1 Down. What is that a picture of?**
- **Ready.** Signal. Student says, *a phone.*
- **That's right. Find the word phone in the list and print it in the boxes for number 1.** Check.
- Repeat for the rest of the words.

> **TASK 10:**
> **AWARDING POINTS**

- Record the total points for Lesson 56 on page 141 of the Workbook.

End of Lesson 56

LESSON 57

- Now you are going to sound out some words. As I touch the sounds, you say them.

- First word.
- **Ready.** Signal.

- What's that word?
- **Ready.** Signal.

- Repeat for each word in the list.

l i f t ing

d a n c e

too

m oa n e d

ēa s y

ambūlanc e

c r aw l

e x p e c t

h ēa l e d

s t r ā n g e

ol d

le ss o n

t r ȳ

pain

e x c i t e

r i p

182

p l <u>ēā</u> s e

✓ If any error occurs, use correction procedure (my turn, do it with me, your turn) as in previous Lessons.

TASK 2: PRACTICING IRREGULAR WORDS

- You are going to read some irregular words you have already learned.

- **Read the first word and spell it.**
- **Ready.** Signal.

- Repeat for each word.

learn

was

climbed

although

tonight

daughter

moved

build

pull

good

break

who

calm

your

of

very

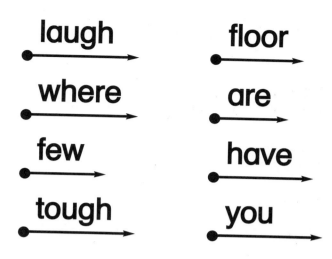

laugh

where

few

tough

floor

are

have

you

✓ If necessary, use correction procedure from previous Lessons.

TASK 3: TEACHING IRREGULAR WORDS

- Say, **Here are some new irregular words.** First I will read the word, then you will read the word and spell it.

- **Listen. The first word is brought.**
- **What word?**
- **Ready.** Signal.
- **Yes, brought.**

- **Spell brought.**
- **Ready.** Signal.

- Repeat for each word.

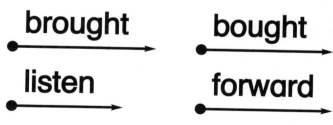

brought

listen

bought

forward

✓ If necessary, use correction procedure from previous Lessons.

- Now you are going to practice reading some words you will see in the story.

- First word.
- **Ready.** Signal.

- Repeat for each word in list.

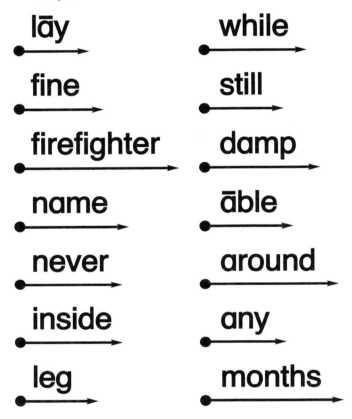

lāy

fine

firefighter

name

never

inside

leg

while

still

damp

āble

around

any

months

✓ If necessary, use correction procedure (my turn, do it with me, your turn) as in previous Lessons.

- Now it's time to find out what happens to Cathy in the old mine shaft. Turn to Lesson 57 on page 69 in your Reader. Check.

- Put your finger on the title.

- **Read the title please.**
- **Ready.** Signal.

- **Now read the story.**
- **Ready.** Signal.

The cave-in - part three

Cathy lay very still on the damp floor of the dark mine shaft.
It was not easy but the woman with Cathy was able to lift the big beam off Cathy's leg.
Cathy moaned and moved a bit. She was coming to.
"Pull your leg out," the small woman said.
Cathy moved her leg.
The pain made her scream.
"Try to be calm," the woman said to Cathy.
We have to get you out of here."
"Where am I?" Cathy asked.
"You are in an old mine shaft.
It fell in on you, but you are going to be fine.
I am going to help you get out of here."
"Who are you? And where is Phil?" Cathy asked.
"Phil is out there. He is too big to crawl in here.
My name is Ann. Let me help you get to the other shaft."
Ann and the firefighters were able to get Cathy out of the mine.
An ambulance had come while they were lifting Cathy up the rope.
In a few months her leg had healed.
But she had learned a good lesson.
She never climbed down strange mine shafts after that.

There is no more to come

 If the student has a problem with any word, have him/her sound it out, say it and then start at the beginning of that sentence again. If the student makes 7 errors, reread the story from the beginning.

TASK 6: SOUND FLUENCY CHECK 11

- Time for another Sound Fluency Check. Turn to page 62 in your Reader. Time student for 30 seconds.

- Record scores for Day 3 of Sound Fluency Check 11 on page 138 of the Workbook.

TASK 7: WORD FLUENCY CHECK 11A

- Time for another Word Fluency Check. Turn to page 63. Time student for 30 seconds.
- Record scores for Day 3 of Word Fluency Check 11A on page 139 of the Workbook.

TASK 8: STORY READING FLUENCY CHECK 10

- Time for another Story Reading Fluency Check. Turn to page 65 in your Reader. Time student for 1 minute.

- Record scores for Day 3 of Story Reading Fluency Check 10 on page 140 of the Workbook.

TASK 9: WORKBOOK EXERCISES

- Say, **Now we are going to do the Workbook Exercises.**
- Open your Workbook to Lesson 57 on page 120. Check.

Exercise 1: Rhyme Time!

- Find Exercise 1 on your worksheet. It's a Rhyme Time! exercise. You are going to print a rhyming word in the blank.
- Read the example.
- **Ready.** Signal. Student reads, *old, cold, bold.*
- That's right. Bold was chosen from the list because it rhymes with old and cold.
- Now read the two words in number 1.
- **Ready.** Signal. Student reads, *too, who.*
- Look in the list and find a word that rhymes with too and who.
- Correct. Print the word blue in the blank and check it off in the list.
- Repeat for numbers 2 to 8.

Exercise 2: Circling Words that Begin with Short Sounds and Crossing Out Words that End with Short Sounds

- Now let's do Exercise 2. You must read each word. Then you will circle any word that begins with a short sound or a short sound combination and cross out any word that ends with a short sound or a short sound combination.
- What's the first word?
- **Ready.** Signal. Student says, *dance.*
- Does dance begin with or end with a short sound or short sound combination?
- Right, it begins with a short sound. Circle the word dance.
- Repeat for each word.

Exercise 3: Making New Words

- In Exercise 3 you are going to make some new words from the letters in the word firefighter.
- Can you see another word that you can make from some of the letters in firefighter?
- Good! Print that word on the first line.
- Monitor the student as s/he prints new words. Be ready to make some suggestions.

Exercise 4: True or False?

- **Find Exercise 4. In this exercise we are going to review Parts 1 and 2 of the story <u>The cave-in</u>. You are going to read each sentence in your Workbook and decide whether it is true or false.**
- **Put your finger on number 1. Read that sentence.**
- **Ready.** Signal. Student reads the sentence.
- **Good reading! Is that sentence true or false?**
- **Ready.** Signal. Student says, *false.*
- **Good. Print an F for False on the line beside the sentence.**
- Repeat for sentences 2 to 8.

Exercise 5: Answering Questions

- **Find Exercise 5. You are going to answer some questions from the story <u>The cave-in - part three</u>. Open your Reader to that story on page 69.**
- **Read the first question in your Workbook.**
- **Ready.** Signal. Student reads, *Where was Cathy?*
- **Part of the answer is done for you. Read that part now please.**
- **Ready.** Signal. Student reads, *Cathy lay very still . . .*
- **Find those words in your Reader and fill in the rest of the sentence to answer the question.** Check.
- **So where was Cathy?**
- **Ready.** Signal. Student reads the whole answer to this question.
- Repeat for questions 2 to 6.

Exercise 6: Circling the Vowel e that Says its Name and Crossing Out the Vowel e that doesn't Say its Name

- **Now let's do Exercise 6. You are going to read a short paragraph. Then you will**

circle any **e** that says its name and cross out any **e** that doesn't say its name. Read the paragraph.
- **Ready.** Signal. Student reads the whole paragraph.
- **Now look at the first word that has an underlined e. What's that word?**
- **Ready.** Signal. Student says, *Edith.*
- **Does the underlined vowel say its name or not?**
- **That's correct, it does say its name. Circle it.**
- Repeat for each underlined vowel.

Exercise 7: Making New Words

- **In Exercise 7 you are going to make some new words from sets of two letters in the word ambulance. The word ambulance is printed down here (point to the word going down) and up here (point to the word going up).**
- **The new words you are going to print must contain the two letters that are printed beside one another. There is a word list here (point to word list on far left) that has the words you will be using.**
- **Let's look at the first set of letters. What letters are they?**
- **Ready.** Signal. Student says, *a and e.*
- **That's right. So you are looking for a word with an a and an e that has seven letters.**
- **Can you find that word in the list?**
- **Good! Print strange on the first line.**
- Repeat for the rest of the words.

```
           TASK 10:
        AWARDING POINTS
```

- Record the total points for Lesson 57 on page 141 of the Workbook.

End of Lesson 57

186

LESSON 58

- You learned that the ending e-d means something happened in the past.
- Usually e-d says the short sound d.
- Sound out these words that end in e-d.

- First word.
- **Ready.** Signal.

- What's that word?
- **Ready.** Signal.
- Yes, that word is **turned.**

- Repeat Task for each word in the list.

turn e d

puzz l e d

ripp e d

star e d

jump e d

- When a word ends in a d or a t and you add the ending e-d, the e-d says ed as in the word <u>ed</u>it.
- Listen as I sound out this word. Sound out the word waited.

- Do that with me.
- **Ready.** Signal.

- Now sound out the word all by yourself.
- **Ready.** Signal.

- What's that word?
- **Ready.** Signal.
- Yes, that word is **waited.**

- Repeat for excited, landed, started and expected.

waited

excited

landed

started

expected

✔ If any error occurs, use correction procedure (my turn, do it with me, your turn) as in previous Lessons.

✔ If any error occurs, use correction procedure (my turn, do it with me, your turn) as in previous Lessons.

- You are going to read some irregular words you have already learned.

- Read the first word and spell it.
- Ready. Signal.

- Repeat for each word.

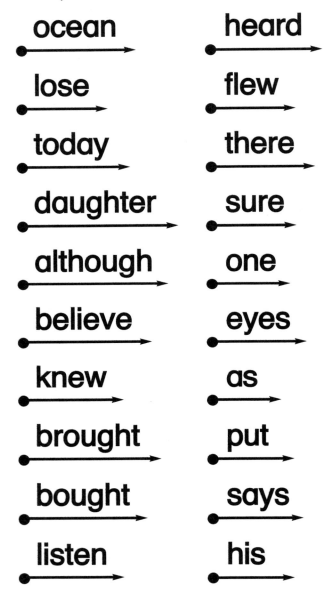

ocean

lose

today

daughter

although

believe

knew

brought

bought

listen

heard

flew

there

sure

one

eyes

as

put

says

his

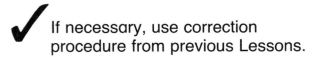

✓ If necessary, use correction procedure from previous Lessons.

- Say, **Here are some new irregular words. First I will read the word, then you will read the word and spell it.**

- **Listen. The first word is shook.**
- **What word?**
- **Ready.** Signal.
- **Yes, shook.**

- **Spell shook.**
- **Ready.** Signal.

- Repeat for each word.

shook

notice

million

grew

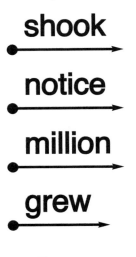

✓ If necessary, use correction procedure from previous Lessons.

- Now you are going to sound out some words. As I touch the sounds, you say them.

- **First word.**
- **Ready.** Signal.

- **Good work. What's that word?**
- **Ready.** Signal.

- Repeat for each word in the list.

contents

dūring

rēally

noise

bed

pair

action

holidāys

mattress

tīny

tent

ōnly

gīant

attention

mission

gēar

ever

✓ If any error occurs, use correction procedure (my turn, do it with me, your turn) as in previous Lessons.

**TASK 5:
READING WORDS**

- Now you are going to practice reading some words you will see in this Lesson's story.

- First word.
- **Ready.** Signal.

- Repeat for each word in list.

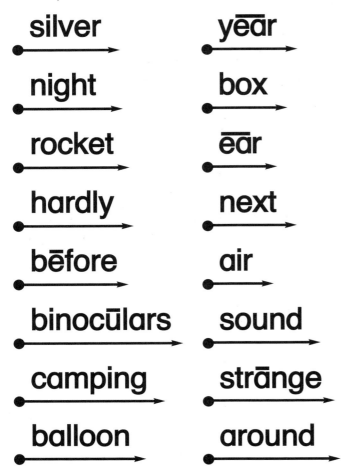

silver   yēar

night   box

rocket   ēar

hardly   next

bēfore   air

binocūlars   sound

camping   strānge

balloon   around

✓ If necessary, use correction procedure (my turn, do it with me, your turn) as in previous Lessons.

TASK 6: SOUNDING OUT WORDS

- Read these words for me.
- **Ready.** Signal. Student reads *don't* and *won't*.

dōn't   wōn't

- Now you are going to sound out some other words like these.

- First word.
- **Ready.** Signal. Student sounds out, *haaadnnnt*

- **What's that word?**
- **Ready.** Signal. Student says, *hadn't*

- Repeat for the rest of the words in the list.

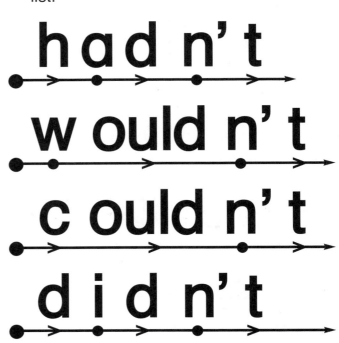

h a d n' t

w ould n' t

c ould n' t

d i d n' t

✓ If necessary, use correction procedure (my turn, do it with me, your turn) as in previous Lessons.

TASK 7: STORY READING

- Now it's time to read a new story. Turn to Lesson 58 on page 71 in your Reader. Check.

- Put your finger on the title.
- Read the title please.
- **Ready.** Signal.

- Now read the story.
- **Ready.** Signal.

Dan the man - part one

When Dan woke up he was really excited.
Today he turned ten.
As he jumped out of bed he noticed a giant box with a big silver balloon on top.
That sure got his attention!
Dan was puzzled. It seemed strange.
The box had not been there the night before.
He hadn't heard any noise during the night.
Dan flew over to the box like a rocket.
He shook it. He put his ear next to it and listened.
There was no sound.
He ripped off the thick tape from around the box.
He stared at the contents of the open box.
Dan couldn't believe his eyes.
Inside was just what he had asked for but never in a million years expected to get.
It was a full set of camping gear - a pup tent, sleeping bag, air mattress and a tiny pair of binoculars.
Although he was only ten, Dan felt like a man of action, a man with a mission, a man with a plan.
He could hardly wait for the holidays to begin.
He just knew that this summer would be the best one ever.

More to come

✔ If the student has a problem with any word, have him/her sound it out, say it and then start at the beginning of that sentence again. If the student makes 7 errors, reread the story from the beginning.

TASK 8: SOUND FLUENCY CHECK 11

NOTE: If the student has said 50+ sounds correctly in 1 minute for three consecutive days, s/he may discontinue timings on Sound Fluency Check 11 if s/he so chooses.

- If not, say, **Time for a Sound Fluency Check. Turn to page 62 in your Reader.** Time student for 30 seconds.

- Record scores for Day 4 of Sound Fluency Check 11 on page 138 in the Workbook.

TASK 9: WORD FLUENCY CHECK 11A

NOTE: If the student has read 60+ words correctly in 1 minute for three consecutive days, s/he should continue timings on Word Fluency Check 11B on page 64.

- If not, say, **Time for a Word Fluency Check. Turn to page 63.** Time student for 30 seconds.

- Record scores for Day 4 of Word Fluency Check 11A (or Day 1 for Word Fluency Check 11B) on page 139 in the Workbook.

TASK 10: STORY READING FLUENCY CHECK 10

NOTE: If the student has read 200+ words per minute in the story three consecutive times, s/he has reached fluency and does not need to try again on this Lesson unless s/he chooses to do so. Encourage student to do timings on other stories in his/her Reader.

- If the student has not yet reached fluency, say, **Time for another Story Reading Fluency Check. Turn to page 65 in your Reader.** Time student for one minute.

- Record scores for Day 4 of Story Reading Fluency Check 10 on page 140 of the Workbook.

- Say, **Now we are going to do the Workbook Exercises.**
- **Open your Workbook to Lesson 58 on page 125.** Check.

Exercise 1: Circling the Vowel **i** that Says its Name and Crossing Out the Vowel **i** that doesn't Say its Name

- **In Exercise 1 you are going to read a short paragraph. Then you will circle any i that says its name and cross out any i that doesn't say its name. Read the paragraph.**
- **Ready.** Signal. Student reads the whole paragraph.
- **Now look at the first word with an underlined i. What's that word?**
- **Ready.** Signal. Student says, *I.*
- **Does the underlined vowel say its name or not?**
- **That's correct, it does say its name. Circle it.**
- Repeat for each underlined vowel.

Exercise 2: Saying the Underlined Sound and Reading the Word

- **Put your finger on Exercise 2. You are going to say the underlined sound in sets of two words and then read the words. What's the underlined sound in the first word?**
- **Ready.** Signal. Student says, *nnn.*
- **What's the underlined sound in the word underneath?**
- **Ready.** Signal. Student says, *nnn.*
- **Good. Read those two words.**
- **Ready.** Signal. Student reads, *knock, know.*
- Repeat for each set of two words in the list.

Exercise 3: Making New Words

- **In Exercise 3 you are going to make some new words from the letters in the word holidays.**
- **Can you see another word that you can make from some of the letters in holidays?**
- **Good! Print that word on the first line.**
- Monitor the student as s/he prints new words. Be ready to make some suggestions.

Exercise 4: Vowel Power!

- **Now let's look at Exercise 4. It's a Vowel Power! exercise. You have to fill in the blanks with vowels to make a word that completes the sentences from the story Dan the man - part one. Turn to that story on page 71 in your Reader.**
- **Read the first sentence. Now look in your Reader for the missing word. What vowels go in the blanks?**
- **Ready.** Signal. Student responds, *e-i-e.*
- **Yes. Print those vowels in the blanks.** Check.
- **Now read the sentence again.**
- **Ready.** Signal. Student reads the sentence.
- Repeat for numbers 2 to 7.

Exercise 5: Answering Questions

- **Find Exercise 5. You are going to answer some questions from the story in your Reader. Read the first question in your Workbook.**
- **Ready.** Signal. Student reads, *How old was Dan that day?*
- **Find the answer in your Reader and fill in the rest of the sentence to answer the question.**
- **So how old was Dan that day?**
- **Ready.** Signal. Student says, *Dan turned ten.*
- Repeat for questions 2 to 5.

Exercise 6: Putting Words in Alphabetical Order

- Find Exercise 6. Read the words.
- **Ready.** Signal. Student reads from landed to pair.
- **In this exercise you are going to print these words in alphabetical order. You must look at the first letter in each word. What first letter in these words** (point to list) **comes first in the alphabet?**
- **Ready.** Signal. Student answers, *ambulance.*
- **That's right! Print ambulance in the blanks. Put a check mark beside it.**
- **What is the word with a first letter that comes next in the alphabet?**
- **Ready.** Signal. Student says, *excited.*
- **Well done. Print excited in the second set of blanks.** Check.
- Repeat for the rest of the words. When the student has finished doing all nine of them, say, **Good work! You just put those nine words in alphabetical order.**
- **Now unscramble the letters that are circled and print them in the blanks below to answer what Dan was celebrating that day.**
- **What was Dan celebrating?**
- **That's right, his birthday.**

Exercise 7: Following a Maze

- Find Exercise 7. In this exercise you are going to go through a maze. Read the instructions.
- **Ready.** Signal. Student reads, *Here is Dan's birthday gift. See how fast you can get into it and out of it!*
- **Good reading! Put your pencil at the top of the bow. Follow the maze through the present and out the bottom. If you run into a wall, start again.**

TASK 12: AWARDING POINTS

- Record the total points for Lesson 58 on page 141 of the Workbook.

End of Lesson 58

LESSON 59

TASK 1: SOUNDING OUT WORDS

- Now you are going to sound out some words. As I touch the sounds, you say them.

- **First word.**
- **Ready.** Signal.

- **Good work. What's that word?**
- **Ready.** Signal.

- Repeat for each word in the list.

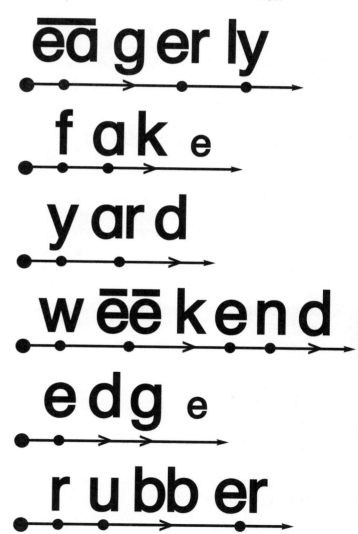

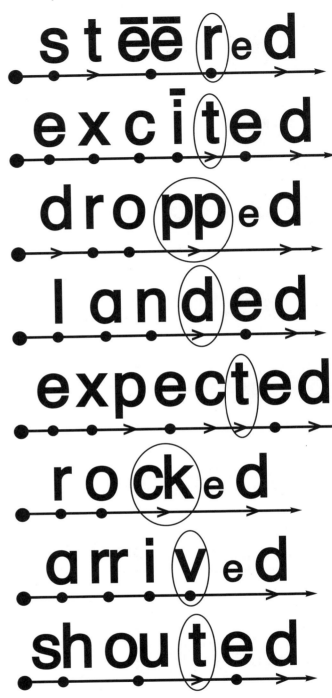

- Repeat Task for each word in the list.

✓ If any error occurs, use correction procedure (my turn, do it with me, your turn) as in previous Lessons.

✓ If any error occurs, use correction procedure (my turn, do it with me, your turn) as in previous Lessons.

TASK 2: SOUNDING OUT WORDS THAT END IN e-d

- Last Lesson you learned that the ending e-d usually says the short sound d.
- But when the word ends in a d or a t and you add the ending e-d, the e-d says ed as in the word <u>ed</u>it.

- Let's practice some words ending in e-d.
- First, look at the circled letter in each word.
- Point to the r in steered.
- Ask, **Is this a d or a t?**
- Student answers, *no.*
- **So will the e-d say d or ed?**
- Student says, *d.*
- **Yes. Sound out that word.**
- **Ready.** Signal.
- Student sounds out, *ssstēēērrrd.*

- **What's that word?**
- **Ready.** Signal.

194

TASK 3: PRACTICING IRREGULAR WORDS

- You are going to read some irregular words you have already learned.

- Read the first word and spell it.
- **Ready.** Signal.

- Repeat for each word.

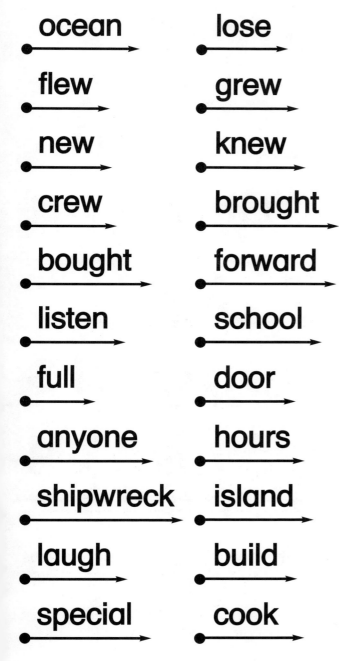

ocean →   lose →

flew →   grew →

new →   knew →

crew →   brought →

bought →   forward →

listen →   school →

full →   door →

anyone →   hours →

shipwreck →   island →

laugh →   build →

special →   cook →

✓ If necessary, use correction procedure from previous Lessons.

TASK 4: TEACHING IRREGULAR WORDS

- Say, **Here are some new irregular words. First I will read the word, then you will read the word and spell it.**

- Listen. The first word is **adventure.**
- **What word?**
- **Ready.** Signal.
- Yes, **adventure.**

- **Spell adventure.**
- **Ready.** Signal.

- Repeat for each word.

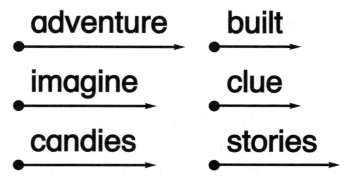

adventure →   built →

imagine →   clue →

candies →   stories →

✓ If necessary, use correction procedure from previous Lessons.

195

- Now you are going to sound out some words that begin with short sounds. Remember to put the sounds together without stopping.

- Sound out the first word.
- **Ready.** Signal.

- What's that word?
- **Ready.** Signal.

- Repeat for each of the words in the list.

holidāys

dūr ing

g ir l

c ap t ai n

p er f e c t

d o lphi n

d āy

h i m s e l f

g r āy

b o bb ing

c ol d

b oa t

contents

pār e n t s

✓ If the student makes an error or stops between the sounds, use correction procedure (my turn, do it with me, your turn) as in previous Lessons and begin the list again.

- Touch the underlined sound in the first word. Say, **Tell me the underlined sound.**
- **Ready.** Signal.

- **Now tell me the word.**
- **Ready.** Signal.

- Repeat for each of the words in the list.

<u>sh</u>ore	r<u>ea</u>dy
k<u>ēē</u>p	<u>w</u>ater
g<u>ī</u>ant	anoth<u>er</u>
f<u>i</u>n<u>a</u>lly	spe<u>n</u>t
pl<u>ā</u>y	<u>s</u>ank
p<u>ai</u>r	<u>m</u>attress
<u>th</u>r<u>ō</u>wn	w<u>ou</u>ld
sna<u>ke</u>	<u>b</u>ēgin
a<u>wā</u>y	<u>o</u>ften
<u>e</u>lse	b<u>ȳ</u>
str<u>ā</u>nge	everyth<u>ing</u>
fl<u>ȳ</u>	camp<u>ing</u>

 Use correction procedure (my turn, do it with me, your turn) as in previous Lessons if student makes an error.

> **TASK 7: STORY READING**

- **Now it's time to read more about Dan and his summer adventure. Turn to Lesson 59 on page 73 in your Reader.**

- **Put your finger on the title.**
- **Read the title please.**
- **Ready.** Signal.

- **Now read the story.**
- **Ready.** Signal.

<u>Dan the man - part two</u>

Dan waited eagerly for school to end and summer to begin.
With his full set of camping gear, he was all ready for the holidays.
Dan and his father put up the tent in the back yard.
Dan brought out a fake rubber snake from his room.
He put the fake snake at the door of his tent to keep girls or anyone else away.
Dan spent hours and hours in and around his new tent.
He would often play games by himself.
One day he imagined he was in a shipwreck. His boat sank.
Dan and the crew were thrown into the cold water.
Dan was bobbing in the ocean when a small gray dolphin steered him to the shore of a strange island.
Another time Dan was the captain of a plane looking for the shipwreck.
He would fly to the edge of the island and look for a flare or some sign of life.
But he saw only the tent, the fake rubber

snake at the door and no girls.
Summer vacation finally arrived.
One day Dan's parents said he could invite two friends over on the weekend for a cookout and a sleepover in the tent.
Dan got everything ready for this special night. He was very excited.
It would be a perfect summer adventure.

One more to come

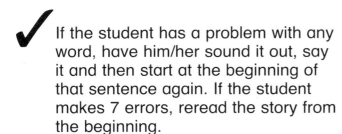 If the student has a problem with any word, have him/her sound it out, say it and then start at the beginning of that sentence again. If the student makes 7 errors, reread the story from the beginning.

TASK 8: SOUND FLUENCY CHECK 11

REMINDER: If the student has said 50+ sounds correctly in 1 minute for any three days of the last four, s/he may discontinue timings on Sound Fluency Check 11 if s/he so chooses.

- If not, say, **Time for a Sound Fluency Check. Turn to page 62 in your Reader.** Check. Time student for 30 seconds.

- Record scores for Day 5 of Sound Fluency Check 11 on page 138 of the Workbook.

TASK 9: WORD FLUENCY CHECK 11A

REMINDER: If the student has read 60+ words correctly in 1 minute for any three days of the last four in Word Fluency Check 11A, s/he should continue timings on Word Fluency Check 11B on page 64.

- If not, say, **Time for a Word Fluency Check. Turn to page 63.** Time student for 30 seconds.

- Record scores for Day 5 of Word Fluency Check 11A (or Day 1 or 2 of Word Fluency Check 11B) on page 139 of the Workbook.

TASK 10: STORY READING FLUENCY CHECK 10

REMINDER: If the student has read 200+ words per minute in the story for three of the last four attempts, s/he has reached fluency and does not need to try again on this Lesson unless s/he chooses to do so. Encourage student to do a timing on a story from Lessons 50 to 58 in his/her Reader.

- If the student has not yet reached fluency, say, **Time for another Story Reading Fluency Check. Turn to page 65 in your Reader.** Time student for one minute.

- Record scores for Day 5 of Story Reading Fluency Check 10 on page 140 of the Workbook.

TASK 11: WORKBOOK EXERCISES

- Say, **Now we are going to do the Workbook part of the Lesson.**
- **Open your Workbook to Lesson 59 on page 129.** Check.

Exercise 1: Practicing the Doubling Rule

- **Find Exercise 1. Read the list of words around the first sun.**
- **Ready.** Signal. Student reads, *flip, cut, set, rub, swim, plan, spin, shop.*
- **Good reading! Now you are going to double the final consonant in each word and then add the ending e-r.**
- **Look at the word flip. What letter are you going to double?**
- **Ready.** Signal.

- Yes, the p.
- On the first line print the word flipper. Check.
- What's that word?
- **Ready.** Signal. Student says, *flipper.*
- Repeat for the rest of the words around the first sun.
- Now read the list of words around the second sun.
- **Ready.** Signal. Student reads, *flip, swim, shop, plan, spin, cut, rub, set.*
- Good reading! Now you are going to double the final consonant in each word and then add the ending i-n-g.
- Look at the word flip. What letter are you going to double?
- **Ready.** Signal.
- Yes, the p.
- On the first line print the word flipping. Check.
- What's that word?
- **Ready.** Signal. Student says, *flipping.*
- Repeat for the rest of the words around the second sun.

Exercise 2: Circling the Vowel o that Says its Name and Crossing Out the Vowel o that doesn't Say its Name

- Now let's do Exercise 2. You are going to read a short paragraph. Then you will circle any o that says its name and cross out any o that doesn't say its name. Read the paragraph.
- **Ready.** Signal. Student reads the whole paragraph.
- Now look at the first word with an underlined o. What's that word?
- **Ready.** Signal. Student says, *took.*
- Do the underlined vowels say their name or not?
- That's correct, they don't say their name. Cross them out.
- Repeat for each underlined vowel.

Exercise 3: Word Search Puzzle

- Find Exercise 3. It's a word search puzzle. Read the first word in the list of the words that you will be looking for.
- **Ready.** Signal. Student reads, *ocean.*
- The arrow beside the word tells you whether the word goes across, up, down or backwards. Look in the puzzle. Go through each row until you find the letters o-c-e-a-n going backwards.
- That's right. Draw a circle around the word ocean.
- Put a check mark beside the word ocean in the list so that you know you have found it.
- If the student is having problems finding the word, repeat steps above for each word in the list. If s/he can do the puzzle independently, allow him/her to do so.

Exercise 4: True or False?

- Find Exercise 4. In this exercise we are going to review the story <u>Dan the man - part one</u>.
- You are going to read each sentence in your Workbook and decide whether it is True or False.
- Put your finger on number 1. Read that sentence.
- **Ready.** Signal. Student reads sentence.
- Good reading! Is that sentence true or false?
- **Ready.** Signal. Student says, *true.*
- Good. Print a T for True on the line beside the sentence.
- Repeat for sentences 2 to 5.

Exercise 5: Answering Questions

- Find Exercise 5. You are going to answer some questions from the story <u>Dan the man - part two</u>. Open your Reader to page 73.
- Now read the first question in your

Workbook.
- **Ready.** Signal. Student reads question.
- **Find the answer to that question in the story. What is the answer?**
- **Ready.** Signal. Student says, *Dan waited eagerly for school to end and summer to begin.*
- **That's correct. Print that answer on the lines under number 1.** Check.
- Repeat for questions 2 to 6.

TASK 12:
AWARDING POINTS

- Record the total points for Lesson 59 on page 141 of the Workbook.

End of Lesson 59

LESSON 60

TASK 1: PRACTICING IRREGULAR WORDS

- You are going to read some irregular words you have already learned.

- Read the first word and spell it.
- **Ready.** Signal.

- Repeat for each word.

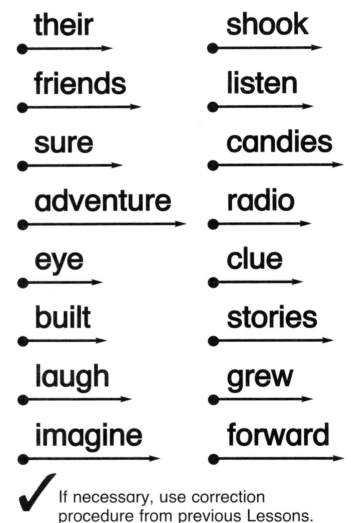

their   shook

friends   listen

sure   candies

adventure   radio

eye   clue

built   stories

laugh   grew

imagine   forward

✓ If necessary, use correction procedure from previous Lessons.

TASK 2: SOUNDING OUT WORDS

- **Now you are going to sound out some words. As I touch the sounds, you say them.**

- **First word.**
- **Ready.** Signal.

- **Good work. What's that word?**
- **Ready.** Signal.

- Repeat for each word in the list.

d i nn er

j or d a n

s c ā r y

a t e

r oa s t e d

a rr i v e d

s i l ly

j o k e

r a cc oo n

b a n g

a w a k e

f a m i ly

s c r a tch ing

r ai d

t r a sh

d r i v e

s qu ēā k

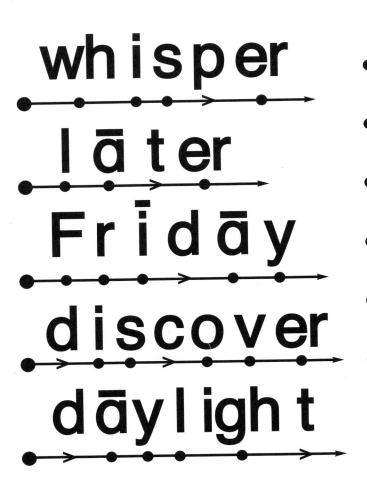

whisper

lāter

Frīdāy

discover

dāylight

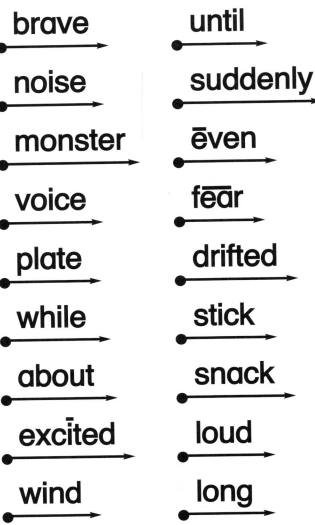

brave

noise

monster

voice

plate

while

about

excīted

wind

until

suddenly

ēven

fēar

drifted

stick

snack

loud

long

✓ If any error occurs, use correction procedure (my turn, do it with me, your turn) as in previous Lessons.

TASK 3:
READING WORDS

- Now you are going to practice reading some other words you will see in the story.

- First word.
- **Ready.** Signal.

- Repeat for each word in list.

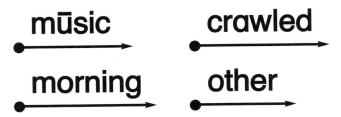

mūsic

morning

crawled

other

✓ If necessary, use correction procedure (my turn, do it with me, your turn) as in previous Lessons.

TASK 4:
STORY READING

- Now it's time to find out more about Dan and his friends at their sleepover. Turn to Lesson 60 on page 75 in your **Reader.** Check.

- Put your finger on the title.
- Read the title please.
- **Ready.** Signal.

- Now read the story.

- **Ready.** Signal.

Dan the man - part three

Dan's two friends arrived on Friday for the sleepover.
Both Matt and Jordan were really excited about the adventure.
Dan's father built a small fire.
For dinner they roasted hot dogs on long sticks.
Later they crawled into their sleeping bags.
While they ate snacks of chips and candies, they listened to music on the radio.
They laughed at silly jokes.
And best of all they told scary monster stories until well after midnight.
At last they drifted off to sleep.
A scratching noise woke Dan up.
He shook his two friends awake.
"Listen!" he whispered to them. "What is that?"
"It's just the wind," answered Jordan. "Go back to sleep."
Suddenly there was a loud BANG.
The boys' eyes grew as big as dinner plates.
"Do you think it's a monster?" Dan asked in a squeaky voice.
Another loud crashing sound sent all three boys flying out of the tent and into the house.
The fake snake at the door sure wouldn't keep a monster out!
The next morning the three boys woke up in Dan's room.
Outside they discovered clues about the midnight monster.
A family of raccoons had raided the trash can.
The boys laughed at their silly fears.
In the daylight they all were much braver.
They looked forward to other nights in the tent.
They all said that even a real monster would not drive them out the next time.
              This is the very end

✔ If the student has a problem with any word, have him/her sound it out, say it and then start at the beginning of

that sentence again. If the student makes 7 errors, reread the story from the beginning.

TASK 5: SOUND FLUENCY CHECK 11

REMINDER: If the student has said 50+ sounds correctly in 1 minute for any three days of the last five, s/he may discontinue timings on Sound Fluency Check 11 if s/he so chooses.

- If not, say, **Time for a Sound Fluency Check. Turn to page 62 in your Reader.** Check. Time student for 30 seconds.

- Record scores in the Additional Practice column for Sound Fluency Check 11 on page 138 of the Workbook.

NOTE: If the student has been unable to say at least 50 sounds correctly per minute at least one time in Sound Fluency Check 11, finish and correct the Workbook Exercises for Lesson 60. In future Lessons include daily practice and timings on Sound Fluency Check 11 on page 62. Record scores in the Additional Practice columns for Sound Fluency Check 11 on page 138 of the Student Workbook until fluency of 50+ sounds per minute is reached. Students should continue to be awarded points for working hard, paying attention, following instructions and doing well on fluency checks.

TASK 6: WORD FLUENCY CHECK 11A

REMINDER: If the student has read 60+ words correctly in 1 minute for any three days of the last five on Fluency Check 11A, s/he should continue timings on Word Fluency Check 11B on page 64.

- If not, say, **Time for a Word Fluency Check. Turn to page 63.** Time student for 30 seconds.

- Record scores in the Additional Practice column for Word Fluency Check 11A (or Day 1, 2 or 3 of Word Fluency Check 11B) on page 139 of the Workbook.

NOTE: If the student has been unable to read at least 60 words correctly in 1 minute at least one time in Word Fluency Check 11A, finish the Workbook Exercises for Lesson 60. Redo Lessons 55 through 60. Include daily practice and timings on Word Fluency Check 11A on page 63. Record scores in the Additional Practice columns for Word Fluency Check 11A on page 139 of the Student Workbook until fluency of 60+ words per minute is reached. Students should continue to be awarded points for working hard, paying attention, following instructions and doing well on fluency checks.

TASK 7: STORY READING FLUENCY CHECK 10

REMINDER: If the student has read 200+ words per minute in the story for three of the last five attempts, s/he has reached fluency and does not need to try again on this Lesson unless s/he chooses to do so. Encourage student to do a timing on a story from Lessons 50 to 59 in his/her Reader.

- If the student has not yet reached fluency, say, **Time for another Story Reading Fluency Check. Turn to page 65 in your Reader.** Time student for one minute.

- Record scores for Story Reading Fluency Check 10 on page 140 of the Workbook.

NOTE: If the student has not yet reached fluency at 200+ words a minute in the same story on at least one timing, finish and correct the Workbook Exercises for Lesson 60. Have the student practice reading the first half of the story until s/he can read it with fewer than 3 L.O.s in 30 seconds. Then practice the next half in the same manner. Combine the two sections and practice until the student can read them fluently in a minute. Record scores in the Additional Practice columns for Story Reading Fluency Check 10. Award points for working hard, paying attention, following instructions and doing well in fluency checks.

TASK 8: WORKBOOK EXERCISES

- Say, **Now we are going to do the last Workbook Exercises for this Level.**
- **Open your Workbook to Lesson 60 on page 133.** Check.

Exercise 1: Making New Words

- **In Exercise 1 you are going to make some new words from the letters in the word adventure.**
- **Can you see another word that you can make from some of the letters in adventure?**
- **Good! Print that word on the first line.**
- Monitor the student as s/he prints new words. Be ready to make some suggestions.

Exercise 2: Circling the Vowel u that Says its Name and Crossing Out the Vowel u that doesn't Say its Name

- **Now let's do Exercise 2. You are going to read a short paragraph. Then you will circle any u that says its name and cross out any u that doesn't say its name. Read the paragraph.**

- **Ready.** Signal. Student reads the whole paragraph.
- **Now look at the first word with an underlined u. What's that word?**
- **Ready.** Signal. Student says, *true*.
- **Does the underlined vowel says its name or not?**
- **That's correct, it doesn't say its name. Cross it out.**
- Repeat for each underlined vowel.

Exercise 3: Crossword Puzzle

- **Exercise 3 is a crossword puzzle.**
- **There are clues under the puzzle to help you know what word to print in the boxes. To help you spell that word there is a word list beside the puzzle.**
- **Look at the first clue in the Across column. It is number 4. Read that clue.**
- **Ready.** Signal. Student reads, *free times*.
- **That's right. Find another word for free times in the word list. What's that word?**
- **Ready.** Signal. Student says, *holidays*.
- **Yes! Print the word holidays in the boxes for number 4 across.** Check.
- Repeat for the rest of the words.

Exercise 4: Putting Story Events in Order

- **Let's do Exercise 4. You are going to review Parts 1 and 2 of the story Dan the man by putting events from those stories in order from 1 to 7.**
- **Read the sentences in your Workbook. Number 1.**
- **Ready.** Signal. Student reads the first sentence.
- Repeat for the rest of the sentences.
- **Which one of these events came first?**
- **Ready.** Signal. Student says, *Dan woke up excited on his birthday.*
- **That's right. Put a number 1 on the line at the beginning of that sentence.**
- Have the student number the rest of the sentences from 2 to 7.

Exercise 5: Answering Questions

- **Find Exercise 5. You are going to answer some questions from the story Dan the man - part three. Open your Reader to page 75.**
- **Now read the first question in your Workbook.**
- **Ready.** Signal. Student reads question.
- **Find the answer to that question in the story. What is the answer?**
- **Ready.** Signal. Student says, *Matt and Jordan were really excited about the adventure.*
- **That's correct. Print that answer on the lines under number 1.** Check.
- Repeat for questions 2 to 8.

Exercise 6: Using Instructions to Draw and Color a Picture

- **Now let's look at Exercise 6. You are going to draw and color a picture.**
- **Read the first sentence.**
- **Ready.** Signal. Student reads, *There is a small fire close to the tent.*
- **That's correct. Draw and color a small fire close to the tent.**
- Have the student read each sentence and then draw or color each part of the picture.

TASK 9: AWARDING POINTS

- Record the total points for Lesson 60 on page 141 of the Workbook.

End of Lesson 60

Congratulations! You have now finished Level 1B! The student is ready to continue in Level 2. S/he is on his/her way to becoming a very competent reader.

Michael Maloney is a teacher, principal and author of the best-selling book, *Teach Your Children Well.* He co-authored Scholastic's Math Tutor, an award-winning software system for teaching arithmetic. Michael has founded or assisted others to found 20 learning centers and schools across North America for children and adults with learning difficulties. He was nominated and was a finalist for the Canada Post National Literacy Awards in 2000.

Michael Maloney, M.A.

Lynne Brearley has taught high school English and Physical Education, as well as elementary school French. When she is not writing or editing,Lynne loves to read, travel, sail, play tennis and rollerblade.

Lynne Brearley, B.A. (Hon)

Judie Preece is a retired high school teacher and administrator. She is the author of another work of non-fiction, *What's in a Name?* Judie enjoys traveling with her husband and friends, reading, rollerblading, painting and the companionship of her dog and three cats.

Judie Preece, B.A.

ACKNOWLEDGMENTS

The authors wish to thank the following people for their effort and support in the creation of *Teach Your Children to Read Well*:

Willi Zaback (graphic artist), Bob House (photographer), Essence Printing, Susan Pearce, Laurel Coo, Lovorka Fabek-Fischer, Mark Bishop, Kay Snedden, Susan Sweet, Patti Clapp, Judy Ruttan and Tammy Belliveau.